A Population History of the United States

This is the first full-scale, one-volume survey of the demographic history of the United States. From the arrival of humans in the Western Hemisphere to the current century, Klein analyzes the basic demographic trends in the growth of the preconquest, colonial, and national populations. He surveys the origin and distribution of the Native Americans, the postconquest free and servile European and African colonial populations, and the variation in regional patterns of fertility and mortality until 1800. He then explores trends in births, deaths, and international and internal migrations during the 19th century, and compares them with contemporary European developments. The profound impact of historic declines in disease and mortality rates on the structure of the late-20th-century population is explained. The unusual patterns of recent urbanization and the rise of suburbia in the late 20th century are examined along with the renewed impact of new massive international migrations on North American society. Finally the late-20th-century changes in family structure, fertility, and mortality are evaluated for their influence on the evolution of the national population for the 21st century and compared with trends in other postdemographic-transition advanced industrial societies in Europe and Asia.

Herbert S. Klein is the Gouverneur Morris Professor of History, Columbia University, and Research Fellow at the Hoover Institution, Stanford University. He is the author of numerous books, including *The Atlantic Slave Trade* (Cambridge, 1999) and *A Concise History of Bolivia* (Cambridge, 2003). He also coedited *The Transatlantic Slave Trade: 1562–1867: A Database* (Cambridge, 2000) with David Eltis, Stephen D. Behrendt, and David Richardson.

A POPULATION
HISTORY OF THE
UNITED STATES

HERBERT S. KLEIN

Columbia University

CAMBRIDGE
UNIVERSITY PRESS

PUBLISHED BY THE PRESS SYNDICATE OF THE UNIVERSITY OF CAMBRIDGE
The Pitt Building, Trumpington Street, Cambridge, United Kingdom

CAMBRIDGE UNIVERSITY PRESS
The Edinburgh Building, Cambridge CB2 2RU, UK
40 West 20th Street, New York, NY 10011-4211, USA
477 Williamstown Road, Port Melbourne, VIC 3207, Australia
Ruiz de Alarcón 13, 28014 Madrid, Spain
Dock House, The Waterfront, Cape Town 8001, South Africa

http://www.cambridge.org

First published 2004

Printed in the United States of America

Typeface Goudy 11/14 pt.   *System* LATEX 2$_\varepsilon$ [TB]

A catalog record for this book is available from the British Library.

Library of Congress Cataloging in Publication Data
Klein, Herbert S.
A population history of the United States / Herbert S. Klein.
p.   cm.
Includes bibliographical references (p.   ) and index.
ISBN 0-521-78268-6 – ISBN 0-521-78810-2 (pbk.)
1. United States – Population – History.   I. Title.
HB3505.K58   2004
304.6'0973 – dc22   2003061548

ISBN 0 521 78268 6 hardback
ISBN 0 521 78810 2 paperback

To

Stanley M. Elkins,
who first taught me to think critically about the
history of the United States

CONTENTS

GRAPHS, MAPS, AND TABLES

GRAPHS

xi

Maps

TABLES

INTRODUCTION

When my editor, Frank Smith, first suggested the need for this volume, I was rather surprised. Were there not a dozen books on the demographic history of the United States, I asked? No, he replied, not a one, and after a systematic checking I found, to my astonishment, that he was quite right. Most countries in Europe have several such volumes dedicated to their population histories, and even many developing countries have such histories. There were, of course, several important but partial general studies that had been produced in the 20th century from Rossiter's simple statistical compilation (1909), to the full-scale surveys of Thompson and Whelpton (1933) and Taeuber and Taeuber (1971). There were also numerous long-term historical studies on aspects of demographic change, especially related to fertility, but there was no one-volume synthesis that covered the entire history of the United States. Despite the extraordinary amount of research produced by individual scholars and even a recent collection of essays on the subject edited by Haines and Steckel (2000), no one had provided the general reader with a survey.

I myself had worked previously on some aspects of U.S. demographic history, most specifically on slavery, the Atlantic slave trade, and Italian immigration, but most of my research and writing has been involved with the demographic history of Latin America. Given this rather unusual background, I thought that I might be able to provide a viewpoint that was somewhat different from the usual approach, and I felt that I had the skills to interpret the more technical work done by demographers, economists, and sociologists for a broader audience. My aim in this book is twofold: to report on the best of the current research and to summarize the mass of quantitative materials that private persons and public agencies have produced for understanding our society. Although few historians have ventured into this area, except for the colonial and early republican period, this is not an unworked field of research. Demographers, economists, and sociologists have devoted a great deal of time and research to understanding the evolution of the national population in the 19th and 20th centuries and have generated a great many new insights as well as new demographic materials. Even government demographers have written about historical demography as they begin to work through issues that are of contemporary concerns. There is thus a vast body of readily available research and materials that can be used to understand this history.

The demographic history of any country shares many characteristics with other populations and their evolution. I have thus tried to show both the commonality of patterns and changes that the population of the United States shared with other nations, especially those of the North Atlantic world, and also to examine those features that were unique to its evolution. Although all modern industrial societies arrive at roughly the same basic structures in the 21st century, they often took slightly different routes to get there. In the case of the United States, the decline of fertility before the fall of mortality, the existence from the beginning of a multiracial society, and the ongoing impact of foreign immigration have been among the special factors that have helped define some of the unique features of the population history. In the following analysis I have tried to show how these unique features modified the broad demographic changes that all populations of the advanced industrializing countries were experiencing in the past three centuries.

It also might be useful to define some of the terms and indices that I use throughout the book. Demographic change is traditionally determined by three major factors: the births, deaths, and in- and out-migration experienced by a given population. To measure these changes, demographers have established a series of indices that are expressed in ratios – usually to the resident population – and thus comparable across different size populations.[1] In dealing with births, there are a host of measures that are used, such as the total births in a given year as a ratio of the total population in that same year. This is the so-called crude birth rate and is expressed as births per 1,000 resident population. Given the constraints on human fertility, a crude birth rate of 55 births per thousand resident midyear population would be considered a very high rate. Today, the crude birth rate in the United States is on the order of 14 per thousand resident population. But this crude rate is just one of many rates used to measure the births in a population. There are a series of more refined rates that try to take into account the fact that fertile women are the basic unit of analysis and compare total births to women in, say, the ages of 15 to 49 years or even the rate of infant girls born to these women in their fertile years. Further refining estimates are created using the birth order, the age of the mother at first and subsequent births, the spacing between children, and so on. The more refined the ratio, the more carefully it it reflects the actual number of women who survive to produce female children and the better it predicts the fertility changes that will occur in the current and future generations. Given the poor quality of vital statistical registration in the United States until the 20th century, most scholars use the very simple crude rates generated from the census, the child–woman ratio, which is the ratio of children listed in the census under 5 years of age to all women in their fertile years of roughly 15 to 49 years of age (taken from the census rather than from birth registrations), which they then use to estimate the "total fertility rates." These are the total number of children produced by an average women from the given population over the course of her childbearing years. In developing countries today, that total fertility rate could be as high as six or seven children per woman who has completed her fertility, whereas in contemporary advanced industrial societies, that rate usually falls below the replacement level of 2.1 children.

---

[1] The standard manual that defines all of these various measures is Henry S. Shryock, Jacob S. Siegel and Associates, *The Methods and Materials of Demography* (New York: Academic Press, 1976).

Next in importance are the death rates, again with the crude death rate being the most used until well into the 20th century. The "crude death rate" is defined as the total number of people who died in a given year as a ratio of the resident population in that year. Demographers also have created a series of very refined death rates related to age, type of disease, and other factors, all of which are more useful to determine general movements in mortality than the crude death rate. One rate that is a rather sensitive indicator of well-being and change is the "infant mortality rate," which calculates the number of infants dying before age 1 as a ratio of all children born in that year. In many regions and districts of the United States, this infant mortality rate has been calculated for populations before the 20th century, and these numbers are often presented here. In turn, the "child mortality ratio" is also a good indication of the well-being of a population and is calculated from the number of children dying before 5 years of age to the number born in a given year. More recently, the infant mortality rates have included fetal deaths as well as deaths by days and months after birth.

Once death rates have been established for all ages, then a life table can be constructed, which essentially predicts the ratio of a given population at birth dying at each subsequent advancing age. Normally, when demographers say that life expectancy of a given population is 45 years of age, it means that half the population born in, say, 1850 will survive to the age of 45 years in 1895. Like the infant mortality rate, this measure of average life expectancy is much used today to compare world populations in terms of health and well-being. This number is often confused by many people as meaning that few in a society with such a low life expectancy reached old age. But it should be remembered that prior to the second and third decades of the 20th century, the death rates among infants and children were extremely high. This means that those who survived to 5 years of age in any premodern society had an expectation of life that would go well beyond the average life expectancy at birth. Thus, for example, the white male life expectancy at birth in the United States in 1900 was 46 years of age; this at a time when infant and child mortality was still high, with some 23% of the males dying before 5 years of age. For those who survived to 5 years of age, their life expectancy increased to 54 years of age. The half of the men who survived to 46 years of age in 1946 still had, on average, more than 20 years of life left.[2] Thus a low average life expectancy at birth in the pre-modern era did not mean that there was not a significant number of persons in the population reaching advanced ages.

To see if a population will grow or decline, one needs to know not only the birth and death rates but also the rates of migration that this resident population experiences. People can be lost by death and by migration and if they leave their original homes in their fertile years, this will also have a major impact on the reproductive potential of the remaining population. Equally, the age and sex of the immigrants who enter the given population in any year will influence their total numbers as well as their potential growth rate. It is often the case in the North American experience that immigrant women have higher rates of fertility and family size than do the natives of the receiving society.

It should be stressed that social, cultural, and legal norms and institutions that define marriage and the family will also have their impact on demographic change. If births out of wedlock are seriously restricted by the local population for religious or legal reasons, for example, then the marital fertility rate (the birth rate in a given year only to women who were legally married – thus ignoring children born outside of marriage) will become the single most important factor in determining fertility. Thus any changes in the age of marriage for women can influence potential fertility, expanding or contracting it depending on the age women enter marriage. Equally, married couples can practice birth control, so that voluntary constraints on births can also occur. Demographers and historians have attempted to examine this question of voluntary constraints indirectly by looking at the spacing between children and the age when women terminate their childbearing. These measures in months and

---

[2] Data taken from the 1900 U.S. life table found at the University of California, Berkeley, and Max Planck Institute for Demographic Research. *Human Mortality Database*. Accessed at http://www.demog.berkeley.edu/wilmoth/mortality/.

years are often the only evidence we have before modern social surveys of the late 20th century about voluntary controls over natality. There may also be fundamental changes in norms and attitudes that profoundly influence fertility and even mortality. In more recent times, for example, the family no longer plays the dominant role it once played in controlling fertility as societies relax their attitudes toward out-of-wedlock births. Such disparate factors as the costs of education or the increasing entrance of young women into the labor force will also influence demographic variables. All these factors suggest that the demographic measures we use are, in essence, constrained and influenced by a host of nondemographic attitudes, institutions, and events. These nondemographic factors could range from changes in the economy to religious beliefs, wars, ecological change, government social welfare policies, or even housing availability and the level of urbanization. But it is also true that, at times, the increasing number of children or the declining level of mortality will influence nondemographic institutions and force them to change. Employment, wages, marriage partner availability, and even the cost of education immediately come to mind as factors that are themselves influenced by demographic change. Although most often demographic factors are what social scientists call "dependent variables," that is, they are influenced by nondemographic factors, at times they can also be causal or independent variables and directly influence attitudes and institutions within the society itself.

In this work I have also tried to explore two major demographic models and their applicability to the United States. The first is the movement that Richard Easterlin has called the "Mortality Revolution," which began in the late 18th century and continued until the second half of the 20th century and would profoundly influence all world population. The other is the "Demographic Transition," which resulted from this profound change in mortality. The Mortality Revolution took some three centuries to reach all the world's populations. It meant that, for the first time in the history of humanity, death rates stabilized and then began a long-term decline for all ages, both causing more people to survive and reproduce and increasing life expectancy for all age groups in all societies. The Mortality

Revolution resulted in increasing population pressure due to the survival of ever larger numbers of persons. The response – the second part of the Demographic Transition – was to relieve that pressure both through out migration and voluntary fertility restraint. The "push" factor for European migration to the Americas in the 19th and 20th centuries and for Asian and Latin American populations in the late 20th and early 21st centuries was this population growth. In turn, voluntary population restraint occurred in many, although not all, societies as a response to increasing population pressure brought on by the Mortality Revolution. In the classic Demographic Transition model it was England that first responded to increasing population growth in the late 19th century by forcing down the fertility rates, a pattern that occurred in China in the second half of the 20th century and in Mexico by the beginning of the current century. How the United States differed from this fairly common model is also a theme that is dealt with in this survey.

Finally, I am concerned with the question of the demand for labor and its influence in shaping the origins, distribution, structure, and status of the national population. This constant in the history of the Americas would define the origins and status of many migrants who arrived in this hemisphere. In turn, I am also concerned with the spacial distribution of this population. In this work the western frontier will be seen to play a major role in the distribution of population as well as in influencing demographic change. But the spacial distribution of the United States population involved its movement not only across the continent but also from rural areas to urban centers. All modern societies since the transport revolutions of the 18th and 19th centuries have increasingly moved toward creating ever-larger cities. In turn, the increasing industrialization of many societies and the growing mechanization of agriculture have moved populations off the land and into these growing metropolises at an ever more rapid pace. A major demographic theme from the 19th century onward in the United States is this process of urbanization and rural decline, a process that will eventually be repeated in most world societies. But to this question of urbanization was added, in the 20th century, the rather special North American patterns of ghettoization and suburbanization, both of which were much influenced by the ethnic and racial makeup of the national population.

Given the fact that few have ventured on this path before me, I have had to determine the periodization used in this work. As historians will realize, most of the chapters begin and end with major political or military shifts in national history and tend to follow standard chronology for historical texts. Sometimes major demographic shifts occurred at these political turning points, and sometimes they did not. Often, as I followed given demographic themes, several population characteristics changed at different times and I found that these divisions in time served as reasonable endpoints for some of these changes. Equally, much of the standard social history materials tended to follow these breaks as well. That said, there is a great deal of room for alternative groupings. One obvious alternative scheme would be to treat 1790–1880 as one coherent unit, ignoring the break of the Civil War, and organize another section going from 1880 to, say, 1950. In both cases, these larger divisions would better incorporate long-term trends in mortality and fertility but would do less well for immigration, for example. Given the somewhat arbitrary nature of some of these breaks, I have tried to compensate for this by providing the reader with an appendix that covers major demographic indices over the entire period.

I also made the decision to present all graphs timed to fit the dating in each chapter. Occasionally, some graphs will exceed these limits in order to emphasize a point or theme that preceded or followed this period. I therefore decided to present a complete series of the most important data in the Appendix tables so that readers who want to have a broader view of given trends can refer to these graphs at any time. The notes to all graphs and figures are given in short title format and the full citation can be found in the Bibliography.

The research for this work was initially supported by a seed grant from Institute for Social and Economic Research and Policy (ISERP) at Columbia University. Major support was then obtained from the Hoover Institution of Stanford University. I would like to thank Thomas Sowell for sponsoring my application for a visiting fellowship at the Hoover Institute during the academic year

2002–2003. Richard Sousa and John Raisian at Hoover provided me with an excellent working environment, which enabled me to complete this book. I was greatly assisted by the Social Science Data Service staff of Stanford University Library, and one of the greatest debts I owe is to the staffs of the U.S. agencies that have made so much of their material freely available on the Internet. Since the 1990 census, the Census Bureau has maintained full online access to all the census materials it is producing and to many of its recent special studies, which are often the best historical materials currently available. The National Center of Health Statistics of the Centers for Disease Control and Prevention (CDC) equally provides both contemporary and historical vital statistics and allows easy access to its vast storehouse of information. Finally, I would like to thank Dr. Gregory L. Armstrong of the CDC who most kindly made available to me his data on infectious disease mortality in the 20th century.

I owe a special debt to my editor and friend, Frank Smith, who proposed this topic to me, provided bibliographic help along the way, and remained enthusiastic about the whole enterprise until the end. Margo J. Anderson, Myron Gutman, and Stanley Engerman each provided fundamental criticism for improving the manuscript. Daniel Schiffner helped me to understand the literature on human genetics, and Alice Kessler-Harris introduced me to the latest works on women and the family. Dr. Judith Heiser Schiffner patiently explained to me issues related to disease and to medicine in general, and her love for all things historic created a wonderful environment for writing this book.

Menlo Park
July 2003

CHAPTER ONE

Paleo–Indians, Europeans, and the Settlement of America

There is little question that the early demographic history of North America is still one of the most controversial fields in current scholarship. To the older work of archeologists, geologists, and linguists has been added the new work of geneticists and physicists, all of which has often overturned long-established dogmas. The pre-history of North America also remains one of the areas in which all types of enthusiasts have created popular origin myths that still dominate some parts of national thought. In this chapter I will lay out the current state of the debate about the origins of mankind in the Americas and the dating and distribution of the pre-columbian populations over time and space. I will show how this distribution of the American Indian population by 1492 influenced the subsequent European settlement patterns that evolved within the Americas.

The region that today forms the continental boundaries of the United States may have first been settled by humans as early as 30,000 B.P. (or years before the present era), but no later than 15,000 B.P.[1] Homo sapien Neanderthals emerged in eastern Africa some 300,000 to 200,000 years ago. They spread throughout the Euroasian land mass and were slowly replaced by modern Homo sapiens about 40,000 years ago. Given that no Neanderthal remains have been found in the Americas, it is now assumed that human migrations did not occur before this replacement had occurred.[2] It is also generally

---

[1] Michael H. Crawford, *The Origins of Native Americans: Evidence from Anthropological Genetics.* Cambridge: Cambridge University Press, 1998.

[2] William N. Irving, "Context and Chronology of Early Man in the Americas," *American Review of Anthropology* 14 (1985), p. 530.

accepted that mankind and numerous species of animals arrived in America via a land bridge across the Bering Strait, which connected the Americas to the Eurasian continent during the late Pleistocene period. This causeway was intermittently open from 70,000 B.P. until 15,000 B.P. Given the harsh Nordic conditions, people could not survive in these regions until they developed adequate protection. The oldest known clothing in Asia is dated to 25,000 B.P. Those Homo sapiens who migrated into America came fully skilled in making tools, knew fire, and wore clothing made from animal skins. The accumulation of recent genetic evidence suggests that one or more founding migrations separated from their Northeastern Asian origin groups sometime between 30,000 and 20,000 B.P.[3]; dental evidence appears to support a formal separation between Asians and Americans by about 15,000 B.P.[4]

Once across "Beringia," as the land bridge between Siberia and Alaska was called, there were still glacial barriers that covered the northern land mass and blocked access to the southern plains. These glaciers began receding only some 14,000 years ago, permitting a slow opening in the mainland corridor to the south that was most likely exploited by humans a few thousand years later.[5] But it would also appear that small groups of humans may have hugged the ice-free

---

[3] The most recent genetic work on origins includes the study by Jeffry T. Lell, Rem I. Sukernik, Yelena B. Starikovskaya, Bing Su, Li Jin, Theodore G. Schurr, Peter A. Underhill and Douglas C. Wallace. "The Dual Origin and Siberian Affinities of Native American Y Chromosomes," *American Journal of Human Genetics* 70 (2002), pp. 192–206, and arguing for a single migration origin see Eduardo Tarazona Santos and Fabrício R. Santos, "The Peopling of the Americas: A Second Major Migration," *American Journal of Human Genetics* 70 (2002), pp. 1377–80; and Anne C. Stone and Mark Stoneking, "mtDNA Analysis of a Prehistoric Oneota Population: Implications for the Peopling of the New World," *American Journal of Human Genetics* 62 (1998), pp. 1153–70.

[4] See the initial survey on the dental evidence in Joseph H. Greenberg, Christy G. Turner II, and Stephen L. Zegura, "The Settlement of the Americas: A Comparison of the Linguistic, Dental and Genetic Evidence," *Current Anthropology* 27, no. 5 (December 1986), pp. 480–5.

[5] David G. Anderson and J. Christoper Gillam, "Paleoindian Colonization of the Americas: Implications from an Examination of the Physiography, Demography and Artifact Distribution," *American Antiquity* 65, no. 1 (2000), pp. 43–66.

coastline and even used boats to migrate past these glacial barriers at a much earlier period.[6] Humans probably arrived in the Americas in bands of 25 to 50 persons (a size considered the norm among contemporary hunters and gatherers), and once through or around the glaciers, they quickly spread as far south as Patagonia. There are good sites of big game hunting bands in North America from about 13,500 B.P. These hunters mostly used weapons tipped with chipped stone heads called "Clovis points," named for a site in New Mexico.[7] But there are also early sites from at least 12,500 B.P. as far south as Chile showing small game hunters and shellfish gatherers who were not associated with typical Clovis point weapons of North America.[8] The big game hunting model based on the production of stone projectile Clovis points is no longer considered the only culture developed by the earliest Paleo–Indian settlers, even in North America. Thus small game hunters and coastal and riverine food gathering groups were to be found alongside the big mammal hunters, and no one group seems to have dominated.

The end of the last Ice Age brought an end to the Bering crossing and thus closed this migration route between the Americas and Asia. This radical change in climate also resulted in the extinction of the big mammals, including horses and camels, which had until then existed in the Americas. Although earlier writers have suggested that

[6] See Alan G. Fix, "Colonization Models and Initial Genetic Diversity in the Americas," *Human Biology* 74, no. 1 (February 2002), pp. 1–10.

[7] Stuart J. Fiedel, *Prehistory of the Americas* 2nd ed. Cambridge: Cambridge University Press, 1992; pp. 48–9 also see his recent redating findings in Stuart J. Fiedel, "Older Than We Thought: Implications of Corrected Dates for Paleoindians," *American Antiquity* 64, no. 1 (1999), 95–116. For a recent attempt to unqualifiedly defend the old model of the late arrival of Clovis hunters as the first migrants – the "Clovis-First" school – see Gary Haynes, *The Early Settlement of North America: The Clovis Era* (Cambridge: Cambridge University Press, 2003). Unfortunately, this work ignores all the recent genetic studies on the origins questions. A more nuanced approach is found in David J. Meltzer, "Clocking the First Americans," *Annual Review of Anthropology* 24 (1995), pp. 21–45.

[8] Thomas D. Dillehay, *The Settlement of the Americas: A New Prehistory.* New York: Basic Books, 2000; and Joseph F. Powell and Walter A. Neves, "Craniofacial Morphology of the First Americans: Pattern and Process in the Peopling of the New World," *Yearbook of Physical Anthropology* 42 (1999), pp. 153–88.

the extinction of big mammals was due to overhunting by humans, this is no longer the dominant position. It is now assumed that some serious environmental factors were the prime cause of their extinction. Thereafter animal domestication would be very limited in the Americas compared with Old World developments, whereas plant domestication would be quite impressive. With the loss of big game as a major food source, the Paleo–Indians (as these early settlers were called) engaged in plant gathering as a source of food, along with fishing and small game hunting. All this marked the slow decline of random nomadism. Even hunting and gathering now became scheduled and cyclic. Increasing sedentary activity slowly gave rise to village settlements. It is stressed by archeologists that plant domestication in the Americas preceded permanent agricultural settlement – a pattern different from Eurasian developments – and was a long and slow process with diets changing only gradually over decades.[9]

With the closing of the connection to Asia, American Paleo–Indians evolved their own patterns of culture and settlement and developed at a slower pace than did their counterparts in Eurasia. Whereas the agricultural revolution – the domestication of plants and to a lesser extent of animals – began in the Near East basin around 9,000 B.C., if not earlier, the first significant domestication of plants did not occur in the Americas until about 7,000 B.C. Plant domestication proceeded slowly and was most advanced in the Andes and its associated Amazonian flood planes and in central Mexico. From these core areas, beans, maize, potatoes, and a host of consumable plants radiated to the rest of the Americas over several centuries.

As these populations of humans spread across the hemisphere, they began to separate themselves into distinct groupings. In the distribution of populations, those settling in North and Central America tended to be fairly close genetically, but with two well- marked isolates: the Eskimos of Alaska and Northern Canada and the Nan-Dene speakers of the Pacific Northwest coast. Some have suggested that these two groups may have migrated at a later date than

[9] Fiedel, *Prehistory of the Americas* (1992), Chapters 4 and 5.

most of the other Paleo–Indians.[10] From current genetic evidence, it appears that all the North American Paleo–Indian groups rather quickly separated from those south of Panama and in turn there seems to have been a genetic separation within South America on an east–west division. Nevertheless, all American Indian groups show greater genetic affinity to Asian populations than to any other group of humans in the world.[11]

The region that is presently the United States was a relative backwater by New World standards. It contained a mix of hunters and gatherers through most of the northern plains regions and included simple agriculturalists and settled villages in the central and southern zones, which initially imported much of their domesticated plants and new technology from the advanced centers of Meso-America. In this period of early settlement, the North American Great Plains region contained primarily big game hunters with probably a small animal hunting culture on the East Coast. Between 8,000 and 6,000 B.C., the big game hunting culture slowly gave way, in the area north of the Rio Grande river, to a gathering and hunting culture with the slow disappearance of mammoths, and it finally evolved into an at least partially sedentary lifestyle associated with the beginnings of plant domestication.

By about 6,000 B.C. a sophisticated gathering culture dependent on fish and shellfish developed along both the Atlantic and Pacific coasts and in major estuaries and inland rivers. The oldest sites for this culture in the North Atlantic region are large mounds

---

[10] L. Luca Cavalli-Sforza, Paolo Menozzi, and Alberto Piazza, *The History and Geography of Human Genes*. Princeton: Princeton University Press, 1994, p. 337ff. On the latest materials related to the number of migrations see P. A. Underhill, L. Jin, R. Zemans, P. J. Oefner, and L. Luca Cavalli-Sforza, "A Pre-Columbian Y Chromosome-Specific Transition and Its Implications for Human Evolutionary History," *Proceedings of the National Academy of Science USA* 93 (1996), pp. 196–200; and Wilson A. Silva, et al., "Mitochondrial Genome Diversity of Native Americans Supports a Single Early Entry of Founder Populations into America," *American Journal of Human Genetics* 71 (2002), pp. 187–92.

[11] For a survey of this material, see Herbert S. Klein and Daniel C. Schiffner, "The Current Debate About the Origins of the Paleoindians of America," *Journal of Social History* 37, no. 2 (Winter 2003), 483–92.

of abandoned shells that have been found along the Hudson River and in Labrador. Such shellfish "middens," as these mounds are called, were now common along the entire Pacific Coast.[12] The Paleo–Indians also took to the water in boats, and in this period the settlement of the islands of the Caribbean and Tierra del Fuego occurred. In many regions, there now appeared formal burial sites, indicating more complex and stratified societies. The stabilization of the environment by 4,000 B.C. led to a major increase in population and sedentary life. Between around 3,500 B.C. and 2,500 B.C., pottery and cotton weaving appeared throughout Peru and Mexico.[13]

The rise of agriculture and settled village life in this period was also associated with the beginnings of trade, the specialization of tasks (from making weapons, fishing, and seed gathering to shamans or religious specialists), the production of tools used in agriculture and food processing, and formal burials. Trade, in turn, led to the rise of distinctive regional styles in tools and other artifacts. Although agricultural life predominated in most regions by 2,000 B.C., some hunting and gathering often existed alongside settled agricultural village life. There were also regions that developed rather unusual combinations of features. In the northern plains of what is today Canada and the United States and in the Pacific Northwest coast there emerged stratified societies organized in villages with long-distance trade that did not develop agriculture, although the predominant model everywhere else seems to have been domestication of plants followed by village settlements.

Paradoxically, settled village life and dependence on domesticated plants initially had a negative impact on the health of the American populations. Early farmers had a poorer diet than hunters and were more subject to food shortages. Bones of early farmers are smaller than those of contemporary hunters, show more growth crises because of famine, and have poorer teeth because of higher carbohydrate intake. Villagers had higher incidence of diseases because of crowding and contact than was the norm among the migrating and

---

[12] Fiedel, *Prehistory of the Americas* (1992), pp. 94–96.
[13] Fiedel, *Prehistory of the Americas* (1992), Chapter V.

small bands of hunters.[14] Given this paradoxical finding, the question is Why did hunters adopt agriculture? The obvious answer is that they had no choice. Resources of hunters and gatherers were disappearing in the Americas, and increasing population density forced hunters to go more fully into farming. The origins of farming in the New World (though not in the Old World) coincided with end of the last Pleistocene glaciations, which brought an end of the mammoths and the rise of the oceans to their present level. It is now assumed that because of these transformations, the Paleo–Indian populations outgrew their subsistence bases and had to turn to agriculture for food.

By the end of late Archaic period, which archeologists currently date from 4,000 B.C. to 1,700 B.C., settled village life had appeared throughout the Americas, and most of the basic plants and animals in use at the time of the European conquest had been domesticated. Also, most of the basic plants and technologies developed by the Mexican and Andean Paleo–Indians were now diffused throughout large parts of the Americas, north and south. Strong regional variations existed and much hunting and gathering persisted everywhere, although even in this activity surviving projectile points indicate that the hunting of small game was now the norm and was quite different from the hunting known in earlier periods. Agriculture, for all its negative impact on the health of native populations, created guaranteed food sources that permitted much denser populations than previously. There was a major increase in populations everywhere. By now, the general pattern was for most regions to depend primarily on gathered and domesticated plant foods and aquatic sources for their subsistence, with game a supplementary source. One of the last regions to shift in this direction was the Great Plains and the coastal groups occupying North America. But even here, permanent housing remains have been dated as early as 5,000 B.C. at sites in southern Illinois and Virginia and to ca. 4,000 B.C. in northern California. At these sites, significant findings of gathered seeds and plants

---

[14] Clark Spencer Larsen and George R. Milner, eds., *In the Wake of Contact: Biological Responses to Conquest.* New York: Wiley-Liss, 1994.

have been discovered along with some domesticated plants imported from Mexico.[15] Moreover, throughout this late Archaic period, more and more permanent settlements have been discovered in North America. These have been separated roughly into riverine, coastal, forest, and the Great Plains regions, each ecological zone creating different variations of the intensity of settlement and or migratory populations and their consumption patterns. Social stratification had become the norm in these increasing complex societies. The Indian Knoll site in western Kentucky dating from 2,500 B.C. shows the presence, in a small number of elite burial sites, of copper made objects from the Great Lakes regions and marine shells traded from the Gulf of Mexico or even South America.[16] Local ceramic pots could also be found by 2,500 B.C. in the Savannah River and in the southeastern coastal regions of North America. Cultivated Mexico-originated plants appear in Kentucky and Missouri by 2,000 B.C., and South American domesticated tobacco appears by 500 B.C. throughout the Eastern Woodlands region. The first of the Mexican domesticated plants to appear in North America were squash and gourds, with corn arriving later. By 300 B.C., maize, or corn, was grown in the Ohio Valley and in the Illinois Valley a hundred years later, although major use of this plant was not the norm in these regions until ca. 700–800 A.D.[17]

There also appear in this period the first of the major mounds needing large drafts of human labor to complete. The first such large mounds appear in the Northeast (the Adena culture) around 500 B.C., and the most important and advanced of these were constructed by the Hopewell mound builders of Ohio and Illinois between 100 B.C. and 400 A.D. These large public works suggest multi-village associations and the rise of more complex state organizations in parts of North America not that dissimilar from the state formations that were developing in Mexico and the Andes. The Hopewell mound builders of Ohio traded with the Atlantic Gulf Coast cultures

---

[15] Fiedel, *Prehistory of the Americas*, p. 96.
[16] Fiedel, *Prehistory of the Americas*, p. 102.
[17] Fiedel, *Prehistory of the Americas*, p. 113.

and imported objects from the Yellowstone Park area, which suggests a long-distance and complex trading network.

In the western region of North America by 1,000 B.C. to 500 B.C. there already had appeared in the Northwestern coastal region, with its extraordinarily abundant aquatic food sources, populated villages with wealth and status differentiation well defined among its residents. As already noted, agriculture was not very important here. Although the major Mexican crops were known and some were planted locally, the California and Northwestern coastal peoples relied on fishing and seed gathering to maintain their rather complex stratified village settlements – a pattern unique in the Americas. In these rich fishing societies, even slavery was known to have existed by historic times.

Elsewhere in the Western region of North America, climatic changes and increasing population densities seem to have been the cause for long-distance migrations. In the Southwest and Great Plains areas, the most significant of such migrations was that of the Numic speakers (who were the Mono, Paiute, Panamint, Shoshoni, Kawaisu, and Ute peoples) who, beginning in 1,000 A.D., spread out from their origin in southeastern California to cover the whole Great Basin of the Southwest, large parts of the deserts of southern California, and most of the northwestern plains. The introduction of the bow and arrow to this region around 500 A.D. also led to overhunting and increasing dependence on wild and domesticated plants, all of which had a negative impact on the health of these populations by the time of contact.[18] But in contrast to the Pacific coastal cultures, in these regions there were less complex societies created with much less permananet settlements.

The Great Plains also saw little major change in this pre-conquest period. The extinction of mammoths, horses, and camels at the end of the Pleistocene epoch led to a dependence on bison hunting, which created little new evolution in the societies that exploited this animal resource. Migrating bands of hunters followed the herds, and there was little cultural evolution from the pre-Christian era until

[18]   Fiedel, *Prehistory of the Americas*, p. 141.

the arrival of the Europeans in this region. Equally, in most of central and eastern Canada, this same type of hunting and gathering society existed with little exploitation of agriculture.

Thus, on the eve of 1492, the area north of the Rio Grande River contained a large number of American Indian populations at significantly different levels of development, although all at a much less advanced stage of economic and political organization than those cultures that developed south of the river. Clearly, ecological adaptations had created special societies in the Pacific Northwest and the Great Planes, whereas the Great Lakes and central river valleys of North America and the southeastern Atlantic coastal societies seem to have been more closely associated with Meso-American technology and had come to rely far more than other areas on agriculture. Yet there were still large regions where major agricultural activity was absent and some sections of the continent where hunting still predominated.

The evolution of groups and cultures throughout North America can be readily explained by local, regional, and hemispheric patterns, without resorting to the supposed arrival and influence of transoceanic African, Pacific Islanders, or even Chinese as some have suggested. All American social and cultural evolution followed well-defined and coherent paths of evolution, with most of the variations being explained by local ecological conditions. All recent genetic evidence consistently points to a single major Northeast Asian source for all humans in the Americas, with a clearly marked separation of these Americans from Asians at least 25,000 to 15,000 years before the present era. Moreover, all the supposed influences of non-American cultures that have been suggested for explaining American evolution can easily be explained by local evolutions and autonomous convergent developments rather than by diffusion from overseas advanced civilizations. Despite all attempts to discredit it, the autonomous evolution mode remains dominant in American archeology.

The American Indians who were the first ones to be encountered by the arriving Europeans were those tribes and linguistic groups who resided along the Atlantic Coast from Maine southward and those who were to be found on the southern borderlands. The first group was made up essentially of Algonquin, Iroquoian, and Siouan language speaking nations, most of whom engaged in agriculture, part-time fishing, and forest hunting. The more northern the tribe, the more likely they were to engage in hunting; the more southern the tribe, the more likely that agriculture was the dominant activity associated with settled village life. Food staples everywhere were corn, squash, and beans, supplemented by wild animals and fish and shell-fish. In the Southeastern coast, along the Gulf of Mexico area and into the major Ohio and Mississippi Valley regions, were a mixture of other major language groups, almost all of whom primarily engaged in agriculture. This was also the same further west on what would be the northern New Spain (colonial Mexico) frontier, where the Pueblos with their advanced urban centers and irrigated intensive agriculture culture existed. Here also were some of the Athabascan-speaking groups from the Northwest – above all the Navahos and Apaches – who still retained a primarily nomadic existence dependent on hunting and raiding.[19]

Although American Indian towns were numerous throughout the coastal and Southwestern regions and population density could be quite high in local areas, it is estimated that the total population of American Indians in North America was just under 2 million in 1492. There were about half a million on the Atlantic Coast, about 450,000 in the Southwest, and under 400,000 along the Pacific Coast. The rest were found in the Great Plains and in Canada. The highest population densities were on the Pacific Coast where Indian population ranged from 31 persons per 100 km² in California to 43 persons per 100 km² in the Northwest. In contrast, the Atlantic Coast densities were less than half that, at 11 persons per 100 km² in the Northeast and 17 persons per 100 km² in the Southeastern Atlantic Coast.[20] The pattern of North American Indian

[19] Alvin M. Josephy, Jr., *The Indian Heritage of America*. Boston: Houghton Mifflin, 1991, Chapters 10, 11, 16.
[20] Douglas H. Ubelaker, "North American Indian Population Size, A.D. 1500 to 1985," *American Journal of Physical Anthropology* 77 (3) (November 1988), Table 1, p. 291. Ubelaker's careful reconstructions are the best estimates

settlements in the late 15th century suggests that these regions were relatively lightly settled areas compared to most of the Americas. This can be seen in contrast to the populations estimated for the advanced civilization regions of the continent (Map 1.1). Although the numbers are still much debated, it is currently assumed that the Meso-American region may have contained on the order of 10 to 20 million persons and that of the advanced civilizations of the Andes another 5 to 10 million persons.[21]

Although these populations would be compromised by European disease at the time of contact, these precontact American Indian populations were not virgin populations in terms of serious disease or malnutrition. As hunters moved more and more into farming and settled village agricultural life, disease and often malnutrition increased. Studies of pre-conquest American Indian population skeletons show the existence of nutritional crises, high infant mortality, and increased incidence of degenerative, infectious, and parasite-related diseases among these Indian groups. Tuberculosis has been found in prehistoric Paleo–Indian populations. A host of other infectious diseases, including syphilis, were common. Obvious malnutrition also has shown itself in the bones taken from numerous precontact burial sites throughout America. The farther from hunting the Paleo–Indian peoples were, the more likely was the increase of the rates of morbidity and mortality among them. Finally, trauma due to scalping and warfare were found everywhere and again seem to be more common the more dense the population and the more recent its settlement. From tooth caries to parasites, these populations knew

currently available for the native population of North America in 1492. The work of Thornton and Dobyns with their far greater estimates of native populations in 1492 are based on rather questionable assumptions, see Russell Thornton, "Population History of Native North Americas," in Michael R. Haines and Richard H. Steckel, eds., A *Population History of North America*. Cambridge: Cambridge University Press, 2000, pp. 9–50.

[21] These numbers are just suggestive. For a survey of the debate on numbers to 1992, see William Denevan, "Native American Population in 1492: Recent Research and a Revised Hemispheric Estimate," in William M. Denevan, ed., *The Native Population of the Americas in 1492*, 2nd ed. Madison, Wisconsin: University of Wisconsin Press, 1992, pp. xviii–xxxvii.

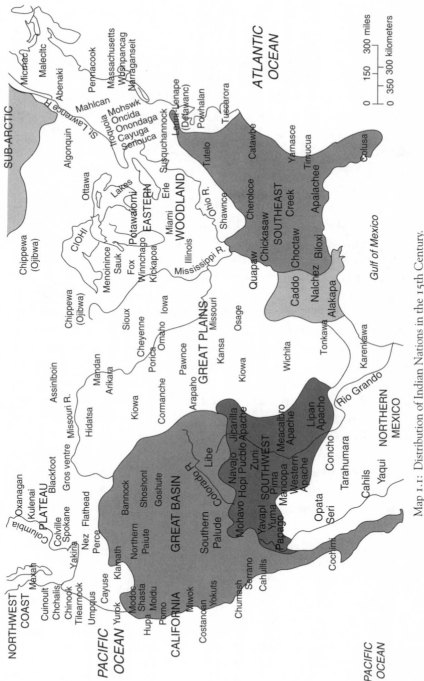

Map 1.1: Distribution of Indian Nations in the 15th Century.

disease and malnutrition and were not living in a paradise, as some have suggested. There were, of course, many new diseases brought to America by the Europeans such as smallpox, measles, and malaria, which were unknown to these peoples but which were endemic to the Europeans and would become epidemic among them after the European invasions. It is also suggested that the infant mortality rates were very high and that life expectancy at birth was 20 years.[22] Although it has been argued that these were comparable to contemporary European rates, this seems to be incorrect. Even people in England in the 16th century were said to have a life expectancy in the mid 30s, and even in the crisis years of the 17th century when death rates equaled birth rates, it never fell below 33 years.[23]

Yet however dense the population became in the Americas, and however advanced their civilizations, these societies remained primarily continental in their expansion and control. Although the Native Americans fully exploited the oceanic resources available to them, ventured to the high seas to settle the islands of the Caribbean and Tierra del Fuego, and exploited offshore islands along the Pacific Coast in quite elaborate boats, they did not explore much beyond the coastal shelf on either coast. By the end of the 15th century, America was still an isolated part of the world with no recent contact with the Eurasian land mass and was virtually unknown in the advanced civilizations of the Eastern Hemisphere. Although several of the nations of Asia and Europe had been using the oceans for many centuries to trade with each other, none of the advanced American civilizations had ventured far from shore either on the Atlantic or Pacific Coasts. Thus, it would be one of these Eurasian societies that would be the one to initiate contact between these two worlds and that would eventually conquer the Americas.

---

[22] Douglas H. Ubelaker, "Patterns of Disease in Early North American Populations," in Michael R. Haines and Richard H. Steckel, eds., A Population History of North America. Cambridge: Cambridge University Press, 2000, pp. 51–98.

[23] E. A. Wrigley and R. S. Schofield, The Population History of England, 1541–1871: A Reconstruction. Cambridge: Cambridge University Press, 1989, Table 7.24, p. 252.

The first Euroasian contact with North America came in the 10th century A.D. In their extraordinary expansion, Scandinavian Vikings had opened up the North Atlantic Islands and Iceland to European settlement by the 9th century. Then Icelandic sailors and explorers in the late 10th century moved on to Greenland and then Newfoundland where they established agricultural colonies. Some of these settlements lasted several hundred years but seem to have been abandoned as the climate worsened in this period. The knowledge of this contact with the Western Hemisphere was limited to a small group of peoples living on the northwestern European coast, and the failure of these colonies to survive and prosper eventually led to the loss of the knowledge of even the existence of these newly encountered regions among the European peoples.[24] The failure of this first contact can be explained by the relative economic and intellectual backwardness of these European peoples at this point in their history, which came at the height of the Middle Ages when Europe itself was divided religiously and its peoples were poorly articulated even within their own region.

But the next time that the Europeans ventured across the Atlantic, they would be coming from a far more coherent society that was in a period of rapid economic, political, and intellectual expansion and integration, and this time they were able to sustain long-term contact and to fully exploit these new American lands for their own advantage. Why it was Europe that conquered America is one of the traditional historical debates. Europe, even in the booming 16th century, was not the wealthiest, the most urban, or even the most advanced civilization of the Eastern Hemisphere, and yet it would come to dominate the world's seas and eventually conquer the Americas and its native populations. In 1500, Europe (less Russia) contained some 66 million peoples, almost double the population of the Americas, but it retained only 14% of the world's population. The Indian subcontinent alone was resident to some

[24] A useful survey of these early Atlantic contacts is found in Seymour Phillips, "The Medieval Background," in Nicolas Canny, ed., *Europeans on the Move: Studies on European Migration, 1500–1800*. Oxford: Clarendon Press, 1994, pp. 9–25.

95 million persons and China some 84 million.[25] Moreover, even within Europe, the two European peoples who led the conquest of the Americas and the domination of the oceans, the Portuguese and the Spanish, in turn held only roughly 6 million persons. Thus in demographic terms, Europe was not the most important region in the world, nor was it even the first to effectively dominate the oceans, although the region was clearly a major sea power from the late Roman period with an intense fishing and merchant fleet in the Mediterranean and North Atlantic waters. Finally, it was not the most advanced in terms of science and technology. In fact, most of its science and technology came from outside its borders. What it did have was an extraordinary ability to generate capital from both private individuals and state sources for its overseas ventures, and it contained populations willing to migrate to new overseas lands in their desire for new wealth and power. Moreover, this ability to raise capital and provide settlers was not confined to any one nation but would prove to be a common response in a large number of leading European states, each one of which in turn proved capable of initiating and sustaining long-term overseas contacts with America and all other parts of the known world.

The causes of the expansion of European peoples has been the subject of enormous debate and multiple interpretations. Everything from its free labor market and its legal systems to the quantitative stress in late Medieval and Renaissance European thought have been suggested as possible causes.[26] One demographic factor that is often cited in explaining Europe's ability to generate capital and expend it on overseas expansion was the so-called European family model. By 1500, most western European Christian societies had developed a system of marriage that indirectly served as a mechanism to control fertility. Europeans developed a set of institutions – legal, cultural, and religious – focused on family formation, which ultimately enabled them to control population growth in the face of

[25] J–N Biraben, "An Essay Concerning Mankind's Evolution," *Population* 4 (1980), pp. 1–13.
[26] See for example, Alfred W. Crosby, *The Measure of Reality: Quantification and Western Society*, 1250–1600. Cambridge: Cambridge University Press, 1997.

declining resources. By this date, most of the western European societies constrained women to have their children within the bonds of marriage – with usually less than 10% of births falling outside marriage. Thus, the experience of married women determined the birth rate of a given society. Then, in turn, marriage was constrained for a series of political, economic, and religious reasons and not all women entered marriage. Depending on the available resources, in most European societies the age of marriage would be delayed or advanced depending on the ability of a married couple to maintain themselves. All this meant that western European women married much later than women in most other world societies. Western Europeans were also unique in the high ratio of women who never gave birth. If independent families could not be maintained because of declining resources, then couples were not permitted to marry, women were withdrawn from the marriage market and placed in religious institutions, and most commonly of all, the age of first marriage would rise for both men and women, thus ensuring the loss of one or more potential children per couple. Once married, the Europeans had the highest recorded marriage fertility rates in the world. By world standards, the Europeans were unusual in both the late age of their marriages and the relatively high ratio of women who never married. Although this mechanism was not consciously and explicitly developed for fertility control and involved complex inheritance patterns and religious beliefs, it was relatively effective in controlling European population growth when resources became limited, just as it was a mechanism for expanding population when resources became abundant. When resources were abundant, the age of first marriage for women declined, total fertility rates rose, and the number of women entering the marriage market reached very high proportions of the women eligible for marriage.[27]

[27] J. Hajnal, "European Marriage Patterns in Perspective," in D. V. Glass and D. E. C. Eversley, eds., *Population in History, Essays in Historical Demography*. London: Edward Arnold, 1965, pp. 101–46; and his essay "Two Kinds of Preindustrial Household Formation System," *Population and Development Review* 8, no. 3. (September, 1982), pp. 449–94; Roger Schofield, "Family Structure, Demographic Behavior, and Economic Growth," in John Walter and Roger

These marriage mechanisms that ultimately had an effect on con-trolling fertility were fairly unique to the western European societies, and it has been suggested that they not only permitted Europeans to exercise voluntary fertility restraints but also were one of the many institutions used by Europeans to create savings.[28] There is also no question that the creation of a free peasantry in most of the western European societies in the centuries previous to the age of discovery had also freed up enormous resources, which gave the Europeans an unusually large population base from which capital and labor could be generated for economic growth and expansion.

These and other factors are often cited to explain the unusual dy-namism of this relatively small world population in 1400, but there is little debate about why Portugal and Spain were the leaders in the European expansion. The Iberians, with their long and intimate contact with advanced Islamic civilization and their recent consol-idation as powerful states with central bureaucracies and substan-tial military resources, were unusually wealthy and powerful by the standards of early modern Europe. Both regimes had long oceanic

Schofield, eds., *Famine, Disease and the Social Order in Modern Society*. Cam-bridge: Cambridge University Press, 1989, pp. 305–30; Michael W. Flinn, *The European Demographic System, 1500–1820*. Baltimore, Md.: Johns Hopkins Uni-versity Press, 1981; and most recently Massimo Livi Bacci, *The Population of Eu-rope: A History*. Oxford : Blackwell, 2000, Chapter 5. It has been argued that by world standards of the mechanisms of positive restraints, the western European family model is fairly unique in that it is imposed by parents in an effort to con-trol labor and resources rather than by the society at large. See Ron Lesthaeghe, "On the Social Control of Human Reproduction," *Population and Development Review* 6, no. 4 (December 1980), pp. 527–48. That this system was not uniform geographically across Europe is stressed by Jack Goody, *The European Family: An Historico-Anthropological Essay*. Oxford: Blackwel, 2000, Chapter 8; and that it varied by class and occupation is emphasized by Jean-Lous Flandrin, *Families in Former Times: Kinship, Household and Sexuality*. Cambridge: Cambridge Univer-sity Press, 1976, Chapter 2.

[28] As Livi Bacci has pointed out, this system was not uniform across Europe and functioned in different ways in different European societies, depending on dif-fering levels of mortality and even of migration, which also had an influence on potential growth and restraint. But all responded to economic restraints by intro-ducing positive checks on potential fertility. Livi Bacci, *The Population of Europe*, Chapter 5.

experience with important naval resources and both had good knowledge of the world beyond their shores because of their long-term contacts with the Islamic states of the Maghreb of North Africa. With long-term military and economic interests in North Africa, it was no accident that the Portuguese directed their caravels to the West African coast in a major move to outflank the increasing powerful Moroccan state, which opposed their North African advances. Once past the Cape of Bodajar, they were able to tap directly into the known sub-Saharan ivory and gold trade, which formerly had been an exclusive monopoly of their archenemies. This extracted wealth in turn enabled them to undertake a continuous set of voyages of exploration, which eventually brought them into the Indian Ocean and enabled them to establish a sea route for carrying the Asian spice and luxury import trades to Europe.

Equally, the Castilian Crown, the last of the major Iberian states to consolidate itself, was able to expand its horizons beyond the peninsula. Not only did it subsidize the Catalan expansion into Italy and the Eastern Mediterranean but also undertook the occupation of the Canary Islands in the Atlantic. Moreover, with the ascension of Charles V (I) in 1516, Castile inherited the wealth of the European Hapsburg empire, which made it the richest state in the continent. It was now able to fight the Protestant Reformation, control the Netherlands, take up much of southern Italy, and even invade Rome. Given its constant rivalry with its Portuguese archenemy, it was inevitable that it too would subsidize explorations – this time toward the West.

That Columbus did not discover America for the Europeans is now well known. Icelandic sailors and explorers had already done that in the 10th and 11th centuries long before the Nina, Pinta, and Santa Maria set sail from the Guadalquiver River. But whatever early contacts may have existed between Europe and America before 1492, there is no question that the Castilians were the ones who were finally able to open up America for European expansion and exploit this opening with a steady input of capital and labor over many centuries, such that the contact was never broken again. Moreover, the existence of the new printing press culture in the rest of Europe guaranteed that all literate Europeans would know of this new land. The letter of Americo Vespucci in 1504 describing his explorations and his evaluation of America as a separate continent was translated into virtually every major European language within a decade of its publication.

The Portuguese response to expansion until the middle of the 16th century was one of commercial domination and trade. Its metropolitan population was small, with only some 1 million persons in 1500, and it initially found itself dealing with well-armed and well-developed states in Africa and Asia. These people were willing to trade, if forced to do so, but could prevent any serious attempts at settlement. Thus, the Portuguese set up trading posts (or factories) everywhere they traded in Africa and Asia, established forts at crucial sites from Africa to Indonesia in order to dominate trade routes and maintained a powerful fleet to deny local groups access to international trade except through Portuguese intermediaries. Given the wealth generated by this international trade monopoly system for Portugal and the Dutch, French, and English who followed them, there was no need to establish settler colonies.

This was the opposite of what would occur in America, even for the Portuguese. Population density in America was probably the lowest in the world at this time and certainly much less than in the Eurasian land mass. Although estimates vary widely, it is currently believed that the total population of the Americas in 1500 was roughly 37 million (a figure most likely on the high side) and that continental Europe – excluding Russia – contained 66 million people. This meant that America held roughly 8% of the estimated 459 million persons then inhabiting the world compared with 14% for Europe.[29]

For the Castilians who followed Columbus, the idea of an elite settler conquest became the norm. Having some 4.7 million in 1500, the continental Spanish populations in the various kingdoms would increase to 6.6 million by 1590, despite a constant out-migration of

---

[29] Biraben, "An Essay Concerning Mankind's Evolution."

population in this period.[30] Spain was in a phase of rapid expansion within and outside its borders in the 16th century. It controlled a vast European and American empire and saw a tremendous growth of its cities, with Seville doubling its population to over 110,000, and a new urban center in Madrid being constructed. Agriculture also flourished in this imperial century, all maintained by a free wage labor force. Finally, the establishment of full-time professional Spanish armies in other European states guaranteed another major area of employment. All this created a large demand for Spanish labor within Spain and its very extensive European possessions. Thus wages for Spanish workers in Europe were high enough to make mass migration to America too costly an operation. In this context, the abundant supply of Indian laborers was crucial to Spanish settlement strategies that would involve the migration to America of a relatively small number of metropolitan residents.

From their base in the West Indies, the Spaniards launched expeditions into the mainland and within half a century controlled most of the advanced Indian peasant societies of the Americas. They had explored a good proportion of the continent from Tierra del Fuego to the northern Great Plains and most of what is today the central and southern United States. Quickly discovering gold and silver in northern Mexico and the Andes, the Spaniards from the beginning were able to use American wealth to subsidize their conquest. Moreover, given the recent nature of the Inca and Aztec empires, they were able to amass large armies of dissident Indians to support their conquests. Finally, given their few numbers, with only some 243,000 Spaniards arriving before 1600,[31] they were able to fully exploit the

---

[30] Jordi Nadal, *La población española (siglos xvi a xx)*, 2nd rev ed. Barcelona: Editorial Ariel, 1986, Table 9, pp. 74–5.

[31] Nicolás Sánchez-Albornoz, *La poblacion de América Latina desde los tiempos precolombinos al año 2025* 2nd ed. Madrid: Alianza Editorial, 1994, Table 4.1, p. 77. For a good survey of the Spanish immigration experience in the period to 1810 see Nicolás Sánchez-Albornoz, "The First Transatlantic Transfer: Spanish Migration to the New World, 1493–1810," in Nicolas Canny, ed., *Europeans on the Move: Studies on European Migration, 1500–1800*. Oxford: Clarendon Press, 1994, pp. 26–38.

peasant Indian labor force through a complex system of indirect rule. Thus, although the Spaniards created a viable settler colony for the first time in the Americas, this colony did not significantly drain the human and capital resources of the metropolitan society. Just the opposite, in fact, was the case. The wealth generated from the conquest of America not only paid for an elaborate colonial administration and defense but also provided surplus funds that enabled Spain to play an active role in European affairs.[32]

Thus, Spain resolved the classic dilemma facing all of the European nations as they attempted to open up colonies in the Americas. In precious metals, they found an abundant resource that could easily be exported to Europe with a high rate of return so as to pay for colonization, and they were able to mobilize a native labor force to work their mines, fields, and factories. This in turn explains why the Spaniards, after fully exploring most of the known hemisphere, abandoned efforts to settle the entire region. Facing hostile and seminomadic Indian frontiers, by the second half of the 16th century they left those frontiers to evangelizing missionary orders to control through missions and also established fortified frontiers to protect their settled areas. With no metals and no easily exploitable Indians, these territories, especially those north of the colony of New Spain, were too costly even for the Spaniards to develop.

In one way or another, each of the European states that would follow the Spaniards in the establishment of settler colonies were forced to resolve the problem of costly labor and the need to export products acceptable in the European or world market. Initially, none who followed the Spaniards to the New World found either the settled Indian peasant populations or the precious metals to pay for the colonization. For this reason, colonization of the Americas would prove a long and costly process for each of the major expanding European states. Even when these Europeans found viable products wanted in the European market, European labor proved too costly to import enough workers to maintain these new American export economies.

[32] Herbert S. Klein, *The American Finances of the Spanish Empire, 1680–1809*. Albuquerque: University of New Mexico Press, 1998.

In their desperate need for labor in the New World the Europeans would eventually turn toward African slaves as the only viable alternative to the lack of native Indian workers or abundant supplies of poor European migrants.

The labor model that would eventually succeed was the one provided by the Portuguese. Although exploring and exploiting Brazil from the beginning of the 16th century, the Portuguese treated this American possession in the same way as they did their other outposts. They initially only traded on an intermittent basis for Brazil wood (for dyes) with the native Tupi-Guarani-speaking tribes along the coast and in fact established a relatively symbiotic relationship with the native population much as the French would create in Canada. But the 17th-century expansion of the northern Europeans and their early attacks on the south Atlantic trade routes of the Portuguese forced the Lisbon government to permanently settle Brazil as a defensive act to eliminate the colonies of French and English who were both attempting settlement and using Brazil as a base to attack the Asian trade routes. Portugal did not want to devote major resources to this operation, however, and decided to settle the region with private fiefdoms granted to rich nationals who were expected to pay for the colonization of poor metropolitan workers. This was a model first used by the Iberians in the eastern Atlantic islands and then adopted by all the early post-Spanish colonizers. But by the middle of the 16th century, this private enterprise had almost totally failed and the Crown decided to create a colonial royal government and put serious resources into establishing a defensible colony.

Even with royal investment, the need for a viable export product and a sizeable labor force to produce it, remained. The Crown decided to expand the few successful colonization experiments that had turned toward sugar and slaves as the only viable means of creating a successful colonization. European demand for sugar, established at the beginning of the Crusades, had progressively expanded, and slowly Portugal had emerged as the largest European producer of this product through its Atlantic islands. In São Tomé and Madeira, the Portuguese planters had used all types of labor, including slaves, and they were able to bring their market experience and their technology with them to Brazil. With its rich soils and three growing seasons per annum, the Brazilian northeast quickly became the world's largest producer of sugar, which in turn became an ever more popularly consumed product as declining prices made it available to ever larger numbers of European consumers.

Faced with a tight labor market at home, the 1 million Portuguese could find few nationals who were willing or able to migrate. Thus, they decided from the beginning to use slave labor. Facing relatively simple American Indian agricultural and hunting societies, they could not use the method of taxation and indirect rule so successfully exploited by the Spaniards with their Andean and Central Mexican Amerindian peasants. Rather, they engaged in massive warfare throughout the region and enslaved all the Amerindian village agriculturalists and nomadic hunters and gatherers whom they could find and used them to produce sugar. As late as 1600, the majority of the enslaved workers producing Brazilian sugar were Indians. But the increasing impact of European disease on these populations slowly eroded their numbers even though the demand for sugar expanded. In this situation, the Portuguese turned toward Africa and began shipping slaves directly from West Africa to America, thus opening up the Atlantic slave trade and compensating for the lack of both Indian and European laborers by involving a third continent in the American colonization scheme.[33]

Like the Spaniards before them, the Portuguese had several advantages denied to those who followed. They already had a thriving sugar industry developing in their overseas Atlantic island possessions, they had capital available from their trade with Asia, and they had excellent trade contacts with West Africa that enabled them to quickly and relatively efficiently introduce African slaves into the American market. None of these factors would be present

[33] This analysis of the origins of African slavery in the Americas is based on the discussion developed in two previous works of mine. See Herbert S. Klein, *African Slavery in Latin America and the Caribbean*. New York: Oxford University Press, 1986; and *The Atlantic Slave Trade*. Cambridge: Cambridge University Press, 1999.

in the French and English settler colonies subsequently founded in the Americas. This explains why these colonies would take so much longer to establish themselves as viable enterprises. To even use slave labor, these colonies would have to establish exportable crops to pay for imported servile workers, and this took years of experimentation and capital to develop. Although all these newer colonizers attempted to enslave the Indians they found, they were never as successful as the Portuguese in creating a viable Indian slave labor force. This explains why these colonizing countries would use religious minorities, convicts, and indentured European migrants in their desperation to create the labor force needed to produce the necessary goods for the European market. Like the Portuguese, however, once a viable product could be found that could be successfully exported to Europe, they used their newfound capital to import African slaves to resolve the unending labor crisis that they faced in the Americas.

The question of why Europeans turned to Africans as slaves at this time had to do with their relatively low cost and abundant supply compared to all other sources of labor, free or enslaved. Although in 1500 there was still no European state that did not retain a few slaves or legally recognize slavery, the use of slave labor in agriculture and manufacturing on a large scale had long disappeared from the continent with the end of the Roman Empire. The emerging power of the European economy was fed by an expanding peasant labor force. Moreover, the increasingly hostile and rigid frontier between Islam and Christianity in Mediterranean Europe progressively reduced the supply of Christians, Jews, and Moors to southern European slave markets. In contrast, the majority of African nations continued to use slavery as a minor institution within largely kin- and lineage-based social systems throughout this period and to trade slaves among themselves and to ship them to Europe and the Middle East.

Initially the Portuguese explorers of the West African coast concentrated on gold, ivory, and other trade goods. Even when they began shipping slaves in the early 1440s, they were mainly sent to Europe to serve as domestic servants. Africans had already arrived at these destinations via the overland Muslim-controlled caravan routes, and thus the new trade was primarily an extension of the older trans-Saharan African slave trade. Until 1500, only some 500 to 1,000 slaves were shipped annually by the Portuguese and a good proportion of these slaves were sold in Africa rather than in Christian Europe. But the settlement of the island depot and plantation center of São Tomé in the Gulf of Guinea and the beginning of trade relations with the Kingdom of the Kongo after 1500 substantially changed the nature of the European slave trade. After 1500, the volume of the trade passed 2,000 slaves per annum, and after the 1530s, these slaves were shipped directly to America. This latter development marked a major shift in sources for African slaves for America. Acculturated and Christianized blacks from the Iberian peninsula had been the first Africans forced to cross the Atlantic. Now it was non-Christian and non-Romance language speakers taken directly from Africa, the *bozales*, who made up the overwhelming majority of slaves coming to America.

But even if slavery was associated with sugar and Africans were now the most common of Europe's slaves, why could not the colonies have been settled by other types of laborers coming from the colonizing nations? The answer to this query rests on an analysis of the labor market within Europe itself. The late 15th to early 16th century was a period of rapid economic growth for western Europe, whose population was still recuperating from the Black Death in the 14th century. Most state governments assumed that their populations were still too few to develop their economies and discouraged out-migration. Cities, with all their opportunities, were expanding throughout Europe, and peasants were opening up many new internal European frontiers in this period. Rising wages within Europe directly reflected the increasing tightness of local labor markets. Finally, the growth of large professional military establishments as a result of the long-term warfare with the Islamic states in the Mediterranean as well as increasing warfare in Europe as a result of the emergence of the schismatic Protestant movement within western European Christianity, also provided a drain on local labor. Added to these local attractions and constraints were the high costs and insecurity of travel to the New World.

Even with the unique attraction of abundant precious metals, Castilians were as much attracted to European emigration as to American migration, and most, in fact, stayed home. Relatively few Castilians and even fewer Portuguese traveled to the New World. Thus, for all intents and purposes, the costs of attracting European workers to America were too high to be able to get major settlement going in the empty lands available to most of the European colonizing powers, especially those who came after Spain and Portugal. Even for the Iberians, slaves were considered essential for the development of their urban centers and African slaves quickly made up half or more of their urban populations. In the context of late 15th century Africa and Europe, it was Africans who could be purchased and transported at a cost that was within the capacity of the American colonizing powers to pay and still make a profit out of their colonies.

CHAPTER TWO

COLONIZATION AND SETTLEMENT OF
NORTH AMERICA

The distribution of the pre-columbian Amerindian population would have as much influence on the settlement patterns of the northwestern Europeans who would colonize the Americas as did the Iberians who had preceded them. Lacking large numbers of Amerindians in settled agricultural villages, it was the Portuguese servile labor plantation model that they adopted, rather than the Spanish multiethnic free labor one. This required the subsidization of the migration of a large servile labor force, both indentured whites and African slaves, in order to produce tropical and semitropical export crops for the European market. It also meant that European immigrants, both free and indentured, were drawn to the economically most viable zones, which in turn were not the healthiest for these migrating persons. The West Indies and the southern North Atlantic continental shore were zones where Europeans often had higher morbidity and mortality rates than in their places of origin and lived much shorter lives than those who migrated to the colder, but poorer northern continental regions. Faced by a constant shortage of labor everywhere, Europeans not only turned to servile laborers but also experimented with new mechanisms of inheritance and marriage patterns in order to retain labor in extended family units. Given the bias of the migrants toward the preponderance of young males, the age of marriage for colonial men would rise above European norms and for colonial women, it would fall below those norms in these new settlements. Paradoxically, in the poorest and coldest colonies, the European immigrants would achieve higher rates of fertility and lower rates of mortality and lived longer and healthier lives than were being experienced in contemporary Europe. Finally, the general availability and abundance of food in these new colonies guaranteed that the North American populations in general would become the best fed and tallest populations in the North Atlantic world.

The first to settle continental North America were the Spaniards, and they did so largely as a defensive measure both against hostile nomadic Indians on their northern frontier and against competing Europeans who tried to use the continent as a base to raid its Mexican and Caribbean settlements. Spanish troops and missionaries established forts and church missions along the Florida and Georgia coasts in the 16th century and set up *presidios* and other fortress-settlements along the northern Mexican frontier in the southwestern United States. This movement involved no more than a few hundred Spanish migrants, mostly troops, their families, and missionaries. In response to French Huguenot attempts to settle Florida, the Spaniards established a permanent settlement at Saint Augustine in 1565, which was maintained by subsidies coming from the central Mexican treasury. In 1598, the Spaniards pushed north from central Mexico and colonized what is today New Mexico, establishing numerous small defensive agricultural settlements in the region, and definitively settled Santa Fe in 1610.

The English and French were the next to arrive, but for a variety of reasons having to do with the European wars of religion and internal European conflicts such as the English Civil Wars, they were unsuccessful in their efforts to establish North American colonies until the early 17th century. Although English and French colonists had arrived in the Americas in the preceding century, for a variety of reasons they could not sustain their colonies. Walter Raleigh's Roanoke settlements in North America in 1585 and 1587 were failures. More substantial efforts were those undertaken midcentury by the French in Florida and Brazil, but these were terminated by Spanish and Portuguese conquest in the late 1560s. It was only with the return of internal peace in Europe by the next century that capital and labor once again became available for colonial adventures. At this point, most Europeans decided to direct their efforts to the less costly settlement of the so-called abandoned regions unclaimed, or at least undefended, by the Spanish or Portuguese. Only the Dutch had the resources to challenge the Iberians directly, and as part of their war of independence against the Spaniards, they succeeded in capturing Pernambuco in Brazil and holding it as a colony from 1630 to 1654. But even they could not oppose the Iberian powers, and Portuguese armadas and armies eventually recaptured Pernambuco and Angola from the Dutch.

The French and the English adopted the procedures used by the Portuguese to establish their new 17th-century North American colonies. Either they contracted out colonization with private individuals who were given quasi-feudal rights of control or they turned to joint stock companies to subsidize the emigration and settlement. In 1607, the Virginia Company established Jamestown, which was to be a company-owned settlement with exclusive ownership of the land and with its male workers held in indenture. This feudal-like arrangement would last until 1620, when the Company finally freed the workers, granted them land, and permitted women to migrate to the colony as well to establish families.[1] In turn, the French established Quebec as a functioning settlement in 1608 along with a feudal arrangement for the arriving colonists. A unique English variation of this pattern of settlement was the establishment of a dissident religious colony at Plymouth, Massachusetts, in 1620 by Pilgrim colonists from England.

The first third of the 17th century also saw a determined effort of the French, English, and Dutch to establish permanent colonies in the lesser Antilles. In 1627, the English settled in Barbados using indentured laborers as their prime workforce and quickly moved to settle the empty Leeward islands of Antigua, St. Kitts, and Nevis by 1632, completing their basic West Indian empire with the conquest of Jamaica in 1655 – the only major Carribean island held by the

---

[1] David W. Galenson, "Settlement and Growth of the Colonies: Population, Labor and Economic Development," in Stanley L. Engerman and Robert E. Gallman, *The Cambridge Economic History of the United States*, 3 vols.; Cambridge: Cambridge University Press, 1996, vol. I, p. 135.

Spaniards to be lost to the northern Europeans. The Dutch quickly took Curaçao from the Spaniards in the 1620s; the French preceded to settle Martinique and Guadeloupe in the same period and, at the end of the century, took and settled the unoccupied half of the island of Hispaniola.

There also was a major effort to colonize continental North America north of the Spanish possessions in Florida. By 1624, the Dutch had established a permanent settlement in New York, and the Swedes succeeded in planting a colony in Delaware in 1638. But it was the English who now made the most sustained effort to settle North America in this region south of the Saint Lawrence River and north of the Spanish possessions. Some 1,000 Puritan immigrants established the colony of Massachusetts Bay in 1630, which in turn was the source for colonists who established New Hampshire, Connecticut, and Rhode Island. There were also proprietary colonies founded by wealthy Catholics (Maryland in 1634), Quakers (Pennsylvania in 1682), and others in the Carolinas in the 1670s. The last of these royally granted proprietary colonies was Georgia, which was founded in 1730.

Thus, a century after the effective colonization of mainland Central and South America and the major islands of the Caribbean, there was finally a successful northern European colonization of both mainland North America and the lesser Antilles. In contrast to the earlier Iberian migrations, this new migration would attract the poorer elements of the metropolitan populations through the use of indentured labor contracts, and these were mostly younger males. Even in the dissident religious migrations, which were the most family oriented of these new European migrations, there were a large number of young single males, and everywhere this demographic group predominated. Thus, the migrants arriving in the New World tended to be much younger, in general, than the resident metropolitan populations from which they came and also far more male than the home populations.[2] All of this was to be expected in a major

[2] On the comparative age and sex of the migrants compared to the resident English population, see Richard Archer, "New England Mosaic: A Demographic

migrant flow and would be the norm from the 16th to the 21st century. This was also the pattern in the Atlantic slave trade as well, for the demand in the New World was for workers and the supply conditions in Africa favored the export of males over females into the Atlantic trade.[3]

These younger migrants were a more healthy population than the nonmigrating Europeans and created a population weighted toward working-age persons, with relatively few older adults and young children. Equally, the biased sex ratio among the migrants also had an effect on marriage rates, pushing down the age of first marriages for women and raising them for men. The age and sex of the migrants also affected the potential growth of the American populations. In most regions experiencing heavy migration, natural growth was either low or negative until such time as the American-born population outnumbered the immigrants. Although the Europeans in this period probably had the highest marital fertility rates in the world, this fertility could not compensate for the biased sex ratios of the initial group of immigrants in most regions. In turn, the emigration of these young workers had a profound negative impact on English population growth in the 17th century, reducing it in the first half of the century and pushing the metropolitan population into negative growth in the second half of the century.[4]

But the youth of the migrants did not protect them from experiencing high rates of disease and mortality. Although New England

Analysis for the Seventeenth Century," *William and Mary Quarterly*, 3d ser., 47, no. 4 (October 1990), pp. 477–502.

[3] See Herbert S. Klein, *The Atlantic Slave Trade*, rev version. Cambridge: Cambridge University Press, 2002; the two essays by David Eltis and Stanley L. Engerman, "Fluctuations in Sex and Age Ratios in the Transatlantic Slave Trade, 1663–1864," *The Economic History Review*, New Series, 46, no. 2 (May 1993), pp. 308–23; and "Was the Slave Trade Dominated by Men?" *Journal of Interdisciplinary History* 23, no. 2 (Autumn 1992), pp. 237–57; and David Geggus, "Sex Ratio, Age and Ethnicity in the Atlantic Slave Trade: Data from French Shipping and Plantation Records," *The Journal of African History* 30, no. 1 (1989), pp. 23–44.

[4] E. A. Wrigley and R. S. Schofield, *The Population History of England, 1541–1871: A Reconstruction*. Cambridge: Cambridge University Press, 1989, p. 187.

shared a climate similar to the mother country, the southern colonies and the West Indies did not. The arrival of malaria from the Mediterranean early in the colonization period guaranteed a difficult adjustment for coastal populations from Maryland to Jamaica. It has been estimated that the crude death rate in these temperate to tropical regions was double that experienced by the New England colonists in the 17th century.[5] But these were not the only mortality rates that the new immigrants suffered. In the 17th century, shipboard mortality for immigrants in the Atlantic crossing was on the order of 10%,[6] probably just below that of the slaves crossing from Africa at this time, which was on the order of 15%.[7] At the same time, in the southern and West Indian colonies there was an initial "seasoning" mortality that could be almost as high as the mortality suffered in the Atlantic crossing.[8] In contrast, new immigrants in the middle and northern colonies apparently experienced little mortality in their first year of residence.[9] It has been estimated that some 15,000 migrants arrived in Virginia between 1625 and 1640 but that the population increased by less than 7,000 in this period, implying a negative growth rate.[10]

---

[5] Henry A. Gemery, "Emigration from the British Isles to the New World: 1630–1700: Inferences from Colonial Populations," *Research in Economic History* 5 (1980), pp. 179–231.

[6] Gemery, "Emigration from the British Isles," p. 187.

[7] Herbert S. Klein and Stanley L. Engerman, "Long Term Trends in African Mortality in the Transatlantic Slave Trade," *Slavery and Abolition* 18, no.1 (April 1997), pp. 59–71; and Herbert S. Klein, Stanley L. Engerman, Robin Haines, and Ralph Schlomowitz, "Transoceanic Mortality: The Slave Trade in Comparative Perspective," *William and Mary Quarterly*, LVIII, no. 1 (January 2001), pp. 93–118.

[8] Henry A. Gemery, "The White Population of the Colonial United States, 1670–1790," in Michael R. Haines and Richard H. Steckel, eds., *A Population History of North America* (Cambridge: Cambridge University Press, 2000), pp. 168–70. On the high death rates of recent immigrants in the South in the 18th century, see John Duffy, "Eighteenth Century Carolina Health Conditions," *The Journal of Southern History*, 18, no. 3 (August 1952), pp. 289–302.

[9] Gemery, "Emigration from the British Isles," p. 190.

[10] Edmund S. Morgan, *American Slavery, American Freedom: The Ordeal of Colonial Virginia*. Boston: W. W. Norton, 1975, p. 159.

Although figures are partial and mostly estimates, there now seems to be general agreement that the crude death rate in the Southern Colonies in the 17th century was in the range of 40 deaths per 1,000 residents, compared with a range of 20 deaths per 1,000 in rural New England for a population of roughly the same age structure.[11] Equally, the fertility rate was somewhat lower and the infant mortality higher in the southern colonies compared to those of New England. In the latter, the birth rate was probably in the range of 40 births per 1,000 resident population and probably much lower in the South. Despite southern women having earlier marriages than those in New England, higher infant and maternal mortality in the South reduced their crude fertility rates to well below those of the northerners, so that child-to-women ratios were consistently lower in the South than in the middle colonies and New England.[12] In the late 17th century in the Tidewater, Virginia, county of Middlesex, average life expectancy at age 20 was 16 years less for men than in late 17th century Andover, Massachusetts. It was even worse for women, being over 22 years less for Virginia women than for women in the New England community of Andover.[13]

Given these two distinct American death and birth patterns, it is assumed (in the lowest bound estimate) that natural growth per annum in the first half of the 17th century was negative at −2.3% per annum for the South, compared to a lower bound estimate of a positive growth of +2.3% per annum for New England in the same period.[14] If the southern colonies could not initially maintain themselves through natural growth, then the only alternative for growth was through immigration. Given the increasing wealth of the southern colonies, compared to the relative poverty of New England, it

---

[11] Gemery, "The White Population of the Colonial United States," pp. 166–67.

[12] Gemery, "Emigration from the British Isles,"and "The White Population of the Colonial United States."

[13] Darrett B. Rutman and Anita H. Rutman, "Of Agues and Fevers: Malaria in the Early Chesapeake," *William and Mary Quarterly*, 3rd ser., 33, no. 1 (January 1976), p. 48.

[14] Gemery, "The White Population of the Colonial United States," Table 5.7, p. 167.

was this zone that attracted the majority of indentured servants, who in·turn made up the overwhelming majority of English and European migrants to North America throughout the 17th century. Starting with a population base of 1,000 persons in 1609, by the 1690s these southern colonies had a resident population of 92,000 persons.[15] Despite the first half century of negative natural growth, the southern population expanded throughout this period primarily because of the migration of something like 132,000 Englishmen to this region in the 17th century.[16]

In contrast, the New England colonies received only 30,000 migrants in this same period, and of these some 20,000 migrated out, leaving a net migrant pool of just 10,000 persons. Nevertheless, because of its lower death and higher fertility rates, the New England population reached the figure of 86,000 persons by the end of the century, most of these added through natural increase. The middle colonies stood between these two extremes, experiencing a similar natural growth rate per annum of over 2% and a steady supply of migrants, so that by the 1690s it had a resident population of 32,400 persons and had absorbed some 29,000 migrants over the course of the century.[17]

Despite its even worse health environment, the British West Indies also drew large numbers of British immigrants in the 17th century. By the 1660s, when the continental colonies numbered about 57,000 white resident population, the British West Indies contained 47,000 English (see Graph 2.1).[18] If the West Indies and the southern colonies were such a negative demographic environment, the question remains as to why they were able to attract the majority of the English who migrated to the New World in the 17th century.

[15] John J. McCusker and Russell R. Menard, *The Economy of British America, 1607–1789* (Chapel Hill: University of North Carolina Press 1985), Tables 6.4 and 8.1, pp. 136, 172.

[16] Gemery, "The White Population of the Colonial United States," Table 5.8, p. 171.

[17] Gemery, "The White Population of the Colonial United States," Tables 5.1 and 5.8, pp. 151, 171.

[18] McCusker and Menard, *The Economy of British America*, Tables 5.1, 6.4, and 7.2, pp. 103, 136, 154.

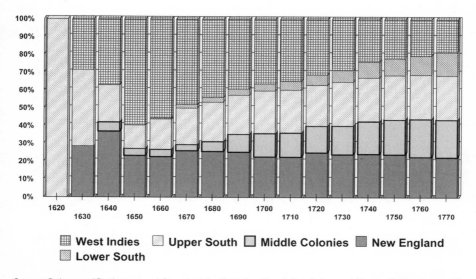

Source: Galenson, "Settlement and Growth of the Colonies: Population, Labor and Economic Development," Table 4.1.

Graph 2.1: Relative Share of Total American Population by British Colonies, 1620–1770.

The answer is obviously economic opportunity.[19] In their search for a viable export to pay for the colonies, Barbados and Virginia had experimented with a host of crops before finally settling on the native American plant of tobacco, which was a lightweight export that soon found a ready market throughout Europe. With the increasing efficiency of Virginia as a producer of tobacco, Barbados would slowly abandon tobacco production, and by the second half of the 17th century would turn toward sugar. In this it was aided by the Dutch who brought the technology, marketing skills, and credit to enable the Barbados planters to start producing sugar with both English

[19] A recent estimate of the relative wealth of free white persons in the various American colonies in 1774 suggests that those in the West Indies were worth 27 times as much as those in New England and those in the Southern Colonies possessed almost two and a half times that of the average of £ (sterling) 38 per capita wealth owned by New Englanders. T. G. Burnard, "'Prodigious Riches': The Wealth of Jamaica Before the American Revolution," *Economic History Review* 54, no. 3 (2001), Table 5, p. 520.

indentured laborers and more and more with African slaves. The expulsion of the Dutch from Pernambuco in 1654 was a catalyst for the transformation of both the English and French West Indies into sugar plantation economies, as the Dutch proved to be the crucial intermediaries enabling these islands to develop the new technology.

For most of the 17th century, the prime labor force used to develop these and all other export crops were indentured servants. The northern Europeans who followed the Iberians to America were unable to develop an extensive Indian slave labor force on the Portuguese model, let alone the complex free Indian labor arrangements developed by the Spaniards. Nor did they have access to precious metals to pay for imported slave labor. But unlike the Iberians of the 16th century, they did have a cheaper and more willing pool of European laborers to exploit, especially in the crisis period of the 17th century. But even for these workers, the costs of transport to America were too high. Subsidizing that passage through selling of one's labor to shippers who in turn sold their indentured contracts to American employers became the major form of colonization in the first half century of northern European settlement in America. The English and the French were the primary users of indentured labor and they were helped by a pool of workers faced by low wages within the European economy. But the rapid growth of the English economy in the last quarter of the century generated a more competitive labor market in Europe and a consequent increase in the costs of indentured laborers to American markets. Thus, the English and the French would also turn to African slaves to sustain their export colonies. With the help of Dutch slave traders who provided both the slaves and the credit to pay for them, the British and French began to bring African slaves into the same regions that had been so attractive to indentured workers, the so-called staple colonies. By 1700, this slave labor force had increased to 115,000 in the West Indies and 31,000 in the British Mainland colonies, the majority of whom could be found in the southern colonies.[20]

---

[20] McClusker & Menard, *The Economy of British America*, Table 7.2, p. 154.

Despite the beginnings of a major African slave trade, the dominant flow of servile labor to North America remained indentured workers from England, Scotland, Ireland, and Germany. It is estimated that one half to two thirds of the European migrants to America before 1700 came as indentured workers.[21] This would mean that of the 160,000 Europeans who crossed the Atlantic to continental North America in the 17th century,[22] between 80,000 and 106,000 came as indentured laborers whose contracts were sold to local free farmers and planters, a figure probably double that of the African slave arrivals during this period.[23] The majority of the indentured in the 17th century went to the Chesapeake Bay, South Carolina, Georgia, and the West Indies, that is, to the richest agricultural regions,[24] and one estimate holds that 75% of all immigrants arriving in Virginia in this century came as indentured servants.[25]

Despite the increasing arrival of Africans and the betterment of wages in England and Europe by the end of the 17th century, this flow of indentured laborers remained steady well into the 18th century. Although there were significant changes in European origins and American receiving markets, this servant migration did not come to an end until the first decades of the 19th century. It is estimated that over half of the some 307,000 European immigrants arriving in British North America from 1700 until the Revolution

[21] David W. Galenson, "The Rise and Fall of Indentured Servitude in the Americas: An Economic Analysis," *The Journal of Economic History* 44, no. 1 (March 1984), p. 1.

[22] Gemery, "The White Population of the Colonial United States," p. 170.

[23] Klein, *The Atlantic Slave Trade*, appendix tables.

[24] Galenson, "The Rise and Fall of Indentured Servitude," p. 10; and James Horn, "Servant Emigration to the Chesapeake in the Seventeenth Century," in Thad W. Tate and David L. Ammerman, eds., *The Chesapeake in the Seventeenth Century*. Boston: W. W. Norton, 1979, pp. 51–95.

[25] Galenson, "The Rise and Fall of Indentured Servitude," p. 9. According to a Virginia census, in 1625, it was estimated that 42% of the resident population was made up of indentured servants, and in Jamaica, such indentured servants were still over half the white population as late as 1730. Robert V. Wells, *The Population of the British Colonies Before 1776. A Survey of the Census Data*. Princeton: Princeton University Press, 1975, pp. 162, 197.

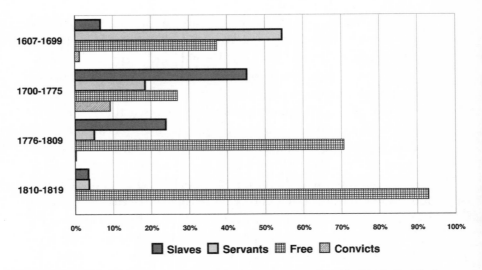

Sources: Fogelman, "From Slaves, Convicts and Servants," Table 1 and Klein, *The Atlantic Slave Trade,* Table A2.

Graph 2.2: Relative Share of Slaves, Convicts, Indentured Servants, and Free Persons among Immigrants Arriving to British North America, 1607–1819.

were indentured laborers, which would have meant that something like 156,000 of them arrived in the period to 1775.[26] Although outpaced by the 251,000 slaves who arrived from Africa to British North America in this same period, the indentured were still a very important immigrant group (see Graph 2.2).[27] But there was also a major change in the flow of immigrants from Europe, as fewer and fewer came as indentured and ever greater numbers were self-paying free immigrants. This steady increase in the volume of free immigrants, along with the arrivals of indentured, meant that despite the

[26] Aaron Fogelman, "From Slaves, Convicts and Servants to Free Passengers: The Transformation of Immigration in the Era of the American Revolution," *Journal of American History* 85, no. 1 (June 1998), Table A3, p. 71; and Aaron Fogelman, "Migrations to the Thirteen British North American Colonies, 1700–1775: New Estimates," *Journal of Interdisciplinary History* XXII, no. 4 (Spring 1992), Table 1, p. 698.

[27] I am here using my lower estimates of slave arrivals rather than the higher rates used by Fogelman.

booming slave trade, Africans represented only about 45% of all immigrants arriving in British North America in this period.[28] Although African slaves replaced indentured workers completely in the West Indies and were also rapidly replacing them on most of the southern plantations, indentured laborers remained important to British North America for most of the 18th century. Because of African slave arrivals, fewer European servile workers now went to the southern colonies, but the Chesapeake remained a major importer, to which was now added the province of Pennsylvania, which proved especially attractive to English and German indentured workers in the 18th century.[29]

Because age, sex, and skills influenced the length of indentured contracts, it was inevitable that young male workers were the shippers' preferred group. But the demographic makeup of these indentured workers changed over time. In the 17th century, it is estimated that under a quarter of the indentured migrants were women, a figure that dropped to under 10% in the 18th century, possibly because of the increasing balance of the sexes in the resident American population and a concomitant lesser demand for women among the purchasers of indentured contracts. The age breakdowns remained the same, with two-thirds of the men and women shipped being between 15 and 25 years of age, with very few below the age of 10 or above the age of 40.[30] These age and sex distortions among the indentured immigrants would have the effect of increasing the economically active population in the New World and reducing the potential reproduction of this arriving cohort because of the relative lack of women. There were, however, changes in skills and occupations. From the 1680s to 1775, the indentured workers were increasingly more skilled and less agricultural.[31] This, in turn, seems to reflect the

[28] Klein, *The Atlantic Slave Trade*, appendix tables.
[29] Galenson, "The Rise and Fall of Indentured Servitude," p. 12. Also see Sharon V. Salinger, *"To Serve Well and Faithfully: Labor and Indentured Servants in Pennsylvania, 1682–1800.* Cambridge: Cambridge University Press, 1987.
[30] David W. Galenson, *White Servitude in Colonial America, An Economic Analysis.* Cambridge: Cambridge University Press, 1981, Chapter 2.
[31] Galenson, *White Servitude in Colonial America*, p. 63.

growing domination of agricultural and unskilled laboring positions by African slaves in the middle and southern colonies.

Although the 18th century saw the increasing importance of Europeans paying their own transportation costs, these free migrants still represented just under half of all nonslave migrants and less than a fifth of all immigrants coming to America. Clearly, the American demand for workers exceeded the European supply of free workers, and this continued dependence of British North America on a white and black servile workforce accounted for the fact that over 80% of all immigrants coming to America from 1700 to 1775 did not pay for their transport.

This same high American demand for labor also had its affect on the demographic structure of even the free immigrants of New England. For those who had access to land, primarily those going to New England and the middle colonies, the tendency was for them to marry earlier and have more children than their contemporaries in England.[32] In New England, the mean age of first marriage for men was 25–26 and for women 22–23 years of age, both two years earlier than both sexes married in England at this time. This resulted in a completed family size of six to eight children, compared to a 17th-century English norm of five children.[33] In British North America in the first generations, and especially in the New England and middle colonies, the European family model, which dominated most of the regions of western Europe, prevailed. This involved a tight control over fertility outside of marriage, with resulting low rates of illegitimate births, and the quick response of age of marriage to negative economic conditions. This had enabled Europeans to respond to food and other crises by cutting down fertility through the combination of raising the age of marriage and withdrawing women from

---

[32] For a good summary of the comparative English and American regional 17th-and 18th-century age of marriage data, see Robert V. Wells, "The Population of England's Colonies in America: Old English or New Americans?" *Population Studies* 46 (1992), Table 1, pp. 88–9.

[33] Gemery, "The White Population of the Colonial United States," p. 152. Also see the comparative table on fertility given in Wells, "The Population of England's Colonies in America: Old English or New Americans?" Table 2, pp. 92–3.

the marriage market altogether as spinsters and nuns. Given their late marriages by world standards, the Europeans also had among the highest known marital fertility rates. Thus, the reduction of the age of marriage, due in this case to access to land in 17th century New England, led to higher fertility than in the mother country.

But New Englanders also experimented with new methods of extended family organization in order to control labor. In the farming community of Andover, Massachusetts, in the mid 17th century, the second-generation age at marriage rose as parents delayed the marriage of their children, especially of their sons, in order to tie their children to their own homesteads. Starting as a nucleated village with open fields surrounding the core population, Andover quickly turned into the later dominant model of rural America – separate and widely dispersed farmsteads with a weak village center. Parents used their control over farming lands, a system of partible inheritance to all sons, and delayed granting of land titles to maintain the labor of their sons on their home farms. In this system, children of the second generation tended to marry a few years later than their parents and establish new homes on their male parent's land. Such new households, in this extended household model, were granted use of the original family lands but did not receive effective title until the parents had died, thus ensuring that their labor was still at the disposition of the original paternal head of household until his death. This was a new and original response to the classic American problem of high cost labor and abundant cheap lands.[34]

Although the Andover response may have been unusual, there is little question that the earlier New England marriage rates began to change at the end of the 17th century. Slowly, the age of marriage began to rise for both women and men and approach the European

---

[34] Philip J. Greven, Jr., "Family Structure in Seventeenth-Century Andover, Massachusetts," *William and Mary Quarterly*, 3d ser., 23, (no. 2) (April 1966), pp. 234–56, and his book, *Four Generations: Population, Land, and Family in Colonial Andover, Massachusetts*. Ithaca, N.Y.: Cornell University Press, 1970. Also see Daniel Scott Smith, "Parental Power and Marriage Patterns: An Analysis of Historical Trends in Hingham, Massachusetts," *Journal of Marriage and the Family* 35, no. 3 (August 1973), pp. 419–28.

norms.[35] This, of course, began to affect natural growth rates in New England, which slowed in the later part of the 17th century and the beginning of the 18th century. This progressive rise in the age of marriage, given the continued constraint on fertility outside of marriage and possibly the decline of fertility within marriages, meant that the size of families was also declining by one or two children over this period.[36] Initially, this slow decline was masked by a rising rate of completed marital fertility in the South due to a declining level of mortality.

Thus, compared to western European populations in this period, the British North American populations of the 17th and 18th centuries showed a surprisingly rapid rate of natural growth of the resident population. Whereas birth and death rates in Europe during most of the 17th century were fairly equal, resulting in a stagnant or very modest population growth, this was not the case in America. In the 17th century especially, death rates in rural New England communities were much lower than those in Europe. Whereas birth rates were only slightly higher in America than in Europe at this time, death rates were far lower – almost half the 40 per thousand rate common to most 17th century European agricultural villages. In Plymouth, Andover, and Ipswich, all agricultural villages of New England that had annual growth rates of over 2% per annum in this period, death rates tended to be quite low for both adults and children. These death rates also varied seasonally (winter being the worst months) rather than in an episodic and/or abrupt pattern, which is a

---

[35] For a summary of these ages at first marriage by sex, see Robert V. Wells, "Quaker Marriage Patterns in a Colonial Perspective," *William and Mary Quarterly*, Third Series, 29, no.3 (July 1972), Table 8, p. 429.

[36] It has been argued that rising ages of first marriage for women accounts for only part of the declining fertility, and that some constraints on fertility within marriage was also occurring in this period, especially toward the end of the 18th century. This argument is based on a sample of Quaker marriage cohorts in the Middle Colonies during the course of the 18th century. See Robert V. Wells, "Family Size and Fertility Control in Eighteenth-Century America: A Study of Quaker Families," *Population Studies* 25, no. 1 (March 1971), pp. 73–82.

clear indication that famine or epidemic crises were not influencing these rates to any serious extent.[37]

These low death rates initially were confined to New England and possibly the Middle Atlantic colonies and were not evident in the other areas of British North America. Both Virginia and Maryland in the 17th and early 18th centuries had far fewer children per household and far greater numbers of orphans than were recorded in these New England rural communities.[38] These smaller household sizes existed despite some evidence that marriage ages for women were much younger here than in rural New England.[39] The death rate in Virginia may have been as high as 50 per thousand even as late as 1700,[40] and there is little question that its child and young adult mortality was much higher than that experienced in New England.[41] Without question, death rates in the southern colonies, if anything, were equal to or exceeded contemporary rates of European rural communities. Clearly, malaria and other health factors, such as

[37] Greven, "Family Structure in Seventeenth Century Andover"; Susan L. Norton, "Population Growth in Colonial America: A Study of Ipswich, Massachusetts," *Population Studies* 25, no. 3 (November 1971), pp. 433–52; and the articles by John Demos, "Families in Colonial Bristol, Rhode Island: An Exercise in Historical Demography," *William and Mary Quarterly*, third series, 25, no. 1 (January 1968), pp. 40–57; and "Notes on Life in Plymouth Colony," *William and Mary Quarterly*, 3d ser., 22, no. 2 (April, 1965), pp. 264–86; and his book *A Little Commonwealth: Family Life in Plymouth Colony*. New York: Oxford University Press, 1970.

[38] Irene W. D. Hecht, "The Virginia Muster of 1624/5 as a Source for Demographic History," *William and Mary Quarterly*, 3d ser., 30, no. 1 (January 1973), pp. 65–92; and Darrett B. Rutman and Anita H. Rutman, "'Non-Wives and Sons-in-Law': Parental Death in a Seventeenth Century Virginia County," in Thad W. Tate and David L. Ammerman, eds., *The Chesapeake in the Seventeenth Century*. Boston: W. W. Norton, 1979, pp. 153–82.

[39] Gemery, "The White Population of the Colonial United States," Table 5.2, pp. 153–54; James M. Gallman, "Determinants of Age at Marriage in Colonial Perquimans County, North Carolina," *William and Mary Quarterly*, 3d ser., 39, no. 1 (January, 1982), p. 179.

[40] Gemery, "The White Population of the Colonial United States," p. 159.

[41] Daniel Blake Smith, "Mortality and Family in the Colonial Chesapeake," *Journal of Interdisciplinary History* 8, no. 3 (Winter 1978), pp. 403–27.

seasonal pollution of tidewater water supplies and consequent out-
breaks of amoebic dysentery and typhoid fever,[42] were influential in
creating a pattern in which deaths equaled or exceeded births and
thus guaranteed a stagnant or even negative growth of the resident
population. Thus, the expansion of the population of these southern
colonies in the 17th century was far more dependent on immigration than in New England, which even lost some of its population
to out-migration in the late 17th and 18th centuries and yet grew
rapidly.

Mortality was also quite high in the cities. Here it was common
for mortality to be in the upper 30s or upper 40s per 1,000 residents.
Given their biased age and sex distributions, along with their higher
rates of mortality, it is not surprising that North American cities consistently experienced negative natural growth, a pattern common to
most urban centers of Europe and America in this period. Boston and
Philadelphia in the 18th century both exhibited these high mortality rates, which were at or above contemporary European rural rates,
with Philadelphia having a higher mortality than Boston.[43] Both also
experienced smallpox and other contagious disease epidemics that
often bypassed the rural areas with their low population densities.
But these "urban centers" (generously defined as containing populations of 8,000 or more persons) accounted for only 3% of the national
population in this period.[44]

---

[42] Carville V. Earle, "Environment, Disease and Mortality in Early Virginia," in
Thad W. Tate and David L. Ammerman, eds., *The Chesapeake in the Seventeenth
Century*. Boston: W. W. Norton, 1979, pp. 96–125.

[43] Gemery, "The White Population of the Colonial United States," Table 5.5,
p. 159; Susan E. Klepp, "Revolutionary Bodies: Women and the Fertility Transition in the Mid-Atlantic Region, 1760–1820," *The Journal of American History*
85, no. 3 (December 1998), pp. 910–45; Billy G. Smith, "Death and Life in a
Colonial Immigrant City: A Demographic Analysis of Philadelphia," *Journal of
Economic History* 37, no. 4 (December 1977); see Table 3, p. 871 for her estimates
of the crude death rates for the city in the 18th century.

[44] Campbell Gibson, "The Population in Large Urban Concentrations in the
United States, 1790–1980: A Delineation Using Highly Urbanized Counties (in
Measurement Issues)," *Demography* 24, no. 4 (November 1987), pp. 601–14.

In contrast to Europe, where famine was still common until the middle of the 18th century,[45] in America, abundant land, animal stocks, and food sources guaranteed a relatively stable source of food consumption. In Andover, Massachusetts, in the 17th century, for example, deaths were spread evenly over the entire year, showing the usual highs in winters and lows in the more temperate periods but never indicating the abrupt spikes of deaths due to a harvest crises. Moreover, all studies of heights of colonial North Americans show them to be 7 centimeters taller than the English by the mid-18th century, a key indication of better food consumption. In fact, 18th century North Americans were only 3 centimeters shorter than North Americans born in 1930.[46]

Nevertheless, over time, mortality was on the increase even in the most favored rural areas of New England because of increasing population densities, which facilitated the spread of epidemic diseases. In the first decades of the 18th century, there was an increase in adult and child mortality in New England. In such New England rural communities as Andover and Plymouth, these mortality rates increased in the first half of the 18th century, with a resulting decline in life expectancy. Increasing densities of populations in the older colonies as well as better communications everywhere meant that the rural communities were less isolated from communicable diseases than earlier. Although the small rural communities of New England had escaped the ravages of smallpox and other epidemics that affected the seaport towns of Boston, New York, and Philadelphia throughout most of the 17th century, by the early 18th century, such

---

[45] See the series of articles by Andrew B. Appleby, "Epidemics and Famine in the Little Ice Age," *Journal of Interdisciplinary History* 10, no. 4 (Spring, 1980), pp. 643–63; "The Disappearance of Plague: A Continuing Puzzle," *The Economic History Review*, New Series, 33, no. 2 (May 1980), pp. 161–73; and "Grain Prices and Subsistence Crises in England and France, 1590–1740," *The Journal of Economic History* 39, no. 4 (December 1979), pp. 865–87. On the impact of the Black Death on Europe see Massimo Livi Bacci, *The Population of Europe: A History*. Oxford: Blackwell, 2000, chapter 4.

[46] Richard H. Steckel, "Nutritional Status in the Colonial American Economy," *William and Mary Quarterly*, 3d ser., 56, no. 1 (January 1999), pp. 40–1.

epidemics began to appear with some regularity in the rural areas. Although death rates still did not approach European norms, they were nevertheless higher than those in the earlier periods.[47]

These changes in rural New England death rates had the effect of reducing the differences between the southern and New England rates. At the same time, although mortality differences between these regions remained until well into the 19th century, there was also a decline in southern mortality as populations progressively moved inland away from the tidewater lowlands with their high incidence of disease. In fact, tidewater regions such as Charles Parish in York County, Virginia, continued to remain unhealthy places through the end of the colonial period, with 18th-century life expectancy as low as that of the 17th century.[48] But movement of populations into the highlands and interior brought regional rates downward for the rural south. Urban death rates also slowly began to decline in the late 18th century, although they would not reach national or rural New England levels until the sanitation revolution at the end of the 19th century.

---

[47] Maris A. Vinovskis, *Fertility in Massachusetts from the Revolution to the Civil War.* New York: Academic Press, 1981, p. 26ff. On the patterns of rising mortality from the 17th century to the 18th century and their relationship to population density in the western Massachusetts region, see R. S. Meindl and A. C. Swedlund, "Secular Trends in Mortality in the Connecticut Valley, 1700–1850," *Human Biology* 49, no. 3 (September 1977), pp. 389–414. Also see the discussion on this for several towns in western Massachusetts in Susan L. Norton, "Population Growth in Colonial America: A Study of Ipswich, Massachusetts," *Population Studies* 25, no. 3 (November 1971), pp. 439–43. It should be noted that demographers have found the reported 17th century rates of infants and children to be much too low and have suggested the results are due to underreporting of these deaths, especially in the much cited case of Andover. See George Alter, "Infant and Child Mortality in the United States and Canada," in Alan Bideau, Bertrand Desjardins, and Héctor Pérez Brignoli, eds., *Infant and Child Mortality in the Past.* Oxford: Clarendon Press, 1997, p. 93.

[48] Smith, "Mortality and Family in the Colonial Chesapeake," p. 405; and Darrett B. Rutman and Anita H. Rutman, "Of Agues and Fevers: Malaria in the Early Chesapeake," *William and Mary Quarterly*, 3d ser., 33, no. 1 (January 1976), pp. 31–60.

Although disease was initially a varying factor affecting growth and life expectancy, declining birth rates were not an epiphenomenon, but rather a long-term pattern that would soon have a profound impact on the growth of the American population. Higher ages of marriage by the end of the 17th and beginning of the 18th century would lead to declining birth rates everywhere in the continental colonies. Initially, the impact of these declining birth rates was tempered by the progressive decline of mortality rates in the south. Although natural growth rates declined somewhat in the 18th century, they were still quite positive for the region as a whole. It has been estimated that more than four-fifths of the growth of the continental population at the end of the 18th century was still accounted for by natural internal growth despite the continuing heavy flow of European and African immigrants.[49]

There was also an ongoing shift of resident population as both immigrant populations and coastal native-born populations moved to the newly opening frontiers. As England expanded its power after the 1660s into the middle colonies through conquest of the Dutch and Swedish settlements in New York and the new lands of Pennsylvania, a whole new region was opened up for expansion. Especially after the formal establishment of a Quaker-led government in the latter colony in the 1680s, Pennsylvania became a major zone of German and English indentured and free immigration because of the abundance of available land. Something like 100,000 German emigrants would reach the colony by the 1770s. The region south of Virginia would also become a new center for population expansion and economic growth in the second half of the 17th century. Beginning in the 1650s colonists from Virginia began to open up the Carolinas, which became a separate colony in the 1680s. By the early part of the 18th century this region along the southern coastline – divided into two colonies in 1710 – was a thriving plantation

[49] Michael R. Haines, "The White Population of the United States, 1790–1920," in Michael R. Haines and Richard H. Steckel, *A Population History of North America*. New York: Cambridge University Press, 2000, Table 8.2, p. 315.

economy producing rice and indigo based on African slave labor.[50] Meanwhile, movement of colonists from South Carolina slowly pushed southward against the Spanish missions, and a determined British royal effort enabled the establishment of a new colony in Georgia in the 1730s. Although initially founded as a proprietary colony with a prohibition of slavery, the colony, by the late 18th century, was fully a part of the southern plantation slave labor system and with the Carolinas formed the new and expanding Lower South Atlantic colonies.

Whereas to 1699, an estimated 198,000 immigrants, free and slave, convict and indentured, had arrived in British North America, the figure jumped to an estimated 586,000 of such immigrants in the period from 1700 to 1775. This migration also became ever more African and, over time, the slave trade accounted for an increasing share of immigrants, going from less than a quarter in the 17th century to just under half in the 18th century.[51] Given the increasing level of economic activity of the continental colonies, these Africans, who formerly had come from the West Indies, now came more and more directly from Africa itself.[52]

There was also a great deal of movement by native-born Americans. Both in the last decades of the 17th century and in most decades of the 18th century, more New Englanders left their region than overseas immigrants entered it – this at a time when both the Middle Atlantic and southern colonies were absorbing ever more immigrants from abroad and from other continental regions (see Graph 2.3). Thus, from the 1670s to the 1770s, New England lost some 42,000 persons to out-migration. New England, in which

---

[50] Russell R. Menard, "Financing the Lowcountry Export Boom: Capital and Growth in Early South Carolina," *William and Mary Quarterly*, 3d ser., 51, no. 4 (October 1994), pp. 659–76.

[51] Fogelman, "From Slaves, Convicts and Servants to Free Passengers," Table 1, p. 44.

[52] On the changing origins of the arriving slaves in Virginia, see Herbert S. Klein, *The Middle Passage: Comparative Studies in the Atlantic Slave Trade*. Princeton: Princeton University Press, 1978, Chapter 6; and an addendum to this material in Herbert S. Klein, "Slaves and Shipping in Eighteenth Century Virginia," *Journal of Interdisciplinary History* V (Winter 1975), pp. 383–411.

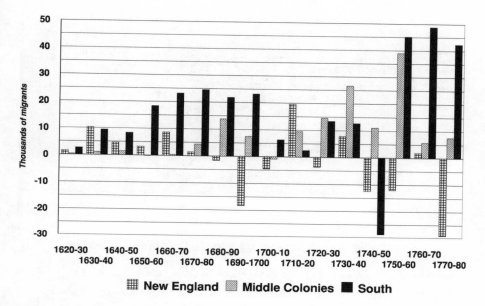

Source: Gemery, "The White Population of the Colonial United States, 1670–1790," Table 5.8.

Graph 2.3: Estimated Net Migration to and from the Regions of North America by Decade, 1620–1780.

resided half of the British North American population in the 1670s, a century later contained just a third of the population of the future republic.[53] In contrast, the Middle Atlantic colonies, which grew from less than 8% to a third of the total continental population in this same century, had a net addition of 140,000 immigrants, and the southern colonies retained 235,000 immigrants in this period – although because of much higher mortality, their share of the total continental population actually declined from 40% to 34% (see Graph 2.4).[54]

There would also be significant internal migration within each region. In New England, New Hampshire, and Connecticut steadily grew at the expense of the once-dominant Massachusetts (see

[53] Gemery, "The White Population of the Colonial United States," p. 171, Table 5.8.

[54] Gemery, "The White Population of the Colonial United States," p. 171, Table 5.8.

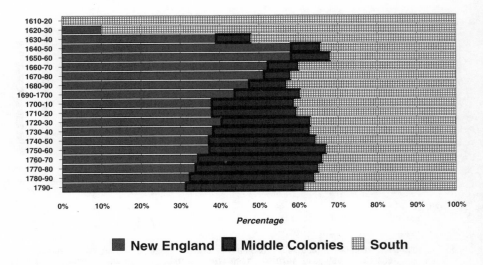

Source: Gemery, "The White Population of the Colonial United States, 1670–1790," Table 5.8.

Graph 2.4: Relative Share of British North American Population by Region by Decade, 1610–1790.

Graph 2.5). In the Middle Atlantic colonies, Pennsylvania, which grew rapidly in the first half of the 18th century along with New Jersey, saw its share of population eaten away by the growth of New York in the second half of the century (see Graph 2.6). As for the Southern Atlantic colonies, the once-dominant Chesapeake colonies of Virginia and Maryland lost ground to the Carolinas and Georgia as the century progressed (see Graph 2.7). In many cases, people moved from the more settled zones of the state with their increasingly restricted access to resources to the more open resources of the frontier, progressively moving to the western parishes of the coastal states and beyond the colonial frontier into new territories. Most estimates suggest an increasing concentration of wealth and resources in the older coastal regions over the course of the late 17th and 18th centuries. This would have an influence on marriage and fertility rates and also be a factor in promoting out-migration. The continued availability of a relatively open frontier with cheap lands and ever improving communications was the major pull factor complementing the push factor of increasing stratification in the older regions.

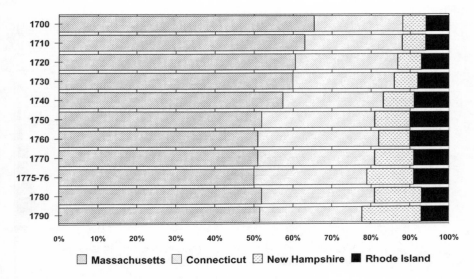

Source: Potter, "The Growth of Population in America,1700–1860," Table 1.

Graph 2.5: Changing Share of New England Population by Colony, 1700–1790.

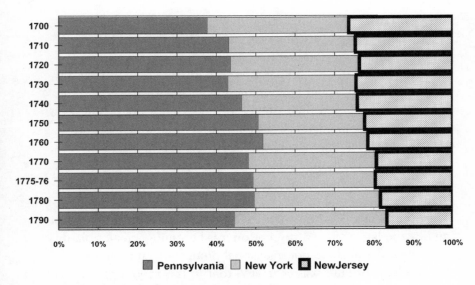

Source: Potter, "The Growth of Population in America, 1700–1860," Table 1.

Graph 2.6: Changing Share of Middle Atlantic Population by Colony, 1700–1790.

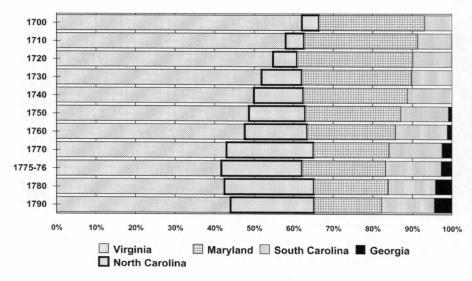

Source: Potter, "The Growth of Population in America, 1700–1860," Table 1.

Graph 2.7: Changing Share of Southern Population by Colony, 1700–1790.

In turn, the international migrations were also related to varying economic growth within America, but in a different way. Given that until the end of the 18th century slave and servile migrations were more important than free migration, the relative economic wealth of a given region would profoundly influence both the type of immigrants arriving and their numbers. The poorer zones were little attractive to any immigrants, the plantation zones were more attractive to the forced migrants and those who came under indentures, and the increasingly prosperous and more open lands of the Middle Atlantic colonies were especially attractive to the free immigrants.

In the South Atlantic colonies, first rice was added to tobacco, and by the late 18th century, cotton was becoming a major plantation crop. All of these nontraditional products found a ready market in Great Britain. It is estimated that in the 1769–1772 period, the value of exports of the southern colonies, over three-fourths of which went to Great Britain and Ireland, was £1.6 million, almost twice what the other two regions produced. In fact, the new Lower South Atlantic colonies of the Carolinas and Georgia alone produced more exports than either the Middle Atlantic or New England colonies. Thus, it is no surprise that despite initially much higher mortality rates for these regions, which even in the 18th century were less healthy than those of the other regions, the southern colonies continued to be attractive to immigrants as well as the prime destination for African slaves. The middle colonies were growing rapidly as they attracted more free immigrants to their extensive fertile lands, which in turn enabled them to produce surplus wheat and other grains not only for the market in the West Indies but also for a growing foodstuffs market in southern Europe, which now took one-third of its exports.[55] For New England, with its poorer soils and shorter growing seasons, the major development would be through its seaports and merchants who would begin to tie the West Indian markets to those of the continent, often in ships built in New England. But these developments were insufficient to attract major flows of immigrants, especially after the close of serious religious migrations in the mid-17th century.

This difference in exports was also reflected in basic differences in personal wealth in these regions. Clearly, the plantation regions were wealthier than the New England or Middle Atlantic colonies. Total wealth per capita for free persons was estimated in the Southern colonies in 1774 at some £93 as compared to £46 for the Middle colonies and just £38 for New England. Moreover, none of these regions could compare with Jamaica, which produced £1,200 per free person in the same period.[56] But in terms of total wealth per capita, the plantation zones, with their slave labor force and larger production units, were wealthier than the family farms of the center and north, although even here the plantation economies of the West Indies were significantly wealthier than those of the mainland Southern colonies.

---

[55] Galenson, "Settlement and Growth of the Colonies," Tables 4.10 and 4.11 pp. 198–99.

[56] Galenson, "Settlement and Growth of the Colonies," Table 4.9, p. 195.

The early 18th century saw a population growing both by high natural rates and by an ever-growing immigration of free and servile labor such that continental British North America finally became the single largest region of the English colonial American empire, reaching an estimated 1.6 million persons by 1770.[57] Moreover, despite the steady growth of the African slave population in the richer West Indies, by the 1770s, just over half the 890,000 African slaves found in the British American empire were resident in the British North American colonies. In turn, the postindependence distribution of these slaves was already very evident in the colonial period. Of the 456,000 estimated British North American slaves, only 11% resided in the middle colonies or New England, the rest were to be found in the upper and lower southern colonies.[58]

What is impressive about this growth of the North American slave population was that it was now based on a positive natural growth of the resident slave population. By the 1770s, the slave trade to North America was reaching its height but was then bringing in only some 5,000 Africans per annum to the ports of North America. But this flow of slaves would not have been sufficient to account for the 456,000 slaves who resided in the continental colonies at this time if the initial negative growth rates had been maintained. Although the Africans in the 17th and early 18th century had experienced the same if not higher mortality than experienced by the whites going to the southern colonies, as they too moved inland their mortality rates began to drop and their fertility rates began to exceed their death rates, giving rise to a steady increase of population. These higher birth rates brought a more balanced sex ratio to the slave population and in turn guaranteed that the native-born slaves would soon outnumber the African arrivals.

The Maryland slave population to 1730, for example, was overwhelmingly African, male, and adult and was clearly a population

---

[57] According to McClusker and Menard, the number was 2.1 million, but 1.6 million according to Gemery, "The White Population of the Colonial United States." Table 5.10, p. 178.

[58] Galenson, "Settlement and Growth of the Colonies," Table 4.3, p. 172.

that had a negative growth rate.[59] It has been estimated that this was the same in Virginia to 1730, but that after that date, the slave population began to experience positive growth rates. These rates, in turn, increased the ratio of native born, children, and women, all of which guaranteed an ever-increasing growth of the resident population. Slave women tended to have their first conceptions while still in their teens and quickly moved to the North European system of breastfeeding, reducing lactation to one year from the typical African pattern of two years. This, in turn, had a major effect on reducing the spacing between children, thus increasing their completed fertility rates.[60] The average number of children produced by resident slave women was about six children, a rate close to that of the modern developing world rates of pretransition populations.[61] Thus, despite the decline or stagnation of the movement of Africans into the colony over the course of the 18th century, the resident slave population began to increase in the second half of the century at an extraordinary natural growth rate of 2.5% per annum, most of which was accounted for by American births.[62]

Although many slave populations in the Americas would experience positive natural growth once the impact of the African immigration, with its predominance of males and adults, had declined, none grew as fast as the North American slave population after 1750. With manumission becoming less common as time went on, there was also less loss of population to the free population. At the same time, the increasing restraints on births felt by free women was absent from the slave population, which was encouraged to maintain high birth rates. In fact, the slave population, by the end of the colonial

[59]   Russell R. Menard, "The Maryland Slave Population, 1658 to 1730: A Demographic Profile of Blacks in Four Counties," *William and Mary Quarterly*, 3d ser., 32, no. 1 (January 1975), pp. 29–54.
[60]   Herbert S. Klein and Stanley Engerman, "Fertility Differentials Between Slaves in the United States and the British West Indies: A Note on Lactation Practices and Their Implications," *William and Mary Quarterly*, XXXV, no. 2 (April 1978), 357–74.
[61]   Allan Kulikoff, "A 'Prolific' People: Black Population Growth in the Chesapeake Colonies, 1700–1790," *Southern Studies* (Winter 1977), p. 408.
[62]   Kulikoff, "A 'Prolific' People," Table 7, p. 413.

period, clearly had reached child–women ratios that were unusual everywhere else in the Americas.

Just as the slave trade was reaching its height in this period, the indentured servant trade was slowly disappearing. Whereas indentured and convict workers made up over half of the nonslave immigrations in the first half of the 18th century, by the last decades, their numbers were declining and their characteristics were changing. Whereas the majority of indentured workers were adult males in the height of the trade, by the last quarter of the 18th century, the majority were women and children. Moreover, the supplementary trade in redemption servant contracts, which were those arranged at the time of landing by immigrants who could not pay their transport, was declining and prepaid or remittance contracts were becoming the norm. Although there was a temporary boom in indentured contracts in the late 1810s just after the end of the Napoleonic wars, the trade was over by 1820. The prime cause of the demise of this once important trade was the decline of the Europeans willing to enter this market. By the early 19th century, there were few arriving immigrants who could neither pay for their own passage nor obtain a prepaid ticket from relatives in America, especially as passage costs after 1830 began a long-term decline in the increasingly active Atlantic shipping trade.[63]

This growth in population was accompanied by a steady growth in wealth in all regions. The latest estimates for the colonial period suggest that per capita wealth was increasing at a steady but moderate rate of between 0.3% to 0.5% per annum,[64] thus keeping ahead of the phenomenal growth of population, which was increasing naturally and through immigration at over 2.5% per annum in this period.[65] Although wealth per capita was still less than a third of the contemporary English rate,[66] it is evident that the distribution of income was.

---

[63] Farley Grubb, "The End of European Immigrant Servitude in the United States: An Economic Analysis of Market Collapse, 1772–1835," *The Journal of Economic History* 54, no. 4 (December 1994), pp. 794–824.

[64] Galenson, "Settlement and Growth of the Colonies," p. 207.

[65] "The White Population of the Colonial United States," Table 5.8.

[66] Galenson, "Settlement and Growth of the Colonies," pp. 190, 192.

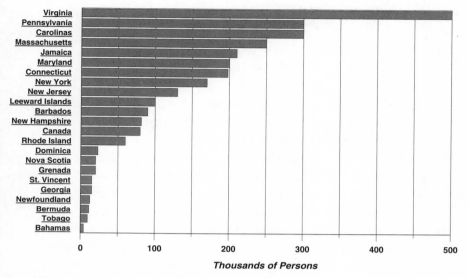

Source: Wells, *The Population of the British Colonies*, Table VII-5.

Graph 2.8: Estimated Population of the British Colonies in America in 1775.

much better in the British North American colonies than in Great Britain. In terms of nutrition and education, the colonies were much better places in which to live, with probably a much higher standard of living than the mother country. In both the 17th and 18th centuries, the overwhelming majority of British North American colonial males were literate and were more literate than contemporary Englishman in the home country.[67] Moreover, by the 18th century the literacy rates in the middle and upper southern colonies quickly approached those of New England and were still above those of contemporary England.[68] Although education levels were the highest in the New England colonies, the height of recruits in the French and Indian wars indicated that the recruits from the southern and middle colonies were taller than those from New England. This would

---

[67] Galenson estimates 75% New England male literacy in the 17th century and 90% in the 18th century compared to an English rate in the late 18th century of 65%.

[68] Galenson, "Settlement and Growth of the Colonies," p. 193.

suggest that nutrition in the southern and middle Colonies was better than that in New England, most probably a reflection of the higher levels of wealth among the free persons of the South.[69]

By the end of the colonial period, the British North American colonies were fully settled along the Atlantic Coast and the local population had made major inroads westward everywhere from New England to the Lower South (see Graph 2.8). The economy of each region was growing, although at different rates, and the level of exports to Europe was increasing. Moreover, an internal market was now evolving that absorbed a large share of local production of foodstuffs and simple manufactures. The increasing wealth of the region was attracting ever more immigrants from across the Atlantic. By the last decades of the 18th century, this immigration was changing as free workers were replacing indentured servants. Thus, the Revolution of 1776 would give birth to a rapidly expanding and economically dynamic republic.

---

[69] Galenson, "Settlement and Growth of the Colonies," p. 202.

CHAPTER THREE

THE EARLY REPUBLIC TO 1860

The first seventy years of the new republic brought some very basic changes in the levels of fertility and mortality from those that had evolved in the 17th and 18th centuries. By 1800, a two-century-long pattern of declining fertility began, with each generation of women producing ever fewer children from the extraordinarily high rates of the late colonial period. At the same time, there was probably a rise in mortality rates, or at least some very sharp shifts, with no clear trends in annual mortality rates until well after the Civil War. There were even some clear indications of malnutrition in the immediate pre-Civil War period, a paradoxical finding given the steady and dramatic growth of the national population. There were also profound changes in migration in this period as the Atlantic slave trade ended in 1808 and the beginnings of mass European immigration to North America began to occur after 1840. It is the causes and consequences of these various factors that I examine in this chapter on the early republic to 1860.

The new republic of the United States began with a census and promised to maintain a periodical population count as part of its normal government operations. Thus began one of the oldest systematic censuses in World History, the decennial counting of the population of the United States. In the period of the 1770s to the 1780s, the political leaders of all the colonies came to the realization that a national census was needed. The movement for independence in the 1770s was accompanied by a major debate on the form that the new postcolonial republican government would take. The Articles of Confederation had already struggled with issues of representation and taxation. The state responsibilities for the public debt as well as of the nature of the state representation in the central government all rested on the question of population size. The individual colonies had been collecting statistics on potential male conscripts and on property for tax purposes and even developed a very rough and haphazard civil registration of births and deaths carried out by the local clergy.[1] But these were random events and all agreed a more systematic registration was needed. All the ideas of 17th and 18th century European writers on "political arithmetic" – the founding science of demographic analysis – were well known to the founding fathers of the republic. Thus, from the earliest deliberations of the revolutionaries in the 1770s there was the awareness of the need to take a census of population. Such simple censuses were not unknown in the colonial period, Virginia having undertaken an official census as early as 1635, and a total of some 38 such official enumerations were recorded in the colonial period.[2] The first Bills of Mortality (death registries), modeled along the line of those taken in London, were published in Boston in 1704.[3] Muster rolls were universally used in all the colonies for creating militias from the 17th to the 18th century, and most states had a sufficient local administration to carry out these surveys. By the time of the Second Continental Congress in 1775, the fragile national government asked all states to carry out a census and tax themselves for the war on the basis of their populations, but only two colonies did so. Then, in the debates about the Articles of Confederation in 1778, an original draft demanded that all colonies should pay taxes into the central treasury proportional to their number of inhabitants based on a proposed triennial census. This was changed, and most states deliberately underreported

---

[1] The most detailed listing of all these colonial censuses is found in Evarts B. Greene and Virginia D. Harrington, *American Population Before the Federal Census of 1790*. New York: Columbia University Press, 1932.
[2] James H. Cassedy, *Demography in Early America. Beginnings of the Statistical Mind, 1600–1800*. Cambridge, Mass.: Harvard University Press, 1969, p. 19; W. S. Rossiter, *A Century of Population Growth. From the First to the Twelfth Census of the United States: 1790–1900*. Washington, D.C. GPO, 1909, p. 4.
[3] Cassedy, *Demography in Early America*, p. 120.

populations and otherwise were less than willing to carry out such formal censuses. Finally, in the Constitutional Convention of 1783, a compromise was worked out on both the taxation issues and the representation of the slaves in the famous proviso that slaves would count as two-thirds of a free person, and thus it was determined that federal rather than state officials would carry out a decennial census for the new republic beginning in 1790, which was formally written into the Constitution as Article 1, Section 2.[4] Unfortunately, civil registration of births and deaths, left in the hands of indifferent state governments, never kept up with the federal development of a national census, which would improve from decade to decade. Although early in terms of a national census, the United States would prove to be late by European standards in developing a national system of vital registration. In fact, it was not until the early 20th century that a national vital registration system was finally established.[5]

The enabling legislation discussed in the first national congress in 1790 provided initially for only a simple enumeration. Although some held that such an enumeration was sufficient, James Madison fought to have a more complete census carried out and was able to

---

[4] Given the poor quality of state response to earlier census demands, the federal government assumed the role of collecting the decennial census. The census was also tied to the crucial question of representation in the House of Representatives, but the issue of how to calculate the relationship between base population and representation was not decided until the enabling legislation of 1792. See Margo J. Anderson, *The American Census: A Social History*. New Haven: Yale University Press, 1988, Chapter 1.

[5] The issue is well summed up by Michael Haines, who notes that the "systematic collection of vital statistics at the federal level only began with the creation of the Death Registration Area in 1900 (comprising at first only ten states and the District of Columbia) and the Birth Registration Area in 1915 (also initially comprising only ten states and the District of Columbia). Both were complete only in 1933 with the admission of Texas. A Marriage Registration Area was only set up in 1957, and a Divorce Registration Area was only created in 1958, although national estimates exist for the period since 1920. The Marriage and Divorce Registration Areas are still not complete." Michael R. Haines, "Ethnic Differences in Demographic Behavior in the United States: Has There Been Convergence?" Cambridge, Mass.: National Bureau of Economic Research Working Paper 9042, July 2002, p. 5

include six breakdowns of the population: "heads of family, free white males over 16, free white males under 16, free white females, other free persons [free colored and Indians], and slaves." Madison wanted to add occupations, but as he wrote to Jefferson in February of 1790, this provision "was thrown out by the Senate as a waste of trouble and [only good for] supplying materials for idle people to make a book."[6] The census itself took 18 months to carry out and found a population of 3.9 million persons living in the new republic, with the exception of the estimated 4,000 persons in the territory northwest of the Ohio river, who were excluded from the count.[7] Thus, from a population of just under 200,000 in the 1690s, the new nation of the United States had grown to eighteen times that number a century later, experiencing an extraordinary growth rate for that time of almost 3% per annum for the century.[8]

The first half of the 19th century was a period of extraordinary changes within the demographic structure of the new republic. The increasing population density of the nation would lead to surprising changes in both the general patterns of fertility and mortality. In a manner unusual for most of the other countries of the North Atlantic world, the population of the United States began to exercise increasing control over its fertility with a resulting long-term decline in the rates of reproduction of the native-born population. At the same time, there would be a slow but steady convergence of mortality rates toward a national norm, but at apparently a higher level of deaths than had been the experience of the healthiest regions in the colonial period. There even appeared in this period a little-understood but real decline in the level of nutrition for the population as a whole. This nutritional crisis, with its impact on declining heights of native-born males and increasing mortality, paradoxically

---

[6] Quoted in Cassedy, *Demography in Early America*, pp. 215–16.

[7] Rossiter, *A Century of Population Growth*, pp. 54–5.

[8] The estimates of the 1690 population ranges from 203,500, given by Rossiter, *A Century of Population Growth*, Table 1, p. 9; to 208,800 generated from John J. McCusker and Russell R. Menard, *The Economy of British America, 1607–1789*. Chapel Hill, N.C.: 1985, Tables 5.1, 6.4, 8.1, and 9.4. For my growth rate calculation I have used the later sum.

was occurring at a time of major economic growth and prosperity in the nation. The combination of these changing demographic patterns created a unique demographic evolution, comparable only to the French experience in this developing world. The population of North America began to experience a long-term trend of declining fertility – the so-called modern demographic transition – long before there was a decline in mortality, a response that was the opposite of what would occur in most countries of the world from the 19th century until today. At the same time, although the level of fertility went into a long-term decline, it was still among the highest in this North Atlantic region and, combined with the beginnings of mass European immigration, guaranteed a population growth rate among the highest in the world in this period.

The new American republic, the geographically largest such representative government created up to that time, began the 19th century as a growing world and hemispheric power. Its population was expanding rapidly, and by 1820 it was almost half the size of the United Kingdom and would have ranked sixth in size among the western European nations at the time (see Graph 3.1). By the middle of the century its leading city, New York, ranked third in size among the cities of the North Atlantic, exceeded only by Paris and London.[9] It was also a nation that was rapidly extending its physical space. By conquest and purchase, the United States would double its territory toward the west by 1820 and double it again in the 1840s (see Graph 3.2 and Map 3.1). North America was also proving very attractive to western Europeans, who had a profound impact on the United States by providing the new nation with a supplemental source of capital and population. What would prove to be a massive European migration after 1830 complemented the still very high rate of natural increase of the resident population.

---

[9] Paul Bairoch, Jean Batou, and Pierre Chèvre, *La population des villes européennes de 800 à 1850*. Geneve: Droz, 1988; and Campbell Gibson, "Population of the 100 Largest Cities and Other Urban Places in the United States: 1790 to 1990," *Population Division Working Paper No. 27* ; Washington, D.C.: Population Division, U.S. Bureau of the Census, June 1998.

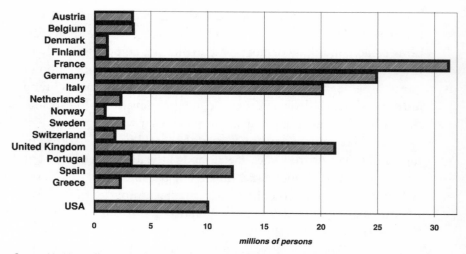

Source: Maddison, *The World Economy: A Millennial Perspective*, Table B-2.

Graph 3.1: United States and European Country Populations in 1820.

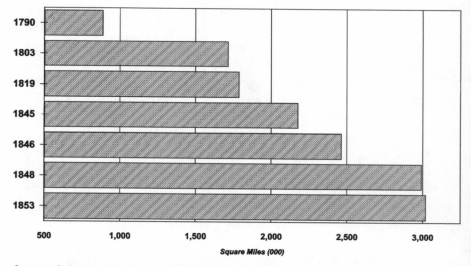

Source: U.S. Bureau of the Census, *Historical Statistics*, Table Series J 1–2.

Graph 3.2: Original Lands in 1790 and Later Conquests/Purchases to 1853.

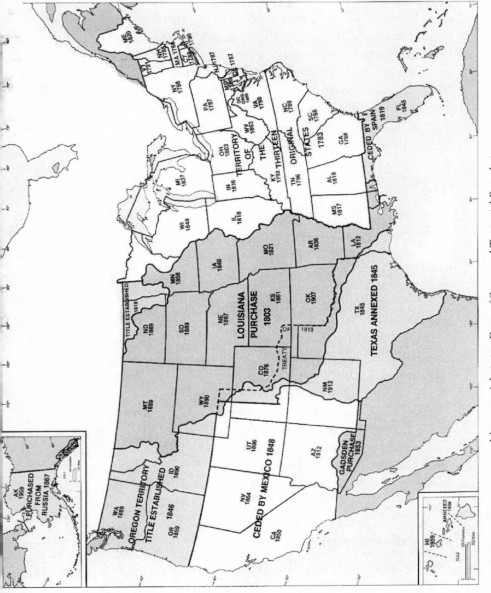

Map 3.1: Admission Dates of States and Territorial Boundaries.

But all this expansion was not a smooth and easy evolution. It came at a cost of continual Indian warfare and relocation of the tribes ever westward and a war with Mexico. Nor did all regions participate equally in this pattern of growth, as the older settled areas began to experience major demographic changes, which differed from those patterns evolving on the ever-expanding frontier. Nor was all moving in a positive direction, for the period before the Civil War would also be a period of increasing malnutrition and higher mortality for this American population, despite major economic growth.

The United States began the 19th century with its really first modern census. Although the census of 1790 provided basic numbers of total population by sex, the simple breakdowns by age excluded female children and, in general, were too limited to be of much use in analyzing the age of the resident population.[10] The categories used in the census of 1800 were also limited, but they did provide the first detailed age breakdowns by sex and this census is usually considered the first to provide fundamental information on at least one of the most highly debated issues in North American population history, that of fertility decline. But even determining fertility rates, more often than not, only indirect measures can be used for the 19th century: specifically the ratio of young children to women in their fertile years is the basic index used.[11] Unfortunately, these age and sex breakdowns of the population in the national census of the 19th century cannot be as effectively used for the other major component of population change, that of mortality. For these reasons, most estimates of mortality are based on state level registrations, samples of populations, or complex estimations based on model life tables and other indirect measures, with substantial debate about the level of underregistration of deaths of children and adults.[12]

---

[10] The 1790 census was based on households rather than persons and only the head of household was listed by name. Anderson, *The American Census*, p. 14.

[11] The classic work in this field is Yasukichi Yasuba, *Birth Rates of the White Population in the United States, 1800–1860: An Economic Study*. Baltimore: Johns Hopkins University, 1962.

[12] For a good example of this, see the estimates used in Peter D. McClelland and Richard J. Zeckhauser, *Demographic Dimensions of the New Republic: American*

In 1800, the United States still had very high fertility rates – higher, in fact, than those of the rest of the western European countries. The crude birth rate was estimated to be approximately 55 births per thousand resident population in 1800, which was equivalent to a total fertility rate of just over seven children per woman who had completed her fertility. At this time, most of the Scandinavian countries and the United Kingdom had a crude birth rate in the upper 20s and lower 30s per thousand population.[13] By 1860, this same resident white population in the United States had reduced its birth rate to 42 births per thousand residents and lowered its total fertility rate to 5.2 children, a decline of over a quarter.[14] This was still a third higher than the equally declining French rate (now at 3.5 children total fertility) but was closing on the relatively high English fertility rate of 4.9 children at that time (see Graph 3.3).[15]

This long-term decline of fertility occurred in a nation that was almost 80% rural and that experienced a death rate that was either stable or rising.[16] In Europe, only France went through this process of declining fertility rates preceding any serious decline in mortality.[17] All other major western European nations imitated the English example, which maintained stable birth rates for most of the 19th century and only began to experience declining fertility long after mortality had begun to decline. Thus, the United States and France

---

Interregional Migration, Vital Statistics and Manumissions, 1800–1860. Cambridge: Cambridge University Press, 1982; and the discussion Clyde L. Pope, "Adult Mortality in America Before 1900: A View from Family Histories," in Claudia Goldin and Hugh Rockoff, Strategic Factors in Nineteenth Century American Economic History. Chicago: University of Chicago Press, 1992, pp. 267–96.

[13] Jean-Claude Chesnais, The Demographic Transition . . . 1720–1984. Oxford: Clarendon Press, 1992, Table A1.2, p. 518ff.

[14] Michael R. Haines, "The White Population of the United States, 1790–1920," in Michael R. Haines and Richard H. Steckel, A Population History of North America. Cambridge: Cambridge University Press, 2000, p. 308; and Ansley J. Coale and Melvin Zelnik, New Estimates of Fertility and Population in the United States. Princeton: Princeton University Press, 1963, Tables 1 and 2, p. 21–23, 36.

[15] Chesnais, The Demographic Transition, Table A1.2 p. 518ff and Table A2.1, p. 543ff.

[16] Coale and Zelnick, New Estimates of Fertility, p. 35.

[17] Chesnais, The Demographic Transition, Chapter 11.

number of children

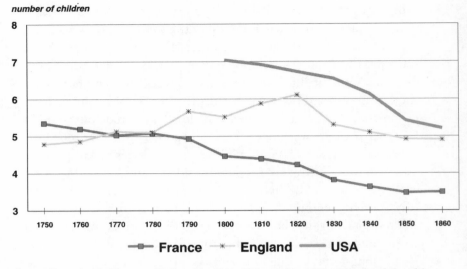

Source: Chesnais, *The Demographic Transition*, Table 11.1 and Haines, "The White Population of the United States," Table 8.2.

Graph 3.3: Total Fertility Rate for France, England, and the United States, 1750–1860.

differed from the pattern that demographers have labeled the "demographic transition" and that was the experience of most world populations from the 19th century to today (see stylized Graph 3.4). In this transition, the experience of the developed nations was for death rates to seriously decline and stabilize at rates lower than fertility rates in the late 18th and early 19th centuries for a variety of reasons related to better nutrition and sanitation. The experience of declining mortality occurred in the developing countries in the mid-20th century and was because of both better sanitation and nutrition and the use of modern medicines after 1950. Initially, the resident population experiencing this change maintains its traditional high levels of fertility, which were associated with higher levels of mortality. It is only after two or three generations that the growing rate of natural increase of the local population – reaching 2% per annum in the developed countries of Europe in the 19th century and over 3% per annum in the developing countries in the late 20th

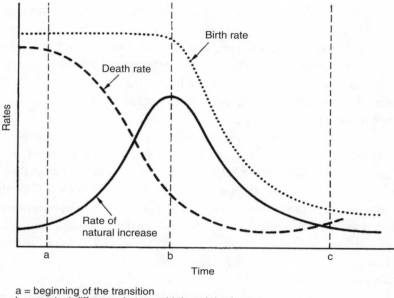

Graph 3.4: Stylized Model of the Demographic Transition.

a = beginning of the transition
b = greatest difference between birth and death rates
c = end of the transition

century – leads most people to begin restraining fertility. As pressure slowly builds on land and resources because of the increasingly rapid growth of the population, natives respond by reducing their fertility rates, which in turn leads to a decline in the natural growth rates. This was the pattern in Europe from the late 19th to the early 20th centuries. It has been the pattern that was repeated in developing countries from the mid-20th century until the early decades of the 21st century. Here, the model society used is England, whose increasing urbanization and population density led the local population to begin to curtail fertility only in the last quarter of the 19th century, long after its late-18th-century decline in mortality. But two major populations in the 19th century did not follow this pattern. One was France and the other was the United States. In these two largely agricultural societies, fertility declines preceded the decline in mortality, seriously cutting the rate of natural increase.

But what could have caused this unusual decline? The answer suggested by demographers is that most of this decline in both countries was related to the increasing pressure of population on land and agricultural resources before 1860. The adoption of partible inheritance under the Napoleonic codes and the increasing subdivisions of agricultural properties are suggested as possible causes in the French situation along with the long and massive wars suffered by the French in the late 18th and early 19th centuries. Paradoxically, declining land availability is also suggested as the primary cause in the case of the United States. Although the American frontier was ever expanding, the majority of the population resided in the old Eastern Seaboard states, and here land resources were on the decline. It was estimated that population density in the original thirteen colonies in 1790 was just nine persons per square mile. By 1820, this had doubled to twenty persons per square mile and doubled again to forty-two persons per square mile by 1860. In contrast, the new frontier areas added to the republic by the 1810s held fewer than one person per square mile and those added subsequent to 1860 never reached the density of the original thirteen colonies in 1790.[18] This density reflects a declining availability of agricultural land, which in turn was the primary factor affecting fertility before the Civil War.[19]   After

[18] W. S. Rossiter, A Century of Population Growth. From the First to the Twelfth Census of the United States: 1790–1900. Washington, D.C.: GPO, 1909, Table 12, p. 59.

[19] See the summary article by Richard A. Easterlin, "Does Human Fertility Adjust to the Environment?" The American Economic Review 61, no. 2 (May 1971), pp. 399–407, as well as his extensive works on this theme cited in note 32 in Chapter 4. The causes for the early 19th century fertility decline have generated an enormous literature dominated by the work Yasukichi Yasuba, Birth Rates of the White Population in the United States, 1800–1860: An Economic Study. Baltimore: Johns Hopkins University, 1962, see especially Chapter 5. Also see the article and book by Morton Owen Schapiro, "Land Availability and Fertility in the United States, 1760–1860," Journal of Economic History, 42, no. 3 (September 1982, pp. 577–600; and Filling Up America: An Economic-Demographic Model of Population Growth and Distribution in the Nineteenth-Century United States. Greenwich, Conn.: JAI Press, 1986; Dan R. Leet, "The Determinants of the Fertility in Antebellum Ohio," Journal of Economic History 36, no. 2 (June 1976), pp. 359–78, and Colin Forster and G. S. L. Tucker, Economic Opportunity and White American Fertility Ratios, 1800–1860. New Haven: Yale University Press, 1972. All

1860, both in France and the United States, the continuing decline in fertility is tied more to the traditional causes suggested in the classic model; increasing urbanization and industrialization in both countries raised the costs of children in terms of housing and education, whereas more possibilities for consumption were opened to adults in the industrializing world.

In the pre-1860 period, when the rural population was still well over 80%, the response of Eastern Seaboard residents to increasingly limited land resources was to marry later and leave a higher ratio of women outside the marriage market. The former action resulted in the decline in marital fertility, which, given the very low rates of illegitimate births, meant a decline in overall fertility rates. The latter cut down on the number of reproducing women in the resident population. This decline in fertility, first noted as early as the late 18th century in New England, began to appear in the Middle Atlantic colonies in the 19th century. On the frontiers, early marriage and high marital fertility were still the norm, but this ever-moving frontier population made up only a small share of the total national population and did not seriously influence the national figures. Not all regions experienced fertility decline at the same rate. The Middle Atlantic colonies received the most foreign immigrants, and these foreign-born immigrants had higher fertility rates than the native born (see Graph 3.5).[20] Thus the rate of decline was slower here than in New England. Of the older coastal seaboard regions, the South declined the least, for here falling mortality rates somewhat made up for a declining fertility, and reproductive rates remained above the national average for the entire period to 1860. But none of these rates,

three studies stress the land availability issue (measured in several ways) as the most important causal factor for fertility decline. One of the few to disagree with this dominant casual model is John Modell, "Family and Fertility on the Indian Frontier, 1820," *American Quarterly* 23, no. 5 (December 1971), 615–34, who stresses occupational factors.

[20] In the best documented analysis of comparative fertility, the foreign-born women of Massachusetts from 1830 to 1870 had almost double the total fertility rate of native-born women. Peter R. Uhlenberg, "A Study of Cohort Life Cycles: Cohorts of Native Born Massachusetts Women, 1830–1920," *Population Studies* 23, no. 3. (November 1969), p. 413.

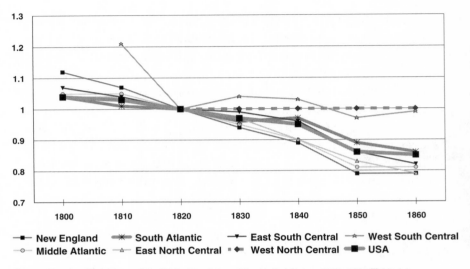

Source: Yasuba, *Birth Rates of the White Population of the United States, 1800–1860:* Table 3.1.

Graph 3.5: Fertility Index of U.S. Regions, 1800–1860 (1820=100).

except for the case of Florida, matched the high levels of fertility experienced on the western frontier in this latter year.[21]

It should be stressed that fertility in the United States, although declining, was still quite high and positive. Its decline, however, quickly translated into lower natural growth rates. In the 1800–1810 period, the rate of natural increase of the resident white population was estimated at 2.92% per annum – a rate that even today would be considered high for a rapidly growing developing nation – but this rate dropped slowly but steadily to 1.99% in the decade of 1850–1860.[22] Had it not been for immigration, it is estimated that the 1860 population would have been a quarter smaller than it was on the eve of the Civil War, but it would still have grown impressively. The post-1830 transoceanic immigration to the United States would

---

[21] Yasukichi Yasuba, *Birth Rates of the White Population of the United States, 1800–1860. An Economic Study.* Baltimore: Johns Hopkins University Press, 1962, Tables II–3, II–7, pp. 55, 61–2.

[22] McClleland and Zeckhauser, *Demographic Dimensions of the New Republic,* Table A-13, p. 100.

turn out to be the largest such oceanic migration in world history, being some five times larger than the Atlantic slave trade, until then
the largest such transoceanic migration. Yet despite its volume, this
international immigration was still secondary in importance to natural growth rates of the resident native population and accounted
for only a quarter of the overall 3% annual growth experienced by
the United States population in the period from the beginning of the
republic up to the Civil War.[23] This rate of growth meant that the
national population was doubling every 23 years.

Equally experiencing high fertility was the African American
slave population. Despite the end of the Atlantic slave trade in 1808,
the African American slave population grew at very high rates. It has
been estimated that this population was growing at 2.2% per annum
and that it had a crude birth rate in the 35–40 range, with an infant
mortality rate estimated in the upper 180s per thousand births and
life expectancy for both sexes in the low 30s.[24] Concentrated overwhelmingly in the South and its expanding southern and western
frontiers, African American slaves had experienced the same high
initial mortality as the whites who migrated to the South. In the
earlier years, in fact, natural growth was negative in many regions.
By the mid-18th century, however, even before the close of the Atlantic slave trade, slaves began experiencing positive rates of natural growth, first in the border areas such as the Upper Chesapeake
Bay region and then throughout the Carolinas and Georgia and into
the new frontier regions. At first, natural growth was slow because
the slaves still suffered higher mortality and lower fertility than the
whites. But by 1808, when the slave trade was formally abolished,
the United States already had a self-sustaining slave population, and
quickly the African-born became a minority of the resident black
population.[25] This pattern of initial negative growth due to high

[23] McClleland and Zeckhauser, *Demographic Dimensions of the New Republic*, p. 15.
[24] Jack E. Eblen, "Growth of the Black Population in Ante Bellum America, 1820–
1860," *Population Studies* 26, no. 2 (July 1972), pp. 283, 288. He estimates the
maximum number of slaves who may have been imported in any illegal slave
trade in the 19th century at 40,000 Africans between 1820 and 1860.
[25] See the earlier discussion on late colonial slave population natural growth rates.
For 19th century rates of growth of this population, see Robert William Fogel

mortality and high adult male ratios among the arriving Africans was the experience of all American regions importing slaves from Africa. In most of these areas, the resident native-born, or creole, slave population slowly began to dominate the local slave population and positive natural rates of growth ensued.[26] But those regions, such as Brazil, Cuba, and the French West Indies, where the slave trade remained intense until well into the 19th century, the Creole population dynamics were overwhelmed by the arrival of new Africans with their biased adult and male ratios. Once the trade ended, even these slave regimes began to experience a positive rate of natural growth.[27]

What was different about the North American experience was that the slave population of the United States achieved positive rates of growth earlier and at higher levels than those obtained in most other large slave populations, and this was due to their fertility rates being the highest achieved by any known slave population in the Americas. Fertility, as measured by "child–women ratios" (number of children under the age of 10 to women 15–45 years of age) was just 10%, on average, less than that of the North American whites, which in turn was much higher than any contemporary European rates. This extraordinarily high slave fertility rate was not due to any better nutrition or even higher life expectancy than other American slaves were experiencing. Nor was it due to U.S. slave women beginning or ending their fertility at earlier or later ages. Unlike the whites, there were no constraints on slave fertility anywhere, thus slave women tended to have their first children at an earlier age than whites. This, in general, compensated for their higher than white mortality rates. The main difference in American slave fertility patterns was primary caused by different

and Stanley L. Engerman, *Time on the Cross: The Economics of American Negro Slavery*. Boston, Mass.: Little, Brown, 1974.

[26] See Jack E. Eblen, "On the Natural Increase of Slave Populations: The Example of the Cuban Black Population, 1775–1900," in Stanley L. Engerman and Eugene Genovese, eds., *Race and Slavery in the Western Hemisphere*. Princeton University Press: Princeton, 1975.

[27] See B. W. Higman, *Slave Populations of the British Caribbean, 1807–1834*. Baltimore: Johns Hopkins University Press, 1984.

patterns of the spacing of births. It has been argued that this difference in spacing – which resulted in more children being born over the life of a fertile women – was due to the adaptation by North American slaves of the practice of breastfeeding children for only one year, which was then the norm for north European whites. In the rest of the Americas, slave women tended to give on demand breastfeeding for up to two years, the African norm, which then resulted in longer spacing between births.[28] Thus, the slave population, which numbered 678,000 in 1790, roughly doubled every 28 years, maintaining a rate of growth overall in this 70-year period of 2.5% per annum. With insignificant migration of illegal African immigrants and only a very moderate out-migration of emancipated slaves, this slave population reached a total 3.9 million persons by 1860 basically through natural growth alone.

Given increasing European immigration, the weight of free and slave African Americans was on the decline, despite their impressive natural growth rates. The African American population went from accounting for 19% of the national population in 1790 to just 14% by 1860. In the South, however, they maintained their relative share of population from census to census. Despite a major growth of the southern white population through natural increase, African Americans consistently accounted for between 35% and 38% of the local population in every pre-Civil War census. In 1860, African Americans made up 40% of the population in the South Atlantic states from Delaware to Florida, they were 35% of the population in the East South Central states of Kentucky, Tennessee, Alabama, and Mississippi, and even in the new cotton states of the West South Central division (which was made up of Arkansas, Louisiana, Oklahoma, and Texas) they were 35% of the population. In every other region and subdivision, their ratio of total population was on the

---

[28] Herbert S. Klein and Stanley Engerman, "Fertility Differentials Between Slaves in the United States and the British West Indies: A Note on Lactation Practices and their Implications," *William and Mary Quarterly* XXXV, no. 2 (April 1978), pp. 357–74.

decline by the 1860s, and what black population did exist in these regions was exclusively free persons of color.[29]

Along with much higher rates of fertility, North American slaves also had lower rates of manumission than those in Cuba and Brazil, if not in the West Indies. Although initially manumission rates in the 18th century probably differed little between Latin America and North America, the 19th century experience was fundamentally different. Reflecting ever increasing rates of manumission, the free colored eventually outnumbered slaves by the middle of the 19th century in Cuba, Brazil, and most of the other slave societies, despite an often intense slave trade. This was the reverse of what occurred in North America in the 19th century. Although the founding fathers expected slavery to disappear with the end of the Atlantic slave trade and the colonial levels of high manumission, the 19th century saw the United States master class turn against manumission in all the southern states that would make up the Confederacy. Because women and children were the most often manumitted slaves everywhere, this decline of out-migrants also helped to keep slave growth rates high in 19th century in North America, despite life expectancies and fertility rates lower than those of the whites.[30] Moreover, by the census of 1830, slave fertility rates finally passed those of the whites for the first time and remained higher than white rates until the end of slavery. Although both whites and slaves experienced declining fertility after that date, the decline was slower among the slaves and slave fertility in 1860 was 12% above the fertility rate of whites. It was also far above the fertility rate of free colored, which was a fifth less than the slave rate as well as lower than that of the whites. The data also confirm that the old tobacco and cotton regions of the Southern Atlantic region consistently maintained the

---

[29] Campbell Gibson and Kay Jung, "Historical Census Statistics on Population Totals by Race, 1790 to 1990, and by Hispanic Origin, 1970 to 1990, for the United States, Regions, Divisions, and States," U. S. Census Bureau, Population Division, Working Paper Series No. 56; Washington, DC, September 2002, Tables 1–14.

[30] For comparative manumission practices in the Americas, see Herbert S. Klein, *African Slavery in Latin America and the Caribbean* (New York: Oxford University Press, 1986).

highest slave fertility rates in the nation throughout the 19th century, suggesting that the old argument about Virginia and the older slave states breeding slaves may have some validity.[31]

For economic and political reasons, this slave population was not uniformly distributed throughout the new republic. In general, it was far more rural than the white population, with only 4% of the slaves living in urban areas in 1860, compared to a fifth of the total population who lived in such centers. In this they sharply differed from the free colored, a third of whom were urban and thus more urbanized than any other group in the nation.[32] Brought to serve in the export agricultural industries – now dominated by cotton – the Africans and their descendants, even before political constraints prohibited their location in the North, tended to reside mostly in the Southern Atlantic and Southwestern states. In 1790, only 6% of the slaves resided outside this zone and none did so after the 1840s. By 1860, the majority of slaves finally resided in the new cotton states of the Southwest, and only 6% of all slave and free African Americans resided outside these two southern regions. Although the 488,000 free colored in 1860 could be found everywhere, even in the West, with a third of them residing in New England and 14% in the Midwest, just over half of them also resided in the South. But because they represented only 11% of the total African American population, they had little impact on the overall distribution of the African American population, of which 94% resided in the slave states in 1860 (see Graph 3.6). The expansion to the far West or the Northwest territories had little impact on this population, the least regionally mobile group within the American population in the 19th century.

In contrast, all other elements of the American population proved to be highly mobile. Noted by all contemporaries as well as later

---

[31] Data taken from Richard H. Steckel, "The African American Population of the United States, 1790–1920," in Michael R. Haines and Richard H. Steckel, eds., *A Population History of North America* (Cambridge : Cambridge University Press, 2000), Tables 10.3 and 10.6, pp. 442, 457.

[32] Steckel, "The African American Population of the United States, 1790–1920," Tables 10.2 and 10.5, pp. 442, 454–5. He defined "urban" as any town over 4,000 population for southern and over 8,000 for northern cities, pp. 439n, 455n.

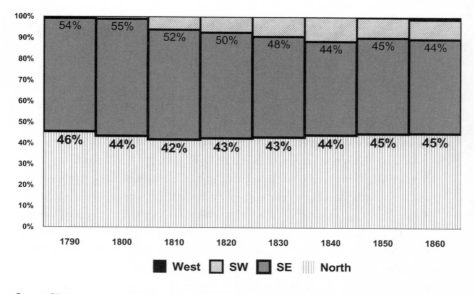

Source: Gibson and Jung, *Historical Census Statistics on Population Totals By Race, 1790 to 1990*, Tables 1–14.

Graph 3.6: Percentage Distribution of the Free Colored Population by Region, 1790–1860.

demographers was the long-term movement of the population of the United States toward the West. The older seaboard states, although containing the majority of the large cities and the bulk of the population, were losing population at a steady rate to the ever-expanding frontier throughout the late 18th and all of the 19th century. This movement in the pre-1860 period was primarily into the Northwest territory, those territories to the north and west of the Ohio River (Ohio, Indiana, Illinois, Michigan, Wisconsin, and parts of Minnesota and North Dakota) and was dominated by young adults, primarily men. There was also a flow of population from the South to the North and, until 1840, a small movement from Canada south into the New England region.[33] By the census of 1860, only 55% of the total population of the United States resided in the original

---

[33] McClleland and Zeckhauser, *Demographic Dimensions of the New Republic*, pp. 18–19.

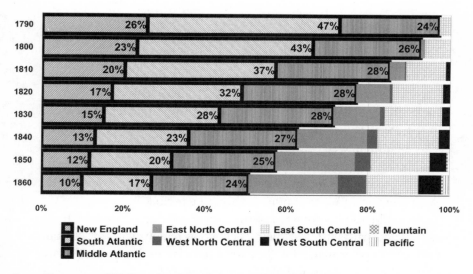

Year	New England	East North Central	East South Central	Mountain
1790	26%	47%	24%	
1800	23%	43%	26%	
1810	20%	37%	28%	
1820	17%	32%	28%	
1830	15%	28%	28%	
1840	13%	23%	27%	
1850	12%	20%	25%	
1860	10%	17%	24%	

New England   **East North Central**   **East South Central**   **Mountain**
South Atlantic   **West North Central**   **West South Central**   **Pacific**
Middle Atlantic

Source: Thompson and Whelpton, *Population Trends in the United States*, Table 6.

Graph 3.7: Declining Importance of Population in the Original Thirteen Colonies, 1790–1860.

thirteen colonies (see Graph 3.7).[34] Although all regions grew rapidly – given both continued high fertility and increasing European immigration – the movement West was so powerful that the new regions being exploited took an ever higher ratio of national population. Although a typical New England state such as Massachusetts grew from 379,000 to 1.2 million between 1790 and 1860, and the quintessential Middle Atlantic state of Pennsylvania grew from 434,000 to 2.9 million in this same sixty-year period, the Northwest territory states saw even more rapid population growth. Ohio went from 230,000 in 1810, when it first entered into the census, to 2.3 million in 1860. Illinois and Indiana entered the census in the next decade and they also experienced major growth, with the former starting its first census with 55,000 persons in 1820 and reaching 1.7 million in 1860, and Indiana, in the same forty-year period, started with 147,000 residents and reached almost 1.4 million persons by the time of the Civil War. Density per square mile went from fewer than

[34] Rossiter, *A Century of Population Growth*, Table 10, p. 56.

5 persons per square mile in these three states to more than 30 persons per square mile by 1860 for Illinois and Indiana and 57 persons per square mile in Ohio – not that different from the 65 persons per square mile in Pennsylvania although still five times less dense than Massachusetts with its 153-person ratio.[35] These new North Central states grew at double to triple the rate of the other regions. Thus, in the 1850–1860 period, this new frontier region was expanding at 5% per annum, well below its earlier rates of increase, but more than double the 2% per annum growth rates of the South and the Northeastern traditional settlement areas, whereas the new states of the West grew by 13% per annum in this same period.[36]

As could also be expected of this newly developing western frontier region, with "frontier" being defined as regions with fewer than two persons per square mile, they attracted a larger than normal share of working age adults and also a higher ratio of men 20 to 40 years of age than the older regions. But the distribution of women by ages was normal and a higher percentage of them were married than in the nation as a whole, guaranteeing higher than national fertility rates in these new frontier zones. The frontier drew most of its immigrants from New England, the Middle Colonies, and neighboring states. Only about 15% of this frontier population before 1860 was foreign born and most of these came from the British Isles. Finally, although there was a larger number of males in working age categories, the fact that women of all ages and conditions tended to be married on the frontier – there were very few widows – guaranteed that the ratio of unmarried males was lower than their overrepresentation in these categories would have suggested.[37] But as frontiers matured and densities went over two persons per square mile, they

[35] U.S. Department of Commerce, Bureau of the Census. *Historical Statistics of the United States, Colonial Times to 1970*, CD edition New York: Cambridge University Press, 1997; original edition (Washington D.C.: U.S. Department of Commerce, Bureau of the Census, 1975), Table Series A195–209.

[36] Calculated from *Historical Statistics*, Table Series A172–194. For a broad survey of the stages of this growth of the west, see Walter Nugent, *Into the West: The Story of Its People*. New York: Alfred A. Knopf, 1999.

[37] Jack E. Eblen, "An Analysis of Nineteenth-Century Frontier Populations," *Demography* 2 (1965), pp. 399–413.

also began to experience declining fertility rates, bringing them in line with the older seaboard regions.

Migration to these regions was constant and population west of the Appalachian Mountains began to grow significantly. By the census of 1860, the original thirteen seaboard states of 1790, which initially contained 97% of the national population, now held only just over half of the total (see Graph 3.7). The East North Central region, that is, the states of Ohio, Indiana, Illinois, Michigan, and Wisconsin, which had no European population in 1790, now accounted for 22% of the national population. This was a vital new farming area that, in many ways, was an extension of the original Middle Atlantic colonies of New York, New Jersey, and Pennsylvania. Another entire new region that developed in the first half of the 19th century was, of course, the new cotton region of the Deep South. This could be divided into the East South Central and West South Central divisions, the former of which consisted of the new states of Kentucky, Tennessee, Alabama, and Mississippi and the latter of which consisted of the states of Arkansas, Louisiana, Oklahoma, and Texas. These two regions by 1860, contained 18% of the total national population and half of the slaves. All of this movement meant that the center of national population now began its inexorable march westward from census to census (see Map 3.2).

The second major migratory movement of the North American population in this period was from both the rural areas and overseas to the newly expanding urban centers. In 1790, there were only six towns in the entire republic with a population of more than 8,000 persons, and the largest city, New York, contained just 33,000 persons[38] and was only a third of the size of Mexico City in the same period.[39] In fact, only 3% of the total national population lived in these cities in the first census. But the booming international trade of the 1790s and early decades of the 19th century brought new wealth

[38] Rossiter, A Century of Population Growth, p. 15, Table 4.
[39] Gibson, "Population of the 100 Largest Cities and Other Urban Places in the United States: 1790 to 1990," Table 2; and Herbert S. Klein, "The Demographic Structure of Mexico City in 1811," Journal of Urban History 23, (1) (November 1996), pp. 66–93.

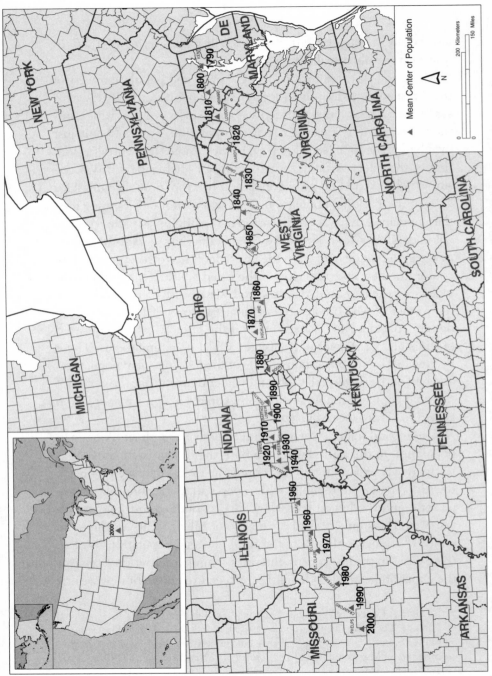

Map 3.2: Mean Center of Population for the United States, 1790–2000.

to these cities, and they expanded faster than the total population. By 1820, the premier city of New York had reached a population of 124,000 persons and numbered over a half a million by midcentury. By the 1830s, it was evident that the new republic had replaced Mexico as the nation with the largest cities in the hemisphere.[40] In contrast to the rural areas, these cities were growing primarily through immigration of the native born and foreign born rather than through natural increase. Given their higher mortality and lower birth rates than the rural areas and their bias of age and sex, the urban populations could not reproduce themselves. As one urban study concluded, "as was the case with virtually all nineteenth-century American cities, very little of Boston's population growth was due to natural increase. Rather it was the product of in-migration."[41] Yet Boston had a crude death rate at roughly mid-20s per thousand, much lower than the mid-30s per thousand of New York or the mid-40s per thousand for Philadelphia.[42] Although the urban population grew as a relative share of total population, the major cities took more time to develop and only in the last decades before the Civil War did the bigger cities begin to dominate the urban population. Thus, towns with fewer than 25,000 persons accounted for 69% of the total urban population of 202,000 persons in 1790, then dropped in the early decades of the 19th century to just over half of the urban residents. But this figure remained steady from 1800 to 1840 and only seriously declined in 1850, when only 42% of the 3.5 million

---

[40] Rossiter, A Century of Population Growth, Table 4, p. 15; and Gibson, "Population of the 100 Largest Cities and Other Urban Places in the United States: 1790 to 1990," Table 9.

[41] Richard A. Meckel, "Immigration, Mortality and Population Growth in Boston, 1840–1880," Journal of Interdisciplinary History XV, no. 3 (Winter 1985), p. 397. In Canada, this same pattern prevailed. In the province of Quebec, the crude death rate was in the mid 20s per 1,000 resident population in the 1800–1860 period, whereas it was in the 40s and 50s in Quebec City and Montreal in the same period. François Pelletier, Jacques Légaré, and Robert Vourbeau, "Mortality in Quebec During the Nineteenth Century: From the State to the Cities," Population Studies 51 (1997), p. 95.

[42] Maris A. Vinovskis, "Mortality Rates and Trends in Massachusetts Before 1860," The Journal of Economic History 32, no. 1 (March 1972), p. 204.

urbanites were found in these small cities.[43] In the next two decades, with the increasing arrival of ever-larger numbers of immigrants from northern Europe, there was a clear shift toward larger towns, which began to dominate the urban sector of the nation. By 1860, over 60% of the 6.2 million persons living in urban area were found in cities with populations of more than 25,000, and 42% of them lived in cities with more than 100,000 persons. As early as 1850, New York was the third largest city in the North Atlantic, just behind Paris and London in size.[44] By 1860, the city reached a population of 814,000 and Philadelphia now counted over half a million persons, and cities over 100,000 alone accounted for 10% of the national population.[45]

The growth of both urban and total population was increasingly fueled by that other major population movement in pre–Civil War America – the arrival of foreign immigrants who paid for their own passage to cross the Atlantic. Although the natural growth rate of the native-born population was a very high 2.5% per annum in this period, it was slowly declining. Yet the population as a whole was growing at over 3% per annum. The cause for this additional growth, was, of course, the beginning of massive European immigration after 1830. This new migration of free workers was due to major changes within Europe itself. There, the natural growth rates were reaching historic proportions and creating population pressure as never before in European history. Countries were rapidly urbanizing and industrializing and were quickly moving their populations off the land and out of agriculture. But until the last decades of the century, the expansion of European employment opportunities could not keep up with this historically new expansion phase of their resident populations. It was quickly perceived in these countries that only an international solution could resolve some of these internal growth

---

43 Warren S. Thompson and P. K. Whelpton, *Population Trends in the United States.* New York: McGraw-Hill Book, 1933, p. 24, table 9.
44 Bairoch, et.al, *La Population des villes européennes.*
45 Campbell Gibson, "Population of the 100 Largest Cities and Other Urban Places in the United States: 1790 to 1990," Washington, D.C.: U.S. Bureau of the Census Population Division Working Paper No. 27, June 1998, Table 9; and *Historical Statistics*, Table Series A 57–72.

problems, and all the major European governments favored out-migration as a crucial safety valve for the basic structural changes that were occurring within their own frontiers. Thus, the 19th century become an unusual period of true globalization in modern history in terms of a truly international Atlantic labor market.

In turn, the classic American equation of extensive lands and scarce labor, along with increasing exports to Europe to satisfy this expanding European population, guaranteed that wages in the Americas remained higher than those in Europe for most of the 19th century. Thus, the "push" and "pull" factors were in place by 1830, and the changing technology and cost of transportation after this date was the last key to getting this entire operation in motion. The development of railroads in Europe and the introduction of steam shipping in the following decades all drove down the cost of migration to the point where large segments of the European population could pay for their own transport. It has been suggested by economic historians that the indentured market would have kept going after 1820 if a supply of laborers from Europe could have been found.[46] But the disappearance of laborers needing to have their passages paid for their them and their replacement by paying passengers led to the total collapse of the system. By 1830, no slave or indentured workers were crossing the Atlantic to supply labor for the United States market. With the expansion of the cotton economy, the ever-expanding production of grains, and the early development of industrial production and mining, the United States was able to maintain wages that could easily compete with the European labor market for most of the 19th century.

The migration of Europeans and others to the United States can be said to have advanced in several stages. From the 1830s to the 1880s, the migrants came essentially from northwestern Europe; from the 1880s to the 1920s the "New Immigrants" came mostly from

---

[46] Farley Grubb, "The End of European Immigrant Servitude in the United States: An Economic Analysis of Market Collapse, 1772–1835," *The Journal of Economic History* 54, no. 4 (December 1994), pp. 794–824; and David W. Galenson, "The Rise and Fall of Indentured Servitude in the Americas: An Economic Analysis," *The Journal of Economic History* 44, no. 1 (March 1984), pp. 1–26.

eastern and southern Europe, with a minor flow of migrants from Asia; and in the post–World War II period, they would come primarily from Asia and Latin America. The numbers of this migration to 1930 were impressive. Overall, from 1821 to 1924 some 44 million Europeans migrated to America, of which 31 million came to the United States.[47] Until 1855, the majority of immigrants crossing the Atlantic came to North America, with the United States predominating as the region of destination. Canada, in the 1826–1835 period, took 40% of all immigrants but quickly declined in relative importance, such that by the post–1836 period, two-thirds were coming to the United States. Moreover, the two other major competitors for trans-Atlantic immigrants, Brazil and Argentina, would not enter the international labor market in a serious way until after 1850. The volume of this trans-Atlantic migration increased overall by 8% per annum in the period from 1821 to the Civil War, although it varied greatly by decade, with the crisis of the 1840s being an especially poor period of migration and the late 1850s seeing an actual decline in total migration. Nevertheless, the numbers are impressive. By the 1831–1835 period, the migrants to the United States were averaging just under 50,000 persons per annum; ten years later, the average was almost double that number, and by 1846–1850, some 250,000 migrants were coming from Europe to eastern U.S. ports each year. Although this volume fluctuated due to European or North American conditions and competing importing markets, by the decade of the 1880s, this international migration averaged just under a half million persons per annum and would eventually rise to close to 1 million persons annually entering the United States by 1901–1905 (see Graph 3.8).

Most of this migration to 1860 was a migration coming from northern Europe, then in the throes of the demographic transition. The Scandinavian countries and the United Kingdom, Ireland, and Scotland all now had population growth rates of over 1% per

---

[47] Imre Ferenczi and Walter Francis Willcox, *International Migrations...*, 2 vols. New York: National Bureau of Economic Research, 1929–1931, vol. 1, pp. 236–37.

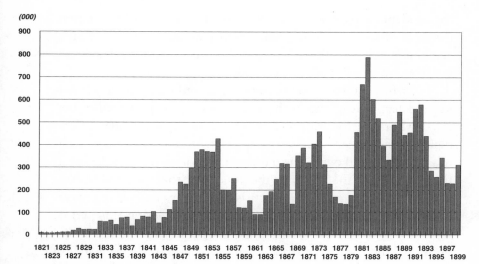

Source: INS, *Statistical Yearbook of the Immigration and Naturalization Service, 2000*, Table 1.

Graph 3.8: Annual Immigration to the United States, 1821–1900.

annum.[48] Although rates of increase varied by country and by decade, the trend was identical in all. By 1800, Sweden was experiencing high birth rates and declining mortality rates and was growing at or above 1% per annum; by the 1830s, the same was occurring in the United Kingdom, and German rates were well over 1% per annum through most of the 19th century.[49] Although many of these foreign immigrants would feed into the growing urban centers, the majority went to work the land. The biggest single area to which they migrated was the Middle Atlantic states, with the old Northwestern states in second place.[50] But in no region, even that of the South, were they absent, and before 1860, it was estimated that 15% of the frontier population was foreign-born. Most of these arriving first-generation immigrants had rates of fertility higher than those of

[48] B. R. Mitchell, *International Historical Statistics: Europe, 1750–1993*, 3rd ed. New York: Stockton Press, 1992, Table A6, pp. 92–101.

[49] Jean-Claude Chesnais, *The Demographic Transition . . . 1720–1984*. Oxford: Clarendon Press, 1992, Chapter 8.

[50] McClleland and Zeckhauser, *Demographic Dimensions of the New Republic*, Table 3.52, p. 44.

the resident native-born population. But by the second generation, the rates of fertility of these immigrant families was also declining and coming close to that of the native-born – a pattern that would be the norm for all subsequent migrations.

As fertility rates were slowly moving toward European levels during the first half of the 19th century, so too were mortality levels slowly rising toward those of some Old World standards. The rapidly growing economy of the thirteen colonies had major periods of growth and overall would expand to an impressive degree in the period from the 1770s to the 1860. But there were also short and sharp periods of economic crisis and major unemployment, especially in the cities and among the artisans. During this period, there were three major wars and various panics and short-term depressions: the wars were those of the Revolution, the Embargo of 1807 and the subsequent War of 1812 with England, the War of 1848 with Mexico, and then the massive Civil War of 1861–1865. Along the way, there were short-term panics in 1812 and 1837 and a major one in 1857, along with a short depression in 1825 and another longer one following the 1857 crisis. Wages declined and unemployment increased.[51] It has been estimated that the general level of income of the future United States fell sharply during the War for Independence and did not regain prewar 1774 levels until the first decade of the 19th century.[52] In turn, the War of 1812 wrecked havoc with North American shipping and badly affected international trade, which in turn created a new depression. Although recovery came in the next decade and the overall economy continued to grow, the 1830s and 1840s were a period of relative stagnation in exports, increasing trade deficits, and falling government revenues, which were primarily based on taxes on trade. Although the gross national product (GNP) grew at the extraordinary rate of

[51] Claudia Goldin and Robert A. Margo, "Wages, Prices, and Labor Markets Before the Civil War," in Claudia Goldin and Hugh Rockoff, *Strategic Factors in Nineteenth Century American Economic History*. Chicago: University of Chicago Press, 1992, pp. 67–104.

[52] Russel R. Menard, "Economic and Social Development of the South," in Stanley L. Engerman and Robert E. Gallman, *The Cambridge Economic History of the United States*, 3 vols., New York: Cambridge University Press, 2000, vol. 1, p. 294.

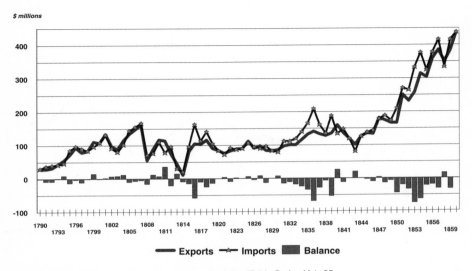

$ millions

Source: U.S. Bureau of the Census, *Historical Statistics*, Table Series U 1–25.

Graph 3.9: Trade Balance and Value of U.S. Exports and Imports, 1790–1860.

4% per annum from 1774 to 1859,[53] a growth only exceeded by Argentina in the late 19th century, actual per capita income did not do as well. This grew by only 0.9% in the same 85-year period, and there were times in the late 18th and early 19th century when per capita GNP was below this overall rate and sometimes even negative (see Graphs 3.9 and 3.10). Thus, in the midst of general growth of both population and the economy, there were severe short-term periods of crisis and a slowing of the pace of national per capita economic growth.

What impact these periodic crises may have had on United States mortality rates and the standard of life in the 19th century is difficult to say. But most of the recent evidence presented seems to suggest a rise in crude mortality rates in the early 19th century to the level that was standard in western Europe and a general decline in

---

53 Robert E. Galman, "Economic Growth and Structural Change in the Long Nineteenth Century," in Stanley L. Engerman and Robert E. Gallman, eds., *The Cambridge Economic History of the United States*, 3 vols., New York: Cambridge University Press, 2000, vol. 11, p. 7.

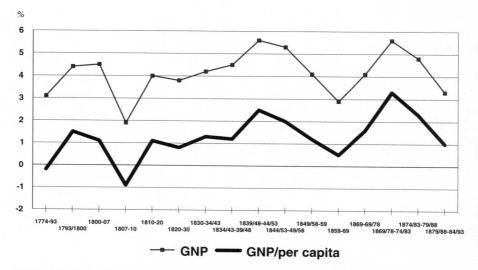

Source: R.E. Gallman, "Economic Growth and Structural Change," Tables 1.3 and 1.7.

Graph 3.10: Annual Rate of Growth of Total Gross National Product and Gross National Product per Capita in 1860 Dollars.

male heights in the general population in the pre-Civil War period – although at levels still higher than was the norm in Europe. Whereas some studies have suggested crude mortality rates under 20 deaths per thousand resident population in the colonial period in such favored places as the New England rural communities, by the 19th century these rates tended to be in the mid-20s range, a rate quite similar to those found in Europe by the mid-19th century.[54] Although urban and southern mortality rates slowly declined, it has been suggested that it was a general increase in mortality in most rural areas – where over 80% of the population still resided in 1860 – that brought overall national rates to a higher level than had existed in the early colonial period. Even rural New England saw its mortality slowly increasing in the 19th century to the mid-20s per thousand. Although regional disparities in mortality had largely disappeared by the 1860s, at least for the Eastern Seaboard region if not in the harsher frontier

[54] McClleland and Zeckhauser, *Demographic Dimensions of the New Republic*, Tables A-18 and A-19, p. 109.

regions, the urban–rural mortality differences remained. Life expectancy in Boston – one of the healthiest urban centers on the Eastern Seaboard – still reached only to the upper 30s at birth for both sexes in the 1830–1860 period, whereas rural Massachusetts towns experienced life expectancy in the mid 40s at birth by this latter period.[55] Philadelphia, as late as 1870, still had a life expectancy at birth for its citizens of less than 40 years,[56] and crude death rates in this decade for the cities of Chicago, Baltimore, and New York were still in the upper 20s per thousand resident population.[57]

With overall mortality apparently increasing before the Civil War, there was a consequent decline in life expectancy. One of the better of the many pre–Civil War estimates suggests that by 1850, the average life expectancy for all persons living in the United States was 36.5 years for men and 38.5 years for women. For whites, it was one year above this national average for both males and females, and for blacks, it must have been below this national average to a larger degree than one year.[58] Another estimate suggests a slightly higher level for whites, giving an average life expectancy at birth in 1850 of 40.4 years for men and 42.9 for women, with nonwhites having a life expectancy of 32.5 years for men and 35.0 for women.[59] These rates were in fact lower than the best rates then occurring in Europe. In Norway, for example, in 1851–1860, average life expectancy at birth was already a high 47 years for men and 50 years for women,

[55] Maris A. Vinovskis, *Fertility in Massachusetts from the Revolution to the Civil War.* New York: Academic Press, 1981, Tables 2.2 and 2.4, pp. 33–4.

[56] Gretchin A. Condram and Rose A. Cheney, "Mortality Trends in Philadelphia: Age- and Cause-Specific Death Rates 1870–1930," *Demography*, 19, no. 1 (February 1982), Table 1, p. 100.

[57] Condran and Cheney, "Mortality Trends," figure 1, p. 98.

[58] Michael R. Haines, "The Use of Model Life Tables to Estimate Mortality for the United States in the Late Nineteenth Century," *Demography*, 16, no. 2 (May 1979), Table 7, p. 307. Haines has suggested a life expectation at birth of 39.5 years for the white population of both sexes in 1850. Michael R. Haines, "The White Population of the United States, 1790–1920," in Michael R. Haines and Richard H. Steckel, eds., *A Population History of North America.* Cambridge: Cambridge University Press, 2000, Table 8.2, p. 308.

[59] S. L. N. Rao, "On Long-Term Mortality Trends in the United States: 1850–1968," *Demography*, 10, no. 3 (August 1973), Table 1, p. 409.

and in Denmark in the same decade it was 44 years for men and 47 years for women.[60]

Thus, in the earliest estimated life tables for the United States and for those of Norway, the longest lived of the Europeans, the difference in average length of life at birth was on the order of almost 10 years. U.S. rates were even below those estimated for the United Kingdom, which in 1850 was 41.01 years for both sexes – with 42.1 years for women and 40.3 years for men.[61] Alternative measures still show these differences. Thus, using a life expectancy model for persons 10 years or older – which avoids the problem of estimating infant and child mortality – which can also be generated from detailed genealogical samples of surviving adults as well as estimated from model life tables, suggests that in 1850–1860, the life expectancy for a resident of the United States at 10 years of age was 46.6 years and 46.7 years more of life respectively for all whites and all native-born whites, (the later being the group with the highest life expectancy of any part of the American population).[62] In contrast, the life expectancy for those in England and Wales – not the most healthy part of northern Europe – was one year more, at 47.7 years for those who had survived to 10 years of age in 1838–1854.[63] Although these numbers, given the paucity of adequate data, are mostly suggestive, they all go in the same direction. This more easily calculated estimation of life at 10 years for native-born white males shows a systematic long-term decline from late 18th century levels that were not made up until the last decades of the 19th century and parallels the findings in declining heights of males.[64]

[60] Jean-Pierre Bardet and Jacques Dupâquier, eds., *Histoire des populations de l'Europe*, 3 vols., Paris: Fayard, 1998, vol. 2, p. 380.

[61] *The Human Mortality Database*, University of California, Berkeley, and Max Planck Institute for Demographic Research.

[62] Robert William Fogel, "Nutrition and the Decline in Mortality Since 1700: Some Preliminary Findings," in Stanley L. Engerman and Robert E. Gallman, eds., *Long-Term Factors in American Economic Growth*. Chicago: University of Chicago Press, 1986, Table 9.5, p. 454.

[63] See Franz Rothenbacher, *The Societies of Europe: The European Population 1845–1945*. New York: Palgrave-MacMillan, 2002, Table EW–5, p. 744.

[64] Fogel, "Nutrition and the Decline in Mortality," Figure 9.1, p. 465.

Life Expectancy in years to live

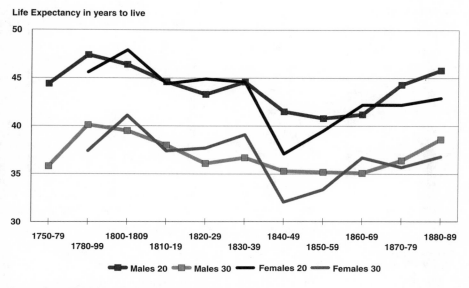

Source: Pope, "Adult Mortality in America before 1900," Table 9.2.

Graph 3.11: Life Expectancy at Ages 20 and 30 Years of Age for Men and Women, 1750–1889.

Although United States rates would eventually change for the better after midcentury, the improvement was rather gradual until the end of the 19th century and it was not until the late 1870s that mortality rates seriously began to decline in the United States.[65] All recent studies of mortality suggest, in fact, that mortality at the end of the 19th century had only returned to the best levels achieved at the end of the 18th century (see Graph 3.11). The two decades before the Civil War were especially harsh, with a serious rise in mortality rates and probably a decline in nutrition.[66] These low rates of life expectancy were, of course, matched by high rates of infant mortality, with most of the rates in the period to 1880 being in the range of 150 to 250 infant deaths per 1,000 live births – a figure higher than the best western European norms in the same period. Until 1880,

---

[65] Haines, "The White Population of the United States, 1790–1920," p. 307.
[66] Pope, "Adult Mortality in America Before 1900," pp. 293–94.

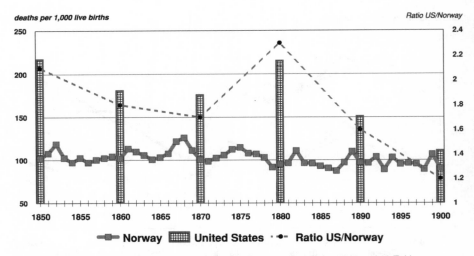

Sources: Rothenbacher, *The Societies of Europe: The European Population 1845—1945*, Table Appendix N4 and Haines, "The Population of the United States, 1790–1920" Table 4.2.

Graph 3.12:   Infant Mortality in Norway and the United States in the 19th Century.

in most decades, Norway's infant mortality rate was half that of the United States (see Graph 3.12).

All this movement of the U.S. population toward the norms of Europe in terms of mortality in the 19th century, along with some increase in the mortality experienced in the immediate pre-1860 period, may have been caused by a variety of factors. It has been suggested that the combination of increasing population density and urbanization, the export of ever higher ratios of domestic food, periodic local economic crises, and the appearance of new diseases on epidemic levels such as yellow fever and especially cholera,[67] helps to explain what some demographic historians have come to call the "Antebellum Paradox" – defined as the marked decline in heights among North Americans that began in the 1830s – which, it is argued, reflected a decline in living standards and nutritional intake

[67] On the three major cholera epidemics that occurred in the United States, see Charles E. Rosenberg, *The Cholera Years: The United States in 1832, 1849 and 1866*, 2nd ed. Chicago: University of Chicago Press, 1987. Of the three epidemics, the most devastating were the first two, both of which occurred throughout the nation.

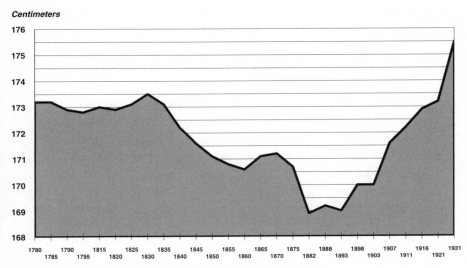

Source: R.E. Gallman, "Economic Growth and Structural Change," Table 1.11.

Graph 3.13: Changing Heights of Americans, 1794–1931 (in Centimeters) by Birth Cohorts.

in the American population.[68] The ultimate height achieved by an adult is a function of both genetics and nutrition. Nutritional deficiencies in early childhood will stunt growth and cause final heights to be less than what might have been expected. From detailed studies of numerous groups of males in the 19th century, it is evident that there was a serious decline in stature from 1835 to the last decades of the century (see Graph 3.13), this despite the fact that the genetic pool was essentially the same for most of the period. In fact, average North American heights do not return to the high levels they achieved in the generation born in 1830 until a century later.

[68] John Komlos, "The Height and Weight of West Point Cadets: Dietary Change in Antebellum America," *The Journal of Economic History* 47, no. 4 (December 1987), pp. 897–927; see also Robert E. Gallman, "Dietary Change in Antebellum America," *The Journal of Economic History* 56, no. 1 (March 1996), pp. 193–201; and the response of John Komlos, "Anomalies in Economic History: Toward a Resolution of the 'Antebellum Puzzle'" *The Journal of Economic History* 56, no. 1. (March 1996), pp. 202–14.

In each generation after that date, there was a decline in heights that did not change direction until the 1880s.

Thus, in the midst of growth and plenty, the United States was becoming like other advanced 19th-century societies – with a mortality rate stabilized at a higher level than in the colonial period. Its fertility rate still remained higher than the European norm, although it was declining ever more rapidly by midcentury and would reach United Kingdom levels by the 1870s. It was also a population progressively moving west along the entire coastline and one that was beginning to achieve European levels of urbanization. Finally, it was a nation that would soon enter a massive Civil War over the definition of one part of its population, that of the African Americans.

CHAPTER FOUR

THE CREATION OF AN INDUSTRIAL
AND URBAN SOCIETY, 1860–1914

The period from 1860 to 1914 was marked by a series of short-term fluctuations and long-term demographic changes in the national population. The Civil War proved to be the most costly in human life of any war suffered by the United States up to this time. This resulted in short-term changes in mortality and fertility. In fact, mortality remained high during most of this period, replicating the patterns of high and fluctuating rates that were the norm for the earlier 19th-century period. But all this would change profoundly after 1870, when death rates in the United States would finally begin a steady and long-term decline. Without question this was to prove to be the most important demographic event in this and the following period. Other trends intensified in this second half of the 19th century and, in turn, were influenced by new evolving forces within national society. Clearly, fertility, which had been on a long-term decline, accelerated that decline at the end of this period and seemed to be more influenced by urban and modern economic factors than had traditionally been the case. Also, the mechanism of controlling natality seem to be changing in important ways in this period, with marital fertility itself declining. These rates also finally reached the low western European levels by the last decade of the century. Abolition of slavery led to profound changes in African American literacy, labor participation, and conditions of health and welfare. Other long-term trends were accelerated in this period, from increased international immigration to rising rates of internal migration. There was a major shift of the national population into urban centers, especially into the large metropolises, as never before. In these various areas of demographic change, many of the trends that had been established earlier in the century were now much accelerated as the United States closed its continental frontier and became a primarily urbanized and industrial society similar to other such societies in the North Atlantic world.

The period opened up with one of the bloodiest wars in American history. The American Civil War, so destructive of life and property in the short run, nevertheless had little impact on long-term trends in American demographic history. Its immediate demographic effects were quite pronounced, however. The conscription of almost half of the eligible young adult males had a negative effect on fertility, and their high rate of deaths had a positive effect on mortality in the first half of the 1860s. It is estimated that the war caused the mobilization of 2.6 million men and that the total number of deaths on both sides was 618,000, with roughly another 472,000 wounded.[1] This was out of a population of 32 million, of whom some 5.8 million were white males aged 15–39 in 1860. This meant that a ratio of 1 in 5 young white males then resident in the country either died or were wounded in the war, which was the highest such ratio ever recorded in an American war. In fact, in no U.S. war, including that of Vietnam, were American causalities so high in absolute numbers.[2] Births declined during the war by an estimated 10%, resulting in half a million lost births, and the first two years of the war were the lowest in terms of the arrival of European immigrants from 1844 to 1931. In all, among deaths, lost births, and lost immigrant population, the war probably led to a deficit of 3 million people in 1870.[3] Although

---

[1] Claudia D. Goldin and Frank D. Lewis, "The Economic Cost of the American Civil War: Estimates and Implications," *The Journal of Economic History* 35, no. 2 (June 1975), pp. 299–326.

[2] In WWI, under 6% of American troops mobilized were killed or wounded, and in WWII, less than 1% of the young male population of the country aged 15 to 44 years were killed or wounded. Colin Clark, *Population Growth and Land Use*, 2nd ed. London: MacMillan Press, 1977, p. 122.

[3] Stanley L. Engerman, "The Economic Impact of the Civil War," in Ralph Andreano, ed., *The Economic Impact of the American Civil War*, 2nd ed. Cambridge, Mass.: Schenkman, 1967, pp. 188–209, and Chester W. Wright, "The More Enduring Economic Consequences of America's Wars," *The Journal of Economic History* 3 (Suppl) (December 1943), pp. 9–26.

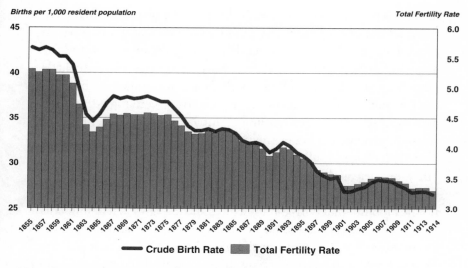

Source: Coale and Zelnik, *New Estimates of Fertility and Population,* Tables 1 and 2.

Graph 4.1: Crude Birth Rate for White Population, 1855–1914.

there was the usual spike in postwar birth rates in the late 1860s and early 1870s, general fertility rates thereafter continued their long-term secular decline for the rest of the century (see Graph 4.1).

The other major demographic effect of the war, of course, was the abolition of slavery. The defeat of the Confederacy led to a basic change in the southern labor force. Whereas the slaves had the highest labor participation ratios ever recorded, with the economically active population being close to 80% of the total population, emancipation led to a massive withdrawal of female and dependent child and aged labor from this agricultural workforce.[4] Women no longer worked in field gangs and children and older persons were no longer made to work as they had before. Thus, among the former slaves, the ratio of economically active to nonactive population now fell to below 60% – the norm for most premodern agricultural populations.[5] But the expected out-migration of ex-slaves from the old plantation

---

[4] On slave labor participation rates, see Robert William Fogel and Stanley L. Engerman, *Time on the Cross: The Economics of American Negro Slavery* (Boston: Little, Brown, 1974), pp. 207–209.

[5] In Latin America, for example, the average of the economically active population (15–64 years) in 1950 was 55% for both Brazil and Bolivia. See United

regions, a pattern that occurred in Brazil and Cuba after emancipation, did not occur here.[6] The promised Republican Party program
of 40 acres and a mule was never delivered to the ex-slaves, and the
majority of them entered freedom without savings and with little
human capital. Ex-slaves had few skills and no literacy to bring to
the free labor market. At the same time, they were forced to compete against better educated immigrant labor everywhere, even in
the southern cities. Finally, the survival of racism from the slave era
placed blockages in all markets against physical and economic mobility for African Americans. This racist reaction of the white population tended to deny African Americans the same physical and economic mobility that native-born whites and foreign-born immigrants
were experiencing and reduced their access to farm lands, especially
in the expanding western frontier. Faced with few alternatives, the
ex-slaves were forced to negotiate sharecropping deals with their old
masters on the traditional estates. In this situation, the majority of
the ex-slaves stayed in the areas in which they were emancipated
and often continued as sharecroppers on the very same farms they
had worked as slaves. Whereas 93% of the African American population, free and slave, had been living in the confederate states in
1860, an extraordinary 91% of this population still lived in these
same states in 1900.[7]

The Civil War also seriously changed the balance of economic
forces by region within the country. The war lowered growth rates
of the economy as a whole in this period, but, most importantly of
all, the emancipation of the slaves, the major property destruction,

Nations: *Demographic Yearbook, Historical Supplement*. New York: United Nations
Publications, 2000, Table 3.

[6] On the comparative experience of emancipation see Herbert S. Klein and Stanley L. Engerman, "The Transition from Slave to Free Labor: Notes on a Comparative Economic Model," in M. Moreno Fraginals, Frank Moya Pons and Stanley L. Engerman, eds., *Between Slavery and Free Labor: The Spanish Speaking
Caribbean in the Nineteenth Century*. Baltimore: Johns Hopkins University Press,
1985, pp. 255–69.

[7] Richard H. Steckel, "The African American Population of the United States,
1790–1920," in Michael R. Haines and Richard H. Steckel, eds., *A Population History of North America*. Cambridge: Cambridge University Press, 2000,
Table 10.7, pp. 462–63.

and the high war costs all had a long-term negative impact on the southern economy.[8] This would turn the South into the most backward region of the nation for another century with a consequent impact on basic demographic indices related to health and the standard of living. But for the nation as a whole, within a decade of the war, the temporary deviation in fertility, mortality, and immigration trends had changed back to long-range patterns, with mortality returning to steady although high levels and fertility continuing a secular decline after a short spike in rates following the war. In both cases, the white part of the American population in the post–Civil War society finally began to move in a rhythm closer to that of the other developing industrial societies of the North Atlantic world. The population became progressively more urban and that urban population was more and more located in ever-larger cities. Fewer workers were now to be found on farms and more were employed in industry than ever before. With these trends in births and deaths the United States by the last quarter of the 19th century finally began to look like England.

But given that North American fertility rates remained higher than the European norm despite their declining trend, the annual natural growth rates of the resident population remained slightly higher than the norm in Europe, even though Europe was now reaching historical growth rate levels in this period. Aside from the fact that the American fertility rates in the early postwar period continued at levels higher than those of most European countries, immigrant workers from Europe continued to arrive in ever larger numbers, so that the total growth rates of the population would remain above the contemporary growth rates experienced by the European populations until the last quarter of the century. Although natural growth rates finally dipped below 3% between 1850 and 1860 and then dropped below 2% per annum between 1880 and 1890, total growth of the national population was sustained at the over 2% per annum level until the end of the century because of the increasing

---

[8] Claudia Dale Goldin, "The Economics of Emancipation," *The Journal of Economic History* 33, no. 1 (March 1973), pp. 66–85; and Engerman, "The Economic Impact of the Civil War."

importance of foreign immigrants, who accounted for as much as a third of total growth in this period.[9]

The one index that would begin to change in profound ways after the Civil War was the mortality rate, which by the late 1870s was finally beginning its long-term secular decline. Mortality in the 19th century, as best as can be estimated without a national vital statistics registration system,[10] was the one rate that exhibited no clear trends until late in the 19th century. Most recent commentators, using small population samples, model life tables, or other indirect measures or estimations, suggest that mortality rose in the first half of the 19th century and then probably stabilized at higher than late-18th-century levels until the last quarter of the 19th century, when these rates finally followed the trends of the European nations and returned to the lower late-18th-century figures. Thus, it would appear that rates of mortality in the United States moved in a direction opposite to those of northern Europe in most of the century. Only after the late 1870s, when the mortality rates in the United States finally began their long-term decline, did these mortality indices come into harmony with the trends in the advanced North Atlantic countries. From declining average male heights to mortality rates estimated from various samples of the population, it was seen that there was an increase in mortality and a decline in life expectancy and the standard of living of the American population from the early 1800s until after the Civil War. It was only a full decade after the war that these indices began to change in a more positive direction.

---

[9] In England, rates were at the 1.2% per annum range for most of the century and especially in the last quarter; see E. A. Wrigley and R. S. Schofield, *The Population History of England, 1541–1871: A Reconstruction.* Cambridge: Cambridge University Press, 1989, p. 187. Rates for the other major countries of Europe were at or below that of England. See Franz Rothenbacher, *The Societies of Europe: The European Population 1845–1945.* New York: Palgrave-MacMillan, 2002, Appendix, national population tables.

[10] The national censuses had only "grossly deficient" data on death and "as late as 1880 only two states, Massachusetts and New Jersey, maintained adequate systems of death registration...." Robert Higgs, "Cycles and Trends of Mortality in 18 Large American Cities, 1871–1900," *Explorations in Economic History* 16, no. 4 (October 1979), p. 382.

As might be expected, the national levels of mortality included wide variation by subsections of the resident population. It has been suggested that although in Europe class and wealth were beginning to influence mortality more than place of residence, in the pre-1900 United States, residence and race were apparently still more influential than economic position in affecting mortality.[11] It is thought that the fact that European countries were far more urbanized than the United States at this time may have been a major cause for this difference.[12] It will be evident when this problem is studied further in the 20th century that place of residence will have less and less significance over time and that occupation and income will become ever more important determinants of mortality differences as the United States moves closer to being a predominantly urban society in the first half of the 20th century.[13] In the second half of the 19th century, regional differences had declined considerably and the spread between urban and rural mortality was declining. But the remaining differences in mortality based on a person's residence still seems to have had a primary influence on morality.

With the urban population doubling from 20% of the national total in 1860 to 40% in 1900, the level of urban mortality began to influence national patterns. There were, of course, some significant changes within urban centers, which began to affect mortality in the late 19th century. The introduction of clean water supplies and the development of modern sanitation facilities all led to a decline in

[11] One of the most complete studies of mortality in the late 19th century, based on a public use sample of individuals in the 1900 census, argued that residence was more important than class in influencing mortality in the late 19th century. See Samuel H. Preston and Michael R. Haines, *Fatal Years, Child Mortality in Late Nineteenth-Century America*. Princeton: Princeton University Press, 1991.

[12] This has been suggested as one of the causal differences, although it has also been suggested that the United States possibly had lesser class inequalities in relation to health. By the turn of the century, England and Wales were 71% urban, compared to only 40% urban in the United States. See Preston and Haines, *Fatal Years*, p. 178, and Michael R. Haines, "Inequality and Childhood Mortality: A Comparison of England and Wales, 1911, and the United States, 1900," *The Journal of Economic History* 45, no. 4 (December 1985), pp. 885–912.

[13] See Robert M. Woodbury, *Infant Mortality and Its Causes*. Baltimore: Williams & Wilkins, 1926, and Chapter 5.

infectious diseases, which most immediately reduced infant and child mortality. It has been estimated that the trend, after a sharp rise in urban mortality in the early 1870s, was downward and that overall crude death rates fell by a fifth from 1870 to 1900 – or from 25 per thousand for some eighteen cities with complete death registration to roughly 20 per thousand in 1900.[14] Nevertheless, the urban–rural differential was still significant until well into the 20th century. In 1900–1902, for example, rural men could expect 54 years of life at birth, whereas those born in the cities had an expectation of only 44 years. For women, the differences were 55 years for rural women and just 48 years for urban women.[15] Moreover, the larger the city, the higher was the mortality.[16]

Another major population group whose death rates remained different from the national average, let alone from the rural population in general, were the African Americans, whose overall mortality remained higher than the national average even though they were the most rural of North American populations. Here, class combined with race would have a more profound impact than urban and rural or regional residence, the factors that most influenced mortality differences in the 19th century. Thus, in terms of both infant mortality and life expectancy, in general, African Americans did worse than white Americans. In 1850, for example, black infant mortality was estimated at 340 deaths per thousand live births that occurred in that year, which was a third higher than the white infant mortality rate of 216 deaths per thousand live births and much higher

[14] Higgs, "Cycles and Trends," p. 391.
[15] Haines suggested that the urban penalty was still 10 years difference in life expectancy in 1900–1902. Michael R. Haines, "The Urban Mortality Transition in the United States, 1800–1940." Cambridge, Mass.: NBER, Historical Research Paper No. 134, July 2001), p. 2. However, Thompson and Whelpton argued that the difference in the combined male and female life expectancy between urban and rural America was just 8.8 years in the same period. See Warren S. Thompson and P. K. Whelpton, *Population Trends in the United States*. New York: McGraw-Hill, 1933, Table 67, p. 242. Also see Michael R. Haines, "The White Population of the United States, 1790–1920," in Michael R. Haines and Richard H. Steckel, eds., *A Population History of North America*. Cambridge: Cambridge University Press, 2000, p. 339.
[16] Haines, "The Urban Mortality Transition in the United States," p. 2.

Years to Live at Birth

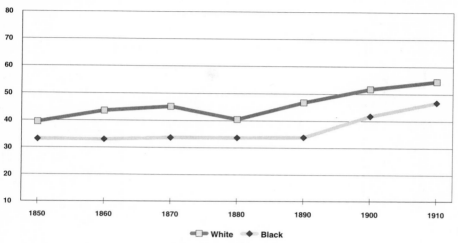

Source: Haines, "The Population of the United States, 1790–1920," Table 4.1 and Eblen "New Estimates of the Vital Rates," p. 309 for 1850–1890 black rates.

Graph 4.2: Life Expectancy of Whites and Blacks in Years, 1800–1910.

than comparable European rates.[17] Life expectancy for black Americans was 23 years compared to 39.5 years for whites in the same year. Nor did this disadvantage change over time. Although both whites and blacks experienced declining mortality after the 1870s, by the end of the 19th century, there was still a 10-year difference in life expectancy between the two groups, and over the course of the next forty years, there was little convergence in these rates by race or in the rates of infant mortality, despite continued improvement in the health of both races (see Graphs 4.2 and 4.3).[18]

Although race, region, and urban–rural differences remained to divide subpopulations, the overall rates for all groups slowly moved

[17] Michael R. Haines, "The Population of the United States, 1880–1990," in Stanley L. Engerman and Robert E. Gallman, eds., *The Cambridge Economic History of the United States*, 3 vols. Cambridge: Cambridge University Press, 1996, vol. II, Table 4.3, p. 158. In Iceland in 1850, the infant mortality rate was 242; in Spain, the infant mortality rate was 171; and in France, England, and Sweden, the infant mortality rate was in the 140s in this same year. Rothenbacher, *The Societies of Europe: The European Population 1845–1945*, Table 3.3, p. 27.

[18] Haines and Steckel, *A Population History of North America*, Appendix Table A2, p. 696.

Deaths per 1,000 live births

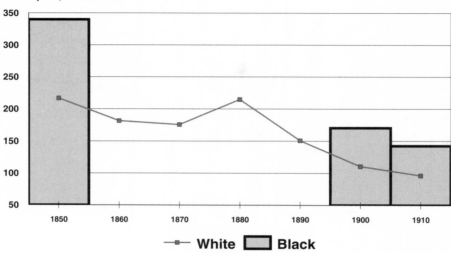

Source: Haines, "Ethnic Differences in Demographic Behavior," Table 3.

Graph 4.3: Infant Mortality of Whites and Blacks, 1850–1910.

downward, matching European trends, in the last quarter of the 19th century. The crude death rate in the second half of the 19th century went from 24 per thousand resident population in the 1870s to 19 per thousand in the 1890s.[19] Infant mortality dropped from over 200 in 1850 to 111 per thousand births by 1900. Consequently, life expectancy grew by over 10 years in this same period from the lower 40s to the lower 50s for the entire population.[20] These were rates that were common in the advanced North Atlantic countries. These declining mortality rates would, of course, have a direct impact on fertility as well. It has been calculated that only 52% of the native-born white women in Massachusetts in 1830 survived to 1874 and were thus able to complete their fertility cycle. But the rate increased to 56% for those who reached 44 years of age in 1894, and for the cohort born in 1870 and completing their fertility in 1914, the survival rate was 60%. Although the total fertility of this group of three generations of native-born white women – born in 1830,

[19] Haines, "The Population of the United States, 1880–1990," Table 4.1, p. 153.
[20] Haines and Steckel, *A Population History of North America*, Appendix Table A2, p. 696.

1850, and 1870 – slowly declined from 3.8 to 3.4 children, because of their lower mortality, the 1870 cohort of women in fact achieved a higher replacement ratio than the earlier cohorts.[21]

The causes for this decline in mortality in the United States in the late 19th century are much in debate. One study shows a high correlation in immigration arrivals and sharp rises in mortality rates. The argument was that immigrants were the poorest element in the society, the ones most likely to go into urban centers, and thus the population with the highest rates of infectious diseases despite their concentration in the working age groups and their lower dependency ratios.[22] Although immigration may explain variations from the trend, it does not explain the causes for the long-term decline of mortality rates that occurred at the end of this period. Moreover, one study of late-19th-century mortality suggests that second-generation immigrant families had a lower level of mortality than did the native-born Americans.[23] Most probably the single major cause both here and abroad for finally forcing down mortality was the sanitation movement that began after 1880, which was responsible for slowly cleaning up the nations' sewage and water supplies. In 1880, few cities had sanitary sewers, but by 1907 every major city in the country had them. In 1875, fewer than 35,000 urban residents had filtered water; by 1910, the number of urbanites with access to such secure water supplies was calculated at 10 million persons.[24] As most medical

---

[21] Peter H. Uhlenberg, "A Study of Cohort Life-Cycles: Cohorts of Native Born Massachusetts Women, 1830–1920," *Population Studies*, 23, no. 3 (November 1969), Tables 2 and A1, pp. 416, 419.

[22] Higgs, "Cycles and Trends." This is also the position taken by Richard A. Meckel, "Immigration, Mortality and Population Growth in Boston, 1840–1880," *Journal of Interdisciplinary History* 15, no. 3 (Winter 1985), p. 416.

[23] Preston and Haines found that when urban size and other factors were added, the influence of immigrant status on child mortality tended to disappear and most certainly was non-influential for the second generation born to immigrant parents. See Preston and Haines, *Fatal Years*, pp. 146–47, 164–65.

[24] Edward Meeker, "The Social Rate of Return on Investment in Public Health, 1880–1910," *Journal of Economic History* 34, no. 2 (June 1974), pp. 392–93. Another estimate holds that 28% of the urban population was drinking filtered water by 1917. K. Celese Gaspari and Arthur G. Woolf, "Income, Public Works and Mortality in Early Twentieth-Century American Cities," *Journal of Economic History* 45, no. 2 (June 1985), p. 356. Gaspari and Woolf, in their study, claimed that

historians have suggested, there were few medical improvements before the end of the 19th century that could have accounted for this massive change.[25] Although the reduction of maternal mortality at birth in the last quarter of the 19th century was fundamental in increasing the life expectancy of adult women, the bulk of the decline in mortality was due to the decline in the rates of infant and child mortality – as it is even today in the developing world. Among this population, the big killers were intestinal and infectious diseases of all kinds, most of them related to poor sanitation. Another factor causing higher rates of morbidity and mortality was nutritional deficiencies. It seems evident from the changes in heights in this period that health was related in many ways to nutritional intake. Although famines had disappeared from Europe and America by the late 18th century – except in the very special government-induced case of Ireland in the 1840s – and food supplies were more than adequate, the variation in heights suggests that dietary limitations could and did affect health in numerous ways. Combined with poor sanitation, these nutritional deficiencies may have had a profound impact on morbidity and mortality rates.[26] Consequently, the rising heights of male cohorts born after the Civil War suggest an improvement in nutritional standards for the American population. With better transportation and better food preservation techniques developing in the second half of the 19th century, the North American populations were better fed than previously, and the food they consumed was less prone to carry disease. These changes in food and water supplies may have helped reduce the level of mortality in the population.

The post–Civil War period was also one in which the birth rates, which had been falling for most of the century, finally reached the

miles of sewer piping had more of an impact on mortality than filtered drinking water.

[25] Henry F. Dowling, *Fighting Infection. Conquests of the Twentieth Century.* Boston: Harvard University Press, 1977, chapter 1.

[26] For the relationship between nutrition status as measured by height and mortality, see Robert William Fogel, "Nutrition and the Decline in Mortality Since 1700: Some Preliminary Findings," in Stanley L. Engerman and Robert E. Gallman, eds., *Long-Term Factors in American Economic Growth.* Chicago: University of Chicago Press, 1986, pp. 439–556.

Number of Children per Woman

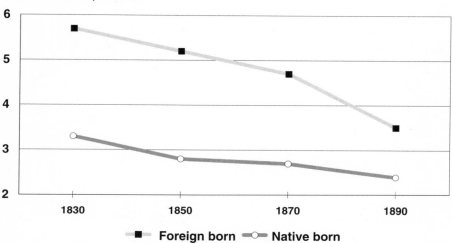

Source: Uhlenberg, "A Study of Cohort Life Cycles," Table 1.

Graph 4.4: Foreign and Native-Born Total Fertility per Woman in Massachusetts for Cohorts Born 1830–1890.

level of the advanced European nations, with the result that the natural growth rates finally fell in line with those of Europe at the end of the 19th century. This declining rate of natural population growth seriously affected total growth rates, despite the increasing volume of European immigration, which now accounted for between a third and a quarter of the total growth in the national population in this last quarter of the century.[27] Although immigrants tended to have higher birth rates than native North Americans in the first generation of arrivals (see Graph 4.4), the experience in the 19th and 20th centuries is that by the second generation, birth rates approached

[27] Although birth registrations in the 19th century were as inadequate as death enumerations and were not really fully developed on a national level until the 1930s when most states entered a Birth Registration Area, demographers have been able to use the child–women ratios – available from the actual census – as a reasonable proxy of fertility, although with the proviso that mortality rates could influence the resulting figures. Given the lack of mortality rates for the various age categories of children and women, most demographers have assumed such rates from hypothetical model life tables developed for known world populations.

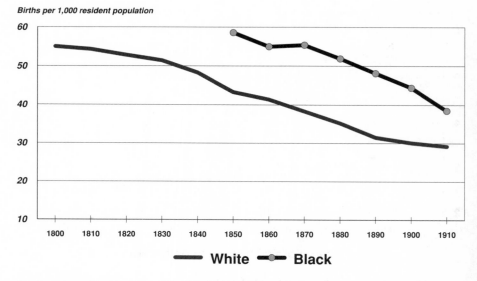

Births per 1,000 resident population

Source: Haines, The Population of the United States,1790—1920, Table 4.2.

Graph 4.5: Crude Birth Rates of Whites and Blacks, 1800–1910.

those of the natives.[28] In any case, given their relatively modest importance within the national population, foreign-born first-
generation residents had only a moderate affect on long-term trends.
The same can be said for the black fertility rates, which remained
higher than those of whites throughout the 19th century (see Graph
4.5) but which accounted for only a small proportion of total births,
because African Americans represented only 14.1% of the population in 1860 and just 11.6% in 1900.

As early as the last years of the 1860s, the total fertility rate
of American women had dropped to a level below that of the advanced Scandinavian countries and England. But this was due to
the impact of the Civil War on the fertility behavior of American
women. The postwar rise in births, a traditional response to the return of the veterans to their families in the age of mass conscription,
moved American rates again to levels above those of Europe. But this

---

[28] For a full discussion of this theme of first and second generation immigrant fertility, see Chapter 5.

children per woman

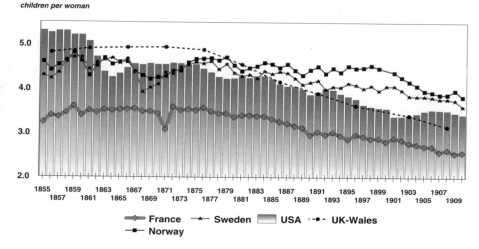

Source: Coale and Zelnik, *New Estimates of Fertility and Population,* Table 2; and Chesnais, *The Demographic Transition,* Table A2.2.

Graph 4.6: Total Fertility Rate of U.S. White Women Compared to Select European Countries, 1855–1910.

reversal of the long-term trend of decline was only temporary, and from the last years of the 1870s, the total fertility rates in the United States dropped to 4.5 children per woman and finally and permanently reached a rate at or below that of the advanced European countries and in line with England itself. The only exception, and a unique one, was that of France, which had the advanced world's lowest rates of reproduction for the entire century (see Graph 4.6).

The cause for this decline in reproduction among American women is probably related to the changes in the demand for education, housing, and employment associated with increasing urbanization and industrialization then occurring in the North American society and economy. The escape valve of the frontier migrations with their usually higher rates of fertility was coming to an end and the frontier would cease to exist altogether by the end of the century. The increasing density of Western settlement began moving Western population fertility rates toward those of the Eastern Seaboard. The movement of the national population off the farms and into the cities was also beginning to affect rates of reproduction quite dramatically, as it did in the rest of the industrialized world. Whereas land tenure was probably the most important factor influencing the trend in declining rates in the first half of the 19th century, by the second half of the century, these new factors of urban residence and non-farm occupations were beginning to have much more of an impact.

By the last decade of the century, the U.S. fertility rates matched those of western Europe, the leaders in the final phase of the demographic transition. In this phase (see Graph 3.4 earlier) the stabilization of death rates in the late 18th and early 19th centuries was not matched by a fall in traditionally high fertility rates, which resulted in ever-increasing annual rates of natural growth. Only at the end of the 19th century did European populations respond to these high growth rates by beginning to curtail their fertility rates. England was one of the first of the western European nations to respond to these changes in the post-1870 period and is held as a model for the transition, which now occurred among all the advanced industrial societies of Europe. This pattern of fertility decline then passed from western Europe to eastern and Mediterranean Europe at the end of the 19th and the beginning of the 20th centuries. In turn, this has been the standard experience of most developing countries in the late 20th century. Only two nations are exceptional to this norm. The first is France, where fertility began to decline at the end of the 18th century, long before mortality rates stabilized and long before growth rates reached unusually high levels. The other, of course, was the United States. Whereas France was at modern levels of low fertility by the 1840s, it would take the United States until the 1890s to reach these low rates.[29] But in both cases, the trend and timing were

[29] By 1845–1849, France reached a total fertility rate of 3.5 children per women who had completed their fertility. Jean-Claude Chesnais, *The Demographic Transition . . . 1720–1984*. Oxford: Clarendon Press, 1992, Table 11.1, p. 323. On the various causes proposed for explaining the unusually early French decline – which include questions of partible inheritance, access to land, population density, wars, revolution, and an early secularization of society – see the discussion in Chesnais, *The Demographic Transition*, pp. 333–40; also see Etienne van de Walle, "Alone in Europe: The French Fertility Decline until 1850," in Charles Tilly, ed., *Historical Studies of Changing Fertility*. Princeton: Princeton University Press, 1978, pp. 257–88.

identical; in both societies, fertility declined before mortality stabilized or declined. Although the initiation of the fertility decline in both France and the United States was tied to questions of land tenure and access to resources in the then primarily rural-agricultural societies, the increased intensity of the fertility decline in the late 19th century is tied to questions of the changing nature of North American society.

In 1860, the United States was still a largely agricultural society. Only 20% of the population resided in towns of 2,500 or more, and 48% of the labor force were still engaged in agriculture. Although manufactures had been growing, industry still absorbed only 18% of the economically active labor force. By 1900, a third of the population resided in towns and cities, and a significant 31% of all persons resided in cities of 100,000 or more population, up from just 10% of the national population in 1860.[30] Equally, the ratio of the economically active population engaged in agriculture now dropped to 37%.[31] Clearly, there was a major shift in the last half of the 19th century, which finally pushed the national population into being defined as primarily nonrural and nonagricultural, with the trends all moving toward further urbanization and a declining importance for rural labor in the national labor force. All of these trends influenced the American populations in their birth, death, and growth rates, making the United States indistinguishable from the other leading industrializing nations of the period.

The dominant hypotheses about this decline have suggested that land availability was the primary concern, along with the desire to maintain family wealth in the face of very large families and the need to accommodate all children.[32] To these traditional rural land tenure

---

[30] Data taken from *Historical Statistics*, Table A 57–72.
[31] Data taken from *Historical Statistics*, Table F 250–261.
[32] Yasukichi Yasuba, *Birth Rates of the White Population in the United States, 1800–1860: An Economic Study*. Baltimore: Johns Hopkins University, 1962, chapter 5; and the essays of Richard A. Easterlin, "Factors in the Decline of Farm Family Fertility in the United States: Some Preliminary Research Results," *The Journal of American History* 63, no.3 (December 1976), pp. 600–14; "Population Change and Farm Settlement in the Northern United States," *The Journal of Economic*

causes, which may have dominated in the first half of the 19th century, were now added the concerns of housing and education costs in the late 19th century, as more families decided that the costs of children were increasing and there was a need for limitations if economic viability of the family was to be maintained.[33] Thus, as one source succinctly stated, "couples strove to provide for a smaller number of expensive, 'high-quality' children."[34] These cost factors and the desire to achieve socioeconomic mobility for their children were factors that were becoming ever more important as ever more families moved off the land to the cities.

But the question is how did this change actually occur? Given the fact that births outside marriage remained low in all Western societies in the 19th century, it was marital fertility that was the crucial area in which changed occurred. In populations in which no contraception was being practiced, one sure way of reducing fertility was to raise the age of marriage for women and have more women reach the end of their fertile years without being married, thus eliminating several years of potential fertility and or reducing the number of potential mothers. From small samples of 19th century population, this seems to have been the case in the earlier period.[35] Another major possibility would have been to lengthen the spacing between births and to terminate fertility at an earlier age, and this appears to be what most influenced changing fertility rates in the second half of the century. Data from the Mormon genealogical records suggest this

History 36, no. 1 (March 1976), pp. 45–75; and Richard A. Easterlin, George Alter, and Gretchen A. Condran, "Farms and Farm Families in Old and New Areas: The Northern States in 1860," in Tamara K. Hareven and Maris A. Vinovskis, eds., *Family and Population in Nineteenth-Century America*. Princeton: Princeton University Press, 1978, pp. 23–84.

33 An interesting study of the costs of children argument can be found in Stephan Thernstrom, *Poverty and Progress: Social Mobility in a Nineteenth Century City.* Cambridge, Mass.: Harvard University Press, 1964.

34 Myron P. Gutmann and Kenneth H. Fliess, "The Determinants of Early Fertility Decline in Texas," *Demography* 30, no. 3 (1993), p. 444.

35 For one such study among many, see Michael B. Katz and Mark J. Stern, "Fertility, Class and Industrial Capitalism, Erie County, New York, 1855–1915," *American Quarterly* 33, no. 1 (Spring 1981), pp. 63–92.

actually occurred among Mormon families in the 19th century.[36] It would appear that once optimal family size was reached, the spacing of children quickly increased and the age of the woman when her last child was born declined.[37] The Mormon data suggest that there was little difference in spacing in the birth of the earliest children, but that when some ideal level was reached, the spacing to the last child increased substantially and the mothers age when she had her last child declined. All this suggests a voluntary attempt to control fertility, which resulted in last children being born to mothers significantly younger than what one could expect on biological grounds alone.

It is evident, as well, that for the reasons suggested by demographic historians, native-born whites were leading the way with a new cultural norm of relatively small families and that this model was quickly adopted by the arriving immigrants as a better model than that which they brought with them from their home countries. It appears, from numerous local studies, that there were uneven rates of change within the population, based on origins, socioeconomic conditions, and religion. Evidently, elites were more concerned with wealth issues than the poor, and initially the Protestants were more willing to control fertility than were the Catholics. Immigrants were slower to change than natives, and rural persons were slower to change than were the urban residents, although all were moving in the same direction throughout the North Atlantic world by the last quarter of the 19th century.[38] It would appear that

[36] Douglas L. Anderton and Lee L. Bean, "Birth Spacing and Fertility Limitation: A Behavioral Analysis of a Nineteenth Century Frontier Population," *Demography* 22, no. 2 (May 1985), pp. 169–83.

[37] In rural western Massachusetts, these were the preferred mechanisms for reducing fertility. See H. Temkin-Greener and A. C. Swedlund, "Fertility Transition in the Connecticut Valley, 1740–1850," *Population Studies* 32, no. 1 (March 1978), pp. 27–41. It has also been suggested that induced abortions may have accounted for just under half of all avoided births by ever-married women in an 1858 cohort. Warren C. Sanderson, "Quantitative Aspects of Marriage Fertility and Family Limitation in Nineteenth Century America: Another Application of the Coale Specifications," *Demography* 16, no. 3 (August 1979), pp. 339–58.

[38] For a detailed case study of ethnicity, origins, residence, and fertility in this period, see Myron P. Gutmann and Kenneth H. Fliess, "The Determinants of Early Fertility Decline in Texas," *Demography* 30, no. 3 (August 1993), pp. 443–57.

the age of first marriage for women was rising through most of the 19th century, although the ratio of women never married was only very moderately increasing in this period. But these changes, especially the ratio of never married (well below 10% for most of the 19th century) in and of themselves were no longer the primary form of control.[39] It has been estimated that three quarters of the decline in fertility in the 19th century came from changes in marital fertility rates (due to changes in child spacing and the earlier termination of fertility among married women) and only about a quarter was due to changes in marriage rates (that is, in the age of marriage and the ratio of women ever married).[40] Rather, the spacing of children became ever more important in controlling fertility. This, in turn, suggests the beginnings of a significant usage of some form of contraceptive method by the North American population well before the end of the 19th century. Also, the decline in fertility was increasing in rapidity in the second half of the 19th century. Whereas the total fertility dropped 25% from 1800 to 1855, it declined by a third between 1855 and 1900.[41] All this influenced the median age of the population, given the declining number of children being born in this period. By 1850, the median age of the resident population recorded in the U.S. census was 18.9 years (up 3 years from 1820), and by 1900, it had risen to 22.9 years.[42] As can be seen when

[39] Michael R. Haines, "Long Term Marriage Patterns in the United States from Colonial Times to the Present" Cambridge, Mass.: NBER, Historical Research Paper No. 80, March 1996), p. 3. It has been estimated that the age of marriage in the United States was 19.5 years in 1800, rose to 21.4 years by 1870, and probably peaked for this period in 1910 at 22.3 years (Sanderson data cited in Table 4 in Haines, "Long Term Marriage Patterns") According to the Bureau of the Census, by 1890 the age of first marriage for women reached a high of 22.0 years and reached its lowest modern level of 20.1 years in 1956. But by today's standards of 25.1 years, this was still not an all-time high figure. See U.S. Census Bureau, "Estimated Median Age at First Marriage, by Sex: 1890 to the Present," Internet Release date: June 29, 2001, Table MS-2.

[40] Warren C. Sanderson, "Quantitative Aspects of Marriage, Fertility and Family Limitation in Nineteenth Century America: Another Application of the Coale Specifications," Demography 16, no. 3 (August 1979), p. 343.

[41] Ansley J. Coale and Melvin Zelnik, New Estimates of Fertility and Population in the United States. Princeton: Princeton University Press, 1963, Table 2, p. 36.

[42] Data taken from Historical Statistics, Table Series A 143–57.

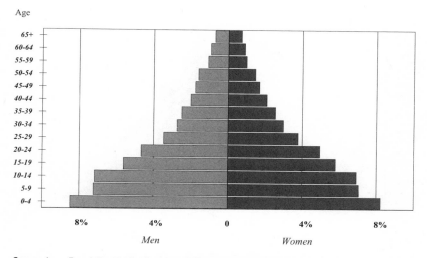

Source: Lee, *Population Redistribution and Economic Growth,* Table 1.1.

Graph 4.7: Age Pyramid of the U.S. Population in 1870.

comparing the age structures of the U.S. population in 1870 and 1900 with that in 1910 (see Graphs 4.7 through 4.9), declining birth rates were having an impact on the structure of the age pyramid, reducing the base of the pyramid and moving the United States slowly to a more modern posttransitional model of age distributions.

During all this period there was also a steady increase in the number of arriving immigrants, with Europeans still predominating as the primary source of these immigrants. Between 1850 and 1915, more than 40 million Europeans migrated to the Americas. Of this number, 28 million would come to the United States, the largest receiving nation in the region (see Graph 4.10).[43] But in the second half of the 19th century, there was a major change in the origin of these European immigrants. Whereas the emigration of northern Europeans, those from the British islands, Scandinavia, and the German regions had predominated up until the 1870s, after 1880 there was a massive arrival of southern and eastern Europeans. As the demographic transition began affecting these regions in the second half of the 19th century, growth rates of the local resident populations

---

[43] Imre Ferenczi and Walter F. Willcox, *International Migrations,* 2 vols. New York: National Bureau of Economic Research, 1929, vol. I, Table 6, pp. 236–37.

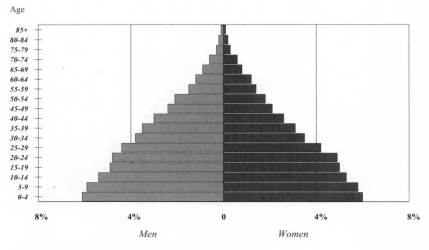

Source: Hobbs and Stoops, *Demographic Trends,* Table A5.

Graph 4.8: Age Pyramid of the U.S. Population in 1900.

of the Iberian Peninsula, Italy, Greece, the Ottoman regions of the
Middle East in the Mediterranean region, and regions of the Russian
empire and Poland in eastern Europe began to outpace the capacity of their newer and growing older cities to absorb this population.
With Argentina, Brazil, and Canada entering the market for workers
along with the United States in this same period and with all initially paying wages higher than those being offered in Europe, there
was an outpouring of immigrant workers from these newer areas of
Europe. At the same time, northern European wages were beginning
to reach Western Hemisphere levels, which resulted in the consequent slowing of emigration from these traditional northern early
19th century sources.[44] The change was rapid. In the decade of the
1870s, the so-called New Immigrants from southern and eastern Europe represented just 6% of all immigrants arriving to ports of the

---

[44] For the latest modeling of this emigration, see Timothy J. Hatton and Jeffrey G.
Williamson, "What Drove the Mass Migrations from Europe in the Late Nineteenth Century?" *Population and Development Review* 20, no. 3 (September 1994),
pp. 533–59.

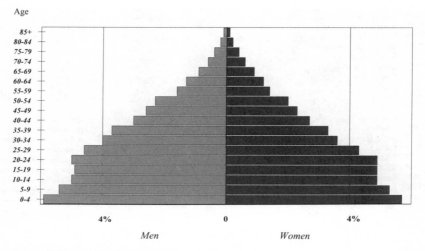

Source: Hobbs and Stoops, Demographic Trends, Table A5.

Graph 4.9: Age Pyramid of the U.S. Population in 1910.

United States. In the next decade, the southern and eastern Europeans jumped to 18% of all migrants and then spurted to over half of all arrivals by the 1890s, far surpassing that of the old northern Europeans. By the first decade of the 20th century, they made up two-thirds of all of all migrants arriving in the ports of the United States (Graph 4.11).[45]

Thus, the period after 1880 would usher in a new period of international migration to the United States, the era of the "New Immigrants." This migration proved to be even more intense than the earlier movements, and it was more urban in direction than the earlier foreign migrations. The intensity of this immigration meant that the relative importance of the foreign-born population within the United States also rapidly increased. In 1850, the 2.2 million foreign born residing in the United States represented only 10% of the

[45] U.S. Department of Justice, Immigration and Naturalization Service, *Statistical Yearbook of the Immigration and Naturalization Service* (1998), p. 19. For the latest survey of this immigration experience, see Walter Nugent, *Crossings: The Great Transatlantic Migrations, 1870–1914*. Bloomington, Ind.: Indiana University Press, 1992.

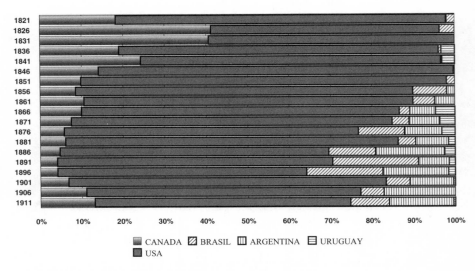

Source: Ferenczi and Wilcox, *International Migrations*, Vol. I, pp. 236–37.

Graph 4.10: Share of European Immigration by American Receiving Country by Quinquenium, 1821–1911.

total resident population, but by 1890, there were 9.2 million such foreign-born persons in the United States and they now accounted for 15% of the population, a ratio that they would roughly maintain until 1910.[46] Of these foreign born in 1850, 92% were coming from Europe, and Europeans still represented 87% of all foreign born in 1910. The next major group of nonnatives were the Canadian immigrants who, throughout the last half of the 19th century and to 1914, represented roughly 10% of all immigrants. By 1910, there were also the first indications of a new migration with 2% of the immigration now coming from Latin America and another percentage and a half coming from Asia.[47]

[46] Campbell J. Gibson and Emily Lennon, "Historical Census Statistics on the Foreign-Born Population of the United States: 1850–1990," Population Division, Working Paper No. 29; U.S. Bureau of the Census, Washington, D.C., February 1999, Table 1.

[47] Gibson and Lennon, "Historical Census Statistics on the Foreign-Born," Table 2.

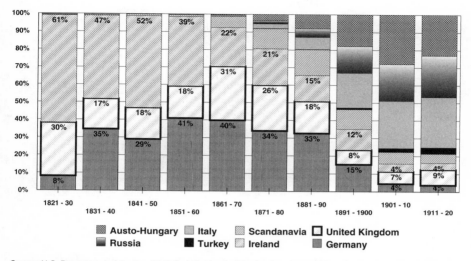

Source: U.S. Department of Justice, *Statistical Yearbook of the Immigration and Naturalization Service, 1998*, Table 2.

Graph 4.11: Origins of Arriving Immigrants to the United States, 1821–1920.

Like all immigrants before or after this period, there were more males among the arriving migrants than females and they were primarily working age adults. But compared to immigrants in the earlier republican period, there were now fewer families, more persons traveling alone, and many fewer children. There were also fewer farmers and far more manual laborers in this post-1880 migration compared to those arriving in the 1830s and 1840s.[48] The median age for both foreign-born men and foreign-born women in 1880 was 38 years of age, over 17 years older than the median age of the national population in that period. Although the median age of the national population by 1910 rose 4 years to 24 years of age and the foreign-born average fell 1 year in this period, they were was still 13 years older, on average, than the national median age in the first decade of the 20th century. Their sex ratio was 119 men to 100 arriving women, compared to the national ratio in 1890 of just 103 males to every

---

[48] Charlotte J. Erickson, "Emigration from the British Isles to the USA in 1841: Part 1. Emigration from the British Isles," *Population Studies* 43 (1989), p. 380. She argued that there is a general consensus about the differences of the migrants of the 1880s from those of the 1830s.

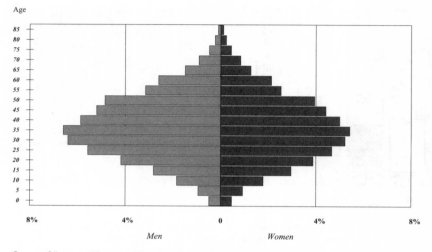

Source: Gibson and Lennon, *Historical Census Statistics on the Foreign-born Population of the United States: 1850–1990*. Table 7.

Graph 4.12: Age Pyramid of the Foreign-Born Population in 1880.

100 females in the national population, and this difference, in fact, increased by 1910 as the arriving immigrants had 131 males for every 100 females, compared to a national total of just 106 males per 100 females.[49] This bias in age and sex can be seen in their age and sex structure in the age pyramids for the foreign-born population in 1880 and in 1910 (see Graphs 4.12 and 4.13). Such an age structure made the reproduction of the arriving population quite difficult to achieve without a constant feeding in of new immigrants and, in this, the post-1880 migration much resembled the earlier African slave migration.

The new immigrants of the post-1880 period were no longer going to the same American regions as the pre-1880 immigrants and they were no longer concentrated on the Eastern Seaboard. Although the old and new European immigrants kept going to the North – 88% were found in the northern states in 1850 and 86% in 1900 – they were now residing farther from the coast. The middle western states, which in 1850 held only 29% of these foreign-born residents, by 1900

[49] Gibson and Lennon, "Historical Census Statistics on the Foreign-Born," Table 7; and *Historical Statistics of the United States*, Table A 143–157 and Table A 119–134.

Age

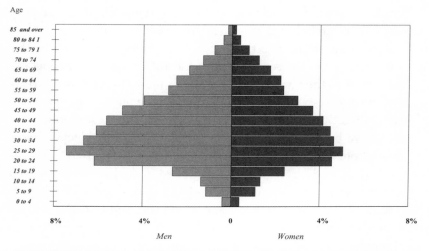

Source: Gibson and Lennon, *Historical Census Statistics on the Foreign-born Population of the United States: 1850–1990. Table 7.*

Graph 4.13: Age Pyramid of the Foreign-Born Population in 1910.

contained some 46% of these foreign born, with their ratio in the Northeast correspondingly declining.[50] These foreign born were also far more urban oriented than the rest of the population, with only a third living in rural areas in 1900 compared to 64% of the native born who declared a rural residence. As early as 1870, over a quarter of them resided in cities of 100,000 or more (compared to just 8% of the native born), and by 1910, some 44% were residing in these large cities (again compared to only 18% of the native-born residents).[51] This far more urban residence, of course, directly affected the mortality rates of the foreign born, who – even controlling for their older ages – had higher mortality rates than the native-born population. But these immigrants also brought with them an experience of higher fertility rates as well, especially as many of them came from the rural areas of Europe. But their predominantly urban residence in the United States would hasten them to adapt to the native-born

[50] Gibson and Lennon, "Historical Census Statistics on the Foreign-Born," Table 14.
[51] Gibson and Lennon, "Historical Census Statistics on the Foreign-Born," Table 18.

fertility and family models and by the second generation, their family sizes were often below that of the native born.

Immigrants were not the only ones moving westward in the United States in the second half of the 19th century. The ongoing movement to the cheaper lands of the frontier also continued to attract the native-born white population. Of the major components of the United States population in this period, the most mobile were the native-born whites and the least mobile were the blacks, almost all of whom were native born in the post–Civil-War period. Whereas the African Americans were concentrated in the South and showed few signs of geographic mobility and immigrants tended to congregate in the northern seacoast states and the Midwest, the native-born whites moved everywhere land and economic opportunity were available.

The movement of the "center" of population in United States reflected this. Until 1800, the center of the national population was estimated to be in Maryland. In 1810, the center moved toward Loudon County in Virginia. From 1810 to 1850, it moved westward through West Virginia and reached just north of Cincinnati, Ohio by 1870. By 1890, it was in eastern Indiana and by 1910, it was centered in Bloomington, Indiana.[52] This reflected a basic change in the regional distribution of the population. The Western states were growing rapidly in the period from 1860 to 1910 and increasing their share of total national population from 15% to 30% by 1910 (see Graph 4.14). But over time, as population densities increased in the new regions and divisions, sex ratios moved toward balance as more locally born populations began to outnumber the recent migrants and the urban centers began to expand to contain an ever increasing share of the population. This urban growth was steady but slow, and the North Central and Western states did not achieve the over-50% urban ratio that the Northeast achieved in 1880 until after 1910 (Graph 4.15). What is most impressive about this movement in all regions, was how little the South changed. Its relative share of the total population remained the same in this period, clearly reflecting

[52] U.S. Bureau of the Census, 1990 Census of Population and Housing, "1990 Population and Housing Unit Counts: United States," (CPH-2).

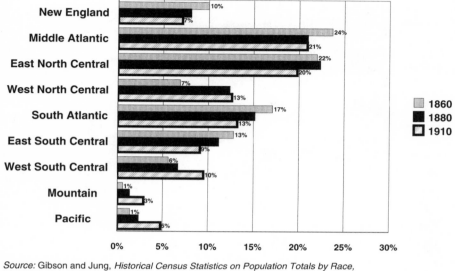

Source: Gibson and Jung, *Historical Census Statistics on Population Totals by Race,* Tables 6–14.

Graph 4.14: Relative Share of Total Population by Division, 1860–1910.

its own rapid native population growth rate. But it was far less urban than the rest of the nation and its urbanization by 1910 was half that of the West or North Central states.

This migration of persons out of their places of birth was a constant in 19th- and 20th-century America. By the end of the century, all the continental states were fully formed and clearly defined regions existed. In terms of the native white population, there was a clear tendency for the Eastern Seaboard to lose population and for the western part of the Middle West and the Mountain and Pacific states to gain population. In comparing the net migration rates of the states at the two ends of this period, those for the decade of 1870–1880 and for 1900–1910, it can be seen that the states that had gained population in the first period lost population in the second as the western migration continued (Maps 4.1 and 4.2).[53] Minnesota,

---

[53] The data on net-migration is taken from the census survival estimates calculated by Everett S. Lee, et al., *Population Redistribution and Economic Growth in the United States, 1870–1950,* 2 vols. Philadelphia: American Philosophical Society, 1957, vol. I Table 1.12, p. 78.

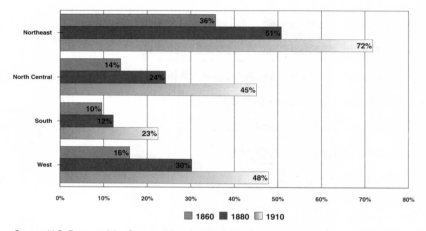

Source: U.S. Bureau of the Census, *Historical Statistics,* Series A 172–94.

Graph 4.15: Percentage of the Population that was Urban by Region, 1860–1910.

for example, was a major gainer in the first period and then began to lose population by the later decade. The same occurred with most of the other states in the West North Central region such as Nebraska, Kansas, and Missouri. In turn, the Mountain and Pacific region states continued to have major net-positive immigrant flows in both periods. But there were also local variations within regions. In New England, Rhode Island had a consistently positive net migration in this period, whereas New Jersey was the only Middle Atlantic state to move toward a positive net migration. Although New Jersey began 1870–1880 with a loss of population, it proceeded to achieve positive net migration ratios in each succeeding decade. In the South, only a few states in the West South Central region (Texas and Oklahoma) consistently gained population, whereas almost all the other southern states lost population through out-migration (see Maps 4.1 and 4.2).

This migration of native-born whites had a direct impact on the overall growth of states. Although all states had a positive rate of growth between 1860 and 1910, the growth rates were much lower in the Eastern Seaboard and increased as one moved inland. New England and the southern Atlantic and East South Central regions

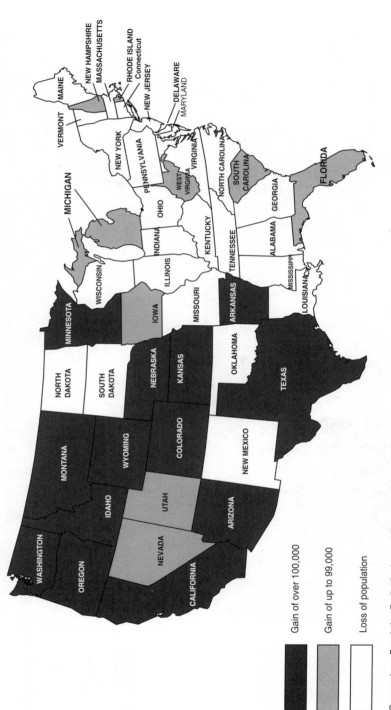

Source: Lee, *Population Redistribution and Economic Growth*, Table 1.12.

Map 4.1: Net Migration by State, 1870–1880 (Census Survival Rate Estimate).

Gain of over 100,000

Gain of up to 99,000

Loss of population

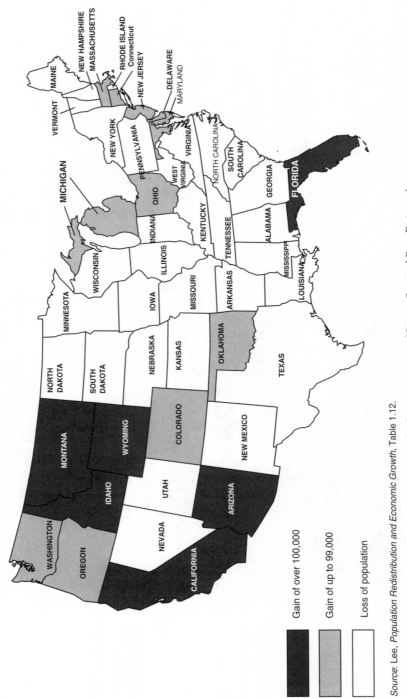

Source: Lee, *Population Redistribution and Economic Growth*, Table 1.12.

Map 4.2: Net Migration by State, 1900–1910 (Census Survival Rate Estimate).

Gain of over 100,000

Gain of up to 99,000

Loss of population

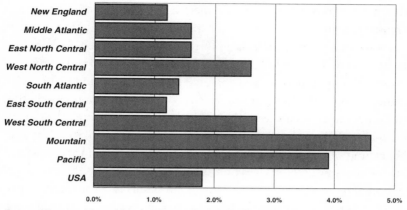

Source: Gibson and Jung, *Historical Census Statistics on Population Totals by Race*, Tables 6–14.

Graph 4.16: Per Annum Growth of Regions, 1860–1910.

all grew at rates well below the national annual average rate of growth, and even the states of the Middle Atlantic and Eastern North Central region barely kept pace with the national average. But the Western, Pacific, and Mountain states all grew at rates well above the national average (see Graph 4.16). This, of course, meant that the relative share of the regions shifted dramatically in accounting for the total national population. In 1860, the Eastern seaboard states from Maine to Florida accounted for over half of the national population, but by 1910, their share had fallen to 41% of the national population. The Western states and those of the Pacific coast, in contrast, went from 14% to 30% of the total population in the same period, and, as noted earlier, these were the fastest growing regions of the nation, so that the shift noted in this period would follow a long-term trend in national population redistribution.

All this western and southwestern expansion came at the cost of the Native American population. These Indian populations had been progressively pushed from their lands by constant warfare throughout the 19th century and were thus exposed to new diseases as they in turn were forced onto reservations or off their traditional lands and faced increasingly harsh environments. Although their decline differed from region to region and was not simultaneous,

the expansion of whites across America was persistent and ever increasing, resulting in ever greater loss of Indian population. Of the
1.9 million Indians inhabiting North America in 1500, only half a
million could be counted by 1900, considered the nadir point for the
Amerindian populations in general. The Northwest and California,
formerly the densest regions of Indian concentration and among the
richest resource areas, were those that were most affected, losing an
estimated 89% and 95% of their original native populations by the
beginning of the 20th century. In contrast, the loss in the Eastern
and Midwestern regions was on the order of 65% to 75% in the same
period. The areas that showed the greatest survivals of Indian population were the southwest and the Alaskan regions, both relatively
isolated from intense white immigration.[54]

In contrast to the whites and even the American Indians in 19th-
century America, blacks were the most geographically immobile
group in North America. The end of slavery found most African
Americans in the South, and they were still residing there in 1910,
although even here they were a minority. In 1850, some 37% of the
southern population was listed as black, with the next most important region of black settlement being the Northeastern states where
they represented only 2.5% of the region's population. Because their
fertility fell behind that of the whites in the post–Civil War period,
the black share of the total population in the South actually fell to
just 29.8% by 1910, even though 91% of American blacks were still
residing in this region in this year. All recent studies have also suggested that black health, in comparison to the rest of the national
population, was worse than any other group and that they suffered
higher rates of mortality and morbidity than any other part of the
national population. Average life expectancy for African American
men and women in the 19th century was in the low 30s and infant
mortality in the mid 200s per 1,000 life births. Moreover, although
female life expectancy was estimated to have risen by only one year

54 Douglas H. Ubelaker, "North American Indian Population Size, AD 1500 to
1985," *American Journal of Physical Anthropology* 77, no. 3 (November 1988),
289–94.

between 1810–1820 and 1901–1910 (to 35.7 years at birth), male life expectancy during this century actually declined by half a year to 32.6 years of life at birth in the later period. The relatively steady level of crude death rates for this population – which remained at around 30 per thousand resident population for the century – was matched by a very significant decline in the rates of reproduction, with the crude birth rate dropping from 22.7 to 14.0 in this same period.[55] Unlike most of the other components of the North American population, the black fertility decline occurred without any movement of the population to urban areas or any significant change of residence or land ownership in this period.[56] Black fertility also declined faster than white fertility and remained below white fertility throughout this period.[57] Some of this decline may have been due to higher levels of illegitimate births, higher ratios of female-headed households, and a higher ratio of children living away from their mothers that occurred among blacks. In 1910, for example, only 7% of households of native-born whites with children were headed by a women, whereas the figure for blacks was 22%.[58] As early as 1880, some 30% of black children lived in households without both parents, compared to just 13% for white children.[59] Although higher black mortality rates somewhat influenced these figures, most studies conclude that social and economic factors such as differential employment opportunities for African American women

[55] Jack Eblen, "New Estimates of the Vital Rates of the United States Black Population During the Nineteenth Century," *Demography* 11, no. 2 (May 1974), Tables 4–6, pp. 307–9.

[56] Stanley L. Engerman, "Changes in Black Fertility, 1880–1940," in Tamara K. Hareven and Maris A. Vinovskis, eds., *Family and Population in Nineteenth-Century America.* Princeton: Princeton University Press, 1978, p. 128.

[57] Reynolds Farley, "The Demographic Rates and Social Institutions of the Nineteenth Century Negro Population: A Stable Population Analysis," *Demography* 2 (1965), p. 387.

[58] S. Philip Morgan, et al., "Racial Differences in Household and Family Structure at the Turn of the Century," *American Journal of Sociology* 98, no. 4 (January 1993), p. 820.

[59] Steven Ruggles, "The Origins of African-American Family Structure," *American Sociological Review* 59, no. 1 (February 1994), Table 2, p. 140.

and men, high levels of poverty, and changing attitudes toward family and marriage among black women in this period may have been the primary causal agents for accounting for these differences in family structure by race so early in the postslavery period. These changing family structures may have influenced black women to reduce their fertility long before they moved off the farms to the cities and long before their mortality experienced changes in any appreciable way. In turn, this declining fertility and the stable rate of mortality go a long way to explaining the declining importance of African Americans even in the South in the half century after the end of the Civil War.

The whole question of the geographic mobility of the resident population of the United States in this period involved two separate spheres. The first was the movement across county, state, and regional boundaries; and the second was the movement from rural areas to urban centers. The physical mobility of the native- and foreign-born populations across regions and states was matched by an internal migration everywhere between urban and rural areas. Thus, the second great geographic mobility that was occurring in late-19th-century America was the growth of urban centers in general and the movement of ever more people off the land to the cities. Between 1850 and 1910, the share of the total national population in cities over 100,000 population went from a third to almost half of the total urban population and their share of the national population climbed from just 6% to 41%. The urban population (that is, persons living in towns of 2,500 or more inhabitants) increased from 15% of the national population in the mid-19th century to 46% of the national population by 1910. Clearly, then, the largest "metropolises" (those with over 100,000 population) were growing faster than the urban population as a whole.

These expanding urban centers included not only those colonial-founded cities of the Eastern Seaboard but also recently founded centers in the middle states of the nation. Cities such as New York, now a world metropolis, numbered close to 5 million persons by 1910; two other cities had over a million population: Chicago, the hub of the Midwest with over 2 million, and Philadelphia, with one and a half million persons.[60] These cities, in turn, were great concentrators of immigrant population and continued to be zones of higher mortality and lower fertility than the rest of the nation and thus continued their dependence on migration of both native-born and foreign-born populations to maintain their growth. Although the death rates of the urban areas were now declining from the 1870s onward, the urban penalty still was sufficiently large to account for the fact that the population of the major cities were not self-sustaining.

Thus the period from the end of the Civil War to the eve of World War I was one of significant demographic change for the United States. The single most important new development was the secular decline in mortality rates for all residents of the nation, which began after the 1870s. Until that time, the death rates in the nation had been high and fluctuating with no clear trend evident after the initial rise at the beginning of the century. The second unusual development in this period was the fact that the black population proved to be so immobile, compared to both the foreign-born and native-born whites. Freedom brought little economic mobility and even less geographic mobility to the ex-slave population. Finally, although the arrival of immigrants continued to grow at a feverish pace for most of this period, reaching its apogee in the last decade of this period, there was a profound change in the origin of these immigrants. Europe was still the home of the overwhelming majority of these immigrants. But in contrast to the earlier period, there was a profound change in the origin of these migrants, from northern Europe to southern and eastern Europe, with only a minor contribution of Asian and Latin American migrants. In contrast to these factors, all the other trends noted in this period tended to continue long-term developments. The urbanization and settlement of the Midwest and western United States all continued apace, especially after the last major incorporation of Mexican territories after the War of 1846–1848. Birth rates, which had been declining throughout the century, in this period declined at an even faster pace so that they

---

[60] Campbell Gibson, "Population of the 100 Largest Cities and Other Urban Places in the United States: 1790 to 1990," Population Division Working Paper No. 27; U.S. Bureau of the Census, Washington, D.C., June 1998, Table 14.

now reached European levels. Finally, this meant that the United States, even with the higher birth rates of the first-generation immigrants, was quickly moving toward the age structure of the advanced European nations. Median age of the resident population was rising steadily, and the ratio of children was declining as older age groups increased their share of the national population.

CHAPTER FIVE

THE EVOLUTION OF A MODERN

POPULATION, 1914–1945

The period from the beginning of World War I to the end of World War II is marked by several major developments. Probably the most profound of these demographic changes is the very rapid and sustained decline in mortality. Mortality rates began to fall in the last decades of the 19th century but then started to decline at an unprecedented pace. This trend was spearheaded by a precipitous drop in deaths from infectious diseases, which affected all groups within the population but was most dramatically experienced by the very youngest persons in the population. Deaths of infants and of young children, previously one of the most vulnerable groups in terms of mortality, declined at a faster rate than for all other age groups. The result of this change in traditional mortality was a steady and rapid rise in life expectancy for every new generation born in this period. The cause for this unprecedented and massive decline in mortality is much debated, but it was undoubtedly related to important changes in sanitation and later to the introduction of new medical practices. Chlorine treatment of water became the norm in this period and proper waste and garbage disposal in the major urban centers was now part of every municipal agenda. Public health campaigns organized by newly founded city and state health departments also led to improvements in the preservation and quality of food, and the pasteurization of milk and other dairy products became standard practice everywhere. Finally, immunization now became a basic part of public health systems. Up to the 1880s, there was only one vaccine available, for smallpox; there now appeared a number of crucial vaccines that were quickly applied to the public. In the last decade of the

19th century vaccines were developed for rabies, typhoid, cholera, and the plague. Then came whooping cough vaccines in 1913 and, in the decade of the 1920s, vaccines for diphtheria, tetanus, and tuberculosis.[1] It now became the norm to vaccinate all children, a process that expanded both nationally and internationally in every subsequent decade.

All these new and important efforts on the infectious disease front resulted in a profound change in mortality patterns by age for the first time in history. The age group that experienced the greatest change in mortality in this initial period was infants and children under 5 years of age, whose mortality dropped precipitously in this period (Graph 5.1). This can be seen in all types of statistics. For example, in the first third of the new century, diarrhea and other intestinal disorders, classic killers of children, moved from being the third leading cause of death in the United States in 1900, outdistanced only by pneumonia/influenza and tuberculosis, to becoming an insignificant killer by 1932, when it no longer appeared on the list of the top 10 killers in the United States (Graph 5.2). The death rate for all age groups declined by only 20% from 1914 to 1955, but that for infants declined 60%, for children 1 to 4 years by an extraordinary 80%,[2] and for youngsters 5 to 14 years by 64%. No other groups experienced this rate of decline. For example, those in the 45–54 age group experienced a decline in age-specific death rates of just over one quarter and those in the 55–64 age group saw their death rates decline by only 18%.[3] In 1915, the infant mortality rate for the

---

[1] Centers for Disease Control and Prevention (CDC), *Morbidity and Mortality Weekly Report* 48, no. 12 (April 2, 1999), Table 1, p. 244. Also see Henry F. Dowling, *Fighting Infection. Conquests of the Twentieth Century*. Boston: Harvard University Press, 1977, Chapters 3 and 4.

[2] The CDC estimated that the decline differed in pace over time. Whereas infant mortality declined 13% in the 1915–1919 period, it dropped 21% in 1920–1929, another 26% in 1930–1939, and an impressive 33% in the decade of the 1940s. CDC, *Morbidity and Mortality Weekly Report* 48, no. 38 (October 1, 1999), pp. 849–58. Also see Gregory L. Armstrong, "Trends in Infectious Disease Mortality in the United States During the 20th century," *Journal of the American Medical Association* 281, no. 1 (January 6, 1999), pp. 61–6.

[3] CDC, National Center for Health Statistics, Data Warehouse, Historical Data, Table "Hist290. Death Rates from Selected Causes, by 10-Year Groups, Race, and Sex: Death-Registration States, 1900–1932, and United States, 1933–1939."

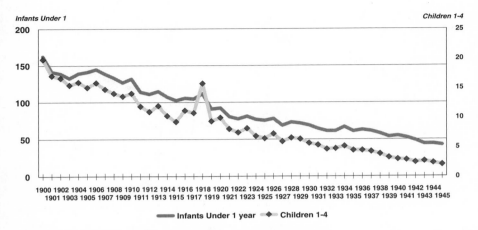

Source: U.S. Bureau of the Census, *Historical Statistics*, Table Series B 182–192.
(pre 1933, for Death Registration Area only).

Graph 5.1: Death Rates of Infants Under 1 Year of Age and Deaths of Children 1 to 4, 1900–1945* (Deaths per 1,000 in Age Group).

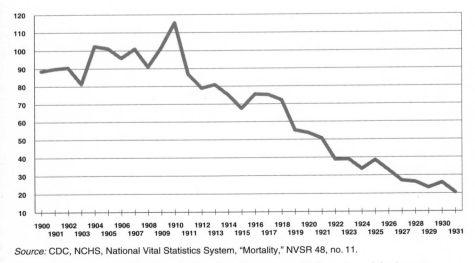

Source: CDC, NCHS, National Vital Statistics System, "Mortality," NVSR 48, no. 11.

Graph 5.2: Mortality Rate for Diarrhea, Enteritis, and Ulceration of the Intestines, 1900–1931 (Deaths per 100,000 Resident Population).

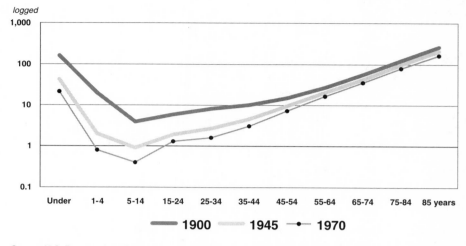

Source: U.S. Bureau of the Census, *Historical Statistics*, Table Series B 182–192.

Graph 5.3: Changing Mortality by Age, 1900, 1945, and 1970 (Deaths per 1,000 in Age Group).

population was 100 deaths per thousand live births, and by 1945 it had reached 38 deaths per thousand live births – a drop of 62%.[4] This decline in the infant and child deaths meant that there was emerging a new mortality pattern within the country and that the traditional "U" style death curve by age was flattening out with only a minor rise in the first few months followed by a steep drop in mortality until the early adult years (see Graph 5.3).

There was also a profound change in the diseases that were considered major killers in this period. The big killers in 1900, for example, were diarrhea, pneumonia/influenza, tuberculosis, and diphtheria, which together accounted for over a third of all deaths in that year.[5] By 1915, diphtheria had dropped off the list of major killers and infectious diseases now accounted for just over a quarter of all deaths. By 1914, heart disease, which had been the fourth leading

[4] U.S. Census Bureau, *Historical Statistics*, Table Series B 136–47.
[5] For a detailed examination of the differential rates of the first two of these diseases in infants and children under 5 years of age compared to the rest of the population, see Warren S. Thompson and P. K. Whelpton, *Population Trends in the United States*. New York: McGraw-Hill, 1933, pp. 251–2.

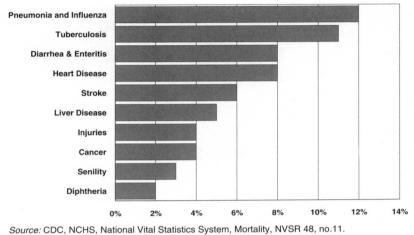

Source: CDC, NCHS, National Vital Statistics System, Mortality, NVSR 48, no.11.

Graph 5.4: The Ten Leading Causes of Death as a Percentage of All Deaths: United States, 1900.

killer at the beginning of the century, moved to its current position of first place, and cancer, which had been in sixth place in 1900, moved to its current second place position, a ranking that would remain unchanged into the 21st century. By 1945, infectious diseases caused just 9% of all deaths registered that year.[6] In fact, accidents of all kinds killed more people than did either of the two leading infectious diseases in that year, and cancer alone killed more than all the infectious diseases combined (see Graphs 5.4, 5.5, and 5.6).

This major shift in the relative importance of infectious diseases, and especially in the decline of their impact on infants and children, had a profound influence on increasing life expectancy. Within the period 1914 to 1945, average life expectancy rose an extraordinary 11 years for both men and women. At the beginning of the period, it was in the low to mid-50s for both sexes and it reached into the upper 60s by 1945.[7] As was typical for most of the late 19th and all of the 20th century, women outdistanced men in life expectancy by

---

[6] CDC, National Center for Health Statistics, Data Warehouse, Historical Data, Table "Leading Causes of Death 1900–1998."

[7] CDC, *National Vital Statistics Report* 50, no. 6 (March 21, 2002), Table 12, p. 33.

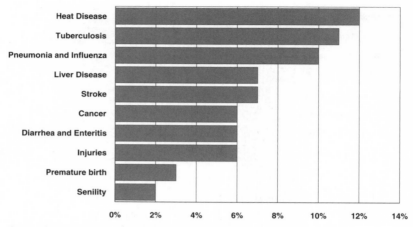

Source: CDC, NCHS, National Vital Statistics System, Mortality, NVSR 48, no.11.

Graph 5.5: The Ten Leading Causes of Death as a Percentage of All Deaths: United States, 1914.

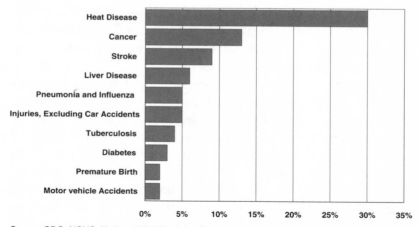

Source: CDC, NCHS, National Vital Statistics System, Mortality, NVSR 48, no.11.

Graph 5.6: The Ten Leading Causes of Death as a Percentage of All Deaths: United States, 1945.

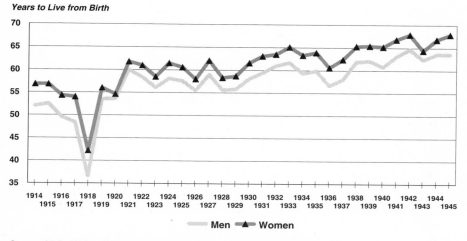

Years to Live from Birth

Source: CDC, *National Vital Statistics Report* 50, no. 6, March 21, 2002, Table 12.
(To 1928 data is for death registration states only - after that date for entire United States).

Graph 5.7: Male and Female Life Expectancy, 1914–1945.*

a significant degree (by a little over four years in both periods) and this difference would increase over time (see Graph 5.7).

Although all elements in North American society experienced falling rates of mortality in the younger age groups and the lessening impact of infectious diseases at all ages, the sharp differences found among races, ethnic groups, and social and economic classes remained. In fact, although region and urban residence seem to have had more impact on mortality than class in the mid- to late-19th century, by the 20th century, the United States was beginning to look more and more like the rest of the advanced industrial world in terms of the association of mortality levels and socioeconomic class. Whether residing in an urban or rural area, the poorer the person, the worse were their disease and mortality experience. Although crowding in cities, with their sharp socioeconomic divisions, still influenced mortality through class, the cities themselves no longer had an infectious disease environment different from the rural areas. Already by 1910–1914, cities (here defined as population centers with over 10,000 persons) had lower rates of mortality for typhoid fever, malaria, and smallpox than did the rural areas of the country. Diphtheria, influenza, and tuberculosis were still more urban than rural killers, with the rates being at least a quarter above those in the rural areas. But by 1926–1929, almost all infectious diseases were equal in the two regions, or even favoring the urban area somewhat, except for influenza/pneumonia, which was now only 14% higher in the urban centers (versus double that rate in the earlier period). Some mortality rates had even steeply reversed their urban–rural relationship. Whereas deaths from diarrhea had been 29% higher in the urban areas in the former period, they were now 23% higher in the rural areas in the later period.[8] Clearly the urban penalty in relationship to mortality was slowly disappearing, and in several diseases most influenced by public health measures, the urban areas were in fact doing better than the rural areas by the late 1920s.[9] Equally, the regional variations in mortality, already declining in the 19th century, were of little consequence by midcentury.[10]

In contrast to the old geographic variations, the influence of class on death was now to be quite clearly marked. Whatever the findings may have suggested about the weak relationship between these two factors in the late 19th and the early 20th centuries, by the middle years of the century, socioeconomic class and mortality were highly correlated. Although the quality of the death records before the middle of the 20th century made analysis of this issue difficult, the data generated since then has confirmed the high correlation between education and wealth and the death rates. It was estimated that at midcentury, there was a 65% higher mortality rate for white men under 64 years of age who had completed fewer than 5 years

[8]   Thompson and Whelpton, *Population Trends in the United States*, Table 73, p. 254.
[9]   By 1929, the infant mortality rate in cities fell below those in the rural areas for the first time and kept declining until 1940. Michael R. Haines, "The Urban Mortality Transition in the United States, 1800–1940," NBER, Working Papers Series, Historical Paper 134 (July 2001), Table 6.
[10] Paul E. Zopf, Jr, *Mortality Patterns and Trends in the United States*. Westport, Conn.: Greenwood Press, 1992, pp. 55–9; also see the discussion in Evelyn M. Kitagawa and Philip M. Hauser, *Differential Mortality in the United States: A Study in Socioeconomic Epidemiology*. Cambridge, Mass.: Harvard University Press, 1973, Chapter 7.

of schooling compared with those who had graduated from college. For women, the difference was even stronger, with white women who were college graduates and had reached 25 years of age living 10 years longer than poorly educated white women in the same age group. This same inverse relation between socioeconomic class and mortality was also found among nonwhites in the population. For all ethnic groups in the population, occupation, status, and mortality were also correlated, as they were in Europe.[11] Moreover, all studies since the mid-20th century have shown that socioeconomic differences and mortality rates have not only remained important but have actually increased over time.[12] Class, especially as measured by education, still clearly shows the same marked differences for all groups.[13] Equally important, the differences in life expectancy between males and females, already apparent at the beginning of the 20th century, increased over time. In 1900, the difference in life expectancy by sex was just 2.1 years in favor of women; by 1914, it was 4.8 years longer for women and would keep rising over time to 5.1 years by 1945 and reach even higher levels in later years.[14]

To these differences in socioeconomic class and sex in terms of mortality can be added the special American division of race. Although blacks experienced as sharp a mortality decline as whites, they never caught up to the life expectancy of whites. In 1914, for example, white males lived, on average, an extraordinary 16 years longer than black males, and white females lived 17 years longer than black females. There is no question that this extreme difference began to decline over time, especially as the African American

---

[11] Kitagawa and Hauser, *Differential Mortality in the United States*, Chapter 2.

[12] Gregory Pappas, Susan Queen, Wilbur Hadden and Gail Fisher, "The Increasing Disparity in Mortality Between Socioeconomic Groups in the United States, 1960 and 1986," *New England Journal of Medicine* 329, no. 2 (July 8, 1993), pp. 103–109; and Robert A. Himmer, Richard G. Rogers, and Isaac W. Eberstein, "Sociodemographic Differentials in Adult Mortality: A Review of Analytical Approaches," *Population and Development Review* 23, no 3 (September 1998), 553–78.

[13] Harriet Orcutt Duleep, "Measuring Socioeconomic Mortality Differentials Over Time," *Demography* 26, no. 2 (May 1989), pp. 345–51.

[14] CDC, *National Vital Statistics Report* 50, no. 6 (March 21, 2002), Table 12, p. 33.

Years to Live from Birth

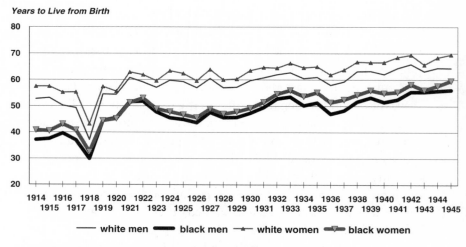

| white men | black men | white women | black women |

Source: CDC, *National Vital Statistics Report* 50, no. 6, March 21, 2002, Table 12.
(To 1928 data is for death registration states only - after that date for entire United States).

Graph 5.8: Male and Female Life Expectancy by Race, 1914–1945.*

population finally begin to migrate out of the South in significant numbers for the first time and have access to better health services in other areas of the country. Slowly, the spread between black and white life expectancy declined over the next 30 years, the difference falling to just 8 years for men and 10 years for women in 1945. (see Graph 5.8). Although the trend was toward equality, it never reached that position, as the migrating black population soon found itself isolated in the North in pockets of extreme poverty known as urban ghettos. Thus, the mortality spread only modesty declined for the rest of the century and black–white differences in all age-related patterns of mortality persisted into the 21st century. From neonatal and infant mortality through maternal mortality and to adult mortality, Blacks still have consistently higher rates than whites to the present day.

Although the secular trend of mortality was downward in this period, there were some significant variations around the trend due to special historical factors. Although World War I would be a high-mortality war, the late incursion of the United States into the war and the fact that it was fought overseas meant that the number of

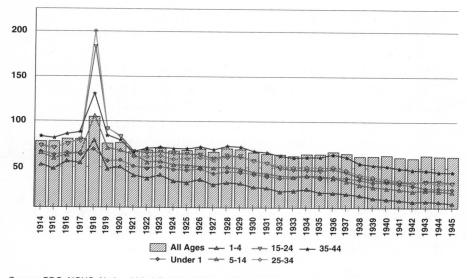

Source: CDC, NCHS, National Vital Statistics System, "Mortality," unpublished tables and National Office of Vital Statistics, *Vital Statistics Special Reports* 43, 1956.

Graph 5.9: Index of Change in Mortality by Age Group, 1914–1945 (1900=100).

U.S. dead and wounded was in fact lower than the total of such in the Civil War and had little impact on influencing national mortality trends. But in 1918, there was a worldwide pandemic of a virulent strain of influenza that became a mass killer, which did, in fact, significantly influence national death rates and even national life expectancy for an entire cohort. Unusual for this type of disease, its impact was greatest among young adults rather than the children and the aged, although all age groups below 55 suffered an increase in mortality (see Graph 5.9).

The trend of declining fertility, which by the late 19th century had brought U.S. rates in line with most of northern Europe, continued to move in the same direction in the new century, but at a slower pace and with some sharp variations around the trend due to external events which would influence attitudes toward reproduction on the part of the resident population. The three most important external factors influencing fertility were the Great Depression and the two major wars fought by the United States in the first half of the

20th century: World War I and World War II. The former economic crisis led to mass unemployment and the decision of many families to postpone childbearing for economic reasons. The two world wars, in turn, extracted a large share of the young males from within the United States and forced their temporary withdrawal from both the marriage and fertility markets. This initially had a negative influence on childbearing decisions of American families. But the return home in the postwar years of millions of young males who had postponed marriage would cause a temporary rise in fertility due to pent-up demand for marriage and children that had been blocked by the war. This was only modestly important in influencing fertility rates after World War I, but was especially important after World War II, which saw the mobilization of over 10 million young adult men into the armed forces in the 1941–1945 period, a figure double that of the men incorporated into the armed forces in World War I.[15]

Thus, in 1914, the total fertility rate was already declining from earlier late-19th-century highs and had fallen to 3.3 children per woman who had completed her fertility – a drop of 0.2 children since 1900. This rate then steadied during the war years and progressively declined through the 1920s. It reached its low point of just 2.1 children – the number of children considered the bare necessity to replenish the resident population – in the middle of the Great Depression in 1936. Fertility would then slowly reverse its long-term decline, but would only climb back to 2.4 children by 1945 (see Graph 5.10). But in the immediate postwar period, as is shown in Chapter VI, a relative boom in births occurred, pushing the fertility rate temporarily back up to very high levels. By 1957, at the peak of the postwar "baby boom," the total fertility rate reached 3.6 children for women who had completed their fertility, a figure even higher than the 1900 rate. But this extraordinary reversal lasted only for a decade, and the century-long trend of decline would continue as economic growth led families to space their children at longer birth intervals or delay first births even later into marriage.

[15] Office of the Chief Military Historian, Center for Military History, *American Military History*. Washington, D.C.: U.S. Army, 1989, pp. 375, 465.

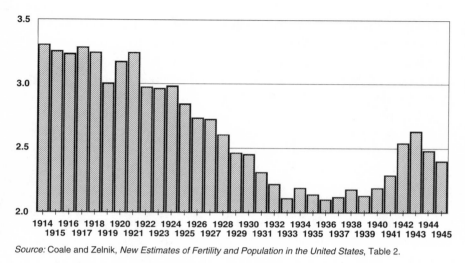

Source: Coale and Zelnik, *New Estimates of Fertility and Population in the United States*, Table 2.

Graph 5.10: Total Fertility Rate for the U.S. White Population, 1914–1945.

The longer spacing between children and delaying of first births explains the surprising finding that this general decline in fertility in the period to 1945 was occurring at the same time as the age of first marriages for women and men was progressively declining. In 1900 for example, age at first marriage for men was 27.6 years and for women 23.9 years – both at the high end compared to 19th-century rates. By 1940, the age at which men married was two years younger than this and for women it was three years less than their 1900 rates. Moreover, these ages at marriage were lower than the norm in Europe at this time except for France.[16] At the same time, the percentage of women never married only modestly changed in this period, slowly rising from 7.8% of the women who reached ages 45 to 54 years in 1910 to peak at 9.1% by 1920, and then declined to just 8.7% in 1940, a trend in declining spinsterhood that would continue to the 1980s. Finally, there was actually a decline in the ratio of males to females in their 20s in the national population – the most important

---

[16] Michael R. Haines, "Long-Term Marriage Patterns in the United States from Colonial Times to the Present," NBER, Working Paper Series, Historical Paper no. 80 (March 1996), Table 3.

age group for first marriages – which went from a majority of males to a majority of females after 1920 because of the declining importance of the foreign born in the population. This should have resulted in a higher age of first marriages for women in this period as male partners became more difficult to find. In fact, it did not influence the trend of declining age of first marriage for women, who would continue to marry at ever younger ages in every decade to 1960, in that year reaching a record-setting level of 20.3 years of age – a level not seen since the colonial period.[17] Given the still quite low rates of illegitimate births (just 8.2% of all births for all women in 1930–1934 and then dropping to 7.0% of all births in 1940–1944),[18] marital fertility itself was seriously declining in this period despite the increasing time women spent in marriages. This was clearly due to the adoption, in this century, of birth control practices within marriage.

As with mortality, the difference between black and white rates in fertility changed little over the period from 1914 to 1945. Although blacks would also experience a significant decline in fertility rates, this decline was too modest to close the gap between the races. In the period to 1945, black fertility kept declining but there was no convergence with white rates. In fact, there was some slight increase in the differences between races. Thus in 1917, the first-year data are available for nonwhites and whites, black births were 15% higher than white births, a difference that slowly increased in the 1920s, took a sharp rise in the depression years of the 1930s, and then slowly declined to 26% above the white rate in 1945 (see Graph 5.11). In fact, convergence between the two rates would not seriously occur until after 1980. But in one area of fertility, black women began to experience change well in anticipation of white women. Already by 1930–1934, almost a third of first births for black women were illegitimate, compared to just 5.9% of all births occurring outside of marriage for white women. Although illegitimate birth rates fell for both races in the period to 1944, after 1945 the rates would reverse

[17] Haines, "Long-Term Marriage Patterns," Table 2.
[18] Amara Bachu, "Trends in Premarital Childbearing, 1930–1994," CPS, Special Report (October 1999), Table 1.

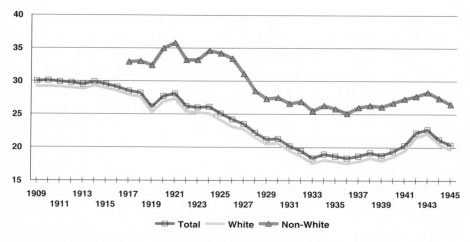

Source: CDC, NCHS, Vital Statistics of the United States, 1997, Vol I "Natality," Table 1.1.

Graph 5.11: Crude Birth Rate by Race, 1909–1945 (Rates per 1,000 Resident Population).

and begin their long steady climb, here in the United States as well as in all the advanced nations of Europe. But the pace of growth was much more rapid among black women than white women and although a slow convergence occurred, rates for whites never reached the level of the steeply rising illegitimacy rates experienced among black women.[19]

One group that was slow to drop its fertility were the Native Americans. Having reached their nadir population of 237,000 by 1900 due to a series of 19th-century wars with the United States and constant forced relocations to newer and ever-poorer reservations, nevertheless, the native Americans still had the highest recorded birth rates of any segment of the national population. Although there was variation among tribes, the Native Americans had the nation's highest level of women ever married and the nation's highest total fertility rate in 1900 – on the order of six to seven children per women who had completed their fertility.[20] But they also had higher mortality

[19] Bachu, "Trends in Premarital Childbearing," Table 1.
[20] Nancy Shoemaker, *American Indian Population Recovery in the Twenteith Century.* Albuquerque: University of New Mexico Press, 1999, Table 3.7, p. 47.

rates than any other group in the population, and their high fertility seemed to be maintained more by early and universal marriage
of women than by higher fertility within marriage. In fact, Indian
women probably had a higher ratio of diseases that affected fertility,
which may account for their very long spacing between childbirths –
much longer than for native whites or blacks.[21] But as their economic
situation finally stabilized with the end of the frontier changes in the
1890s, and as their children and adults were slowly but progressively
immunized in the first decades of the 20th century, their very high
mortality rates finally began to fall and, in turn, would lead to ever-
higher growth rates in the Native American population. Given the
delayed pattern of these mortality changes, fertility decline was also
delayed among the Indians. The result was that population now expanded quite rapidly at 1.33% per annum for the continental Indian
population between 1900 and 1960, when the population was now
double that of the 1900 nadir population.[22] Although fertility slowly
declined, as late as 1940 the total fertility rate was 4.5 children
for Indian women who had completed their fertility – two children
more than black women and almost three more children than white
women had in that year.[23]

In contrast to the black and American Indian patterns, there was
rapid convergence between foreign-born immigrant and native-born
white birth patterns in this period. Immigrants arriving to America throughout most of this migration history were coming from nations that had not completed their fertility transitions. England was
the first to do so, starting a systematic fall in fertility from the last
quarter of the 19th century onward. But in the southern and eastern European countries in this period, as well as in the sending Latin
American nations in a later period, mortality had fallen but fertility

[21] Shoemaker, *American Indian Population*, Chapter 3.
[22] Shoemaker, *American Indian Population*, Table 1.1 and for the 1960 continental Indian population, see Campbell Gibson and Kay Jung, "Historical Census
Statistics on Population Totals by Race, 1790 to 1990, and by Hispanic Origin,
1970 to 1990, for the United States, Regions, Divisions, and States," US Census
Bureau, Population Division, Working Paper Series No. 56; Washington, D.C.,
September 2002, Table B-3.
[23] Shoemaker, *American Indian Population*, Table 5.7, p. 89.

was only just beginning to decline in response to the rapid growth of population. The result was that these immigrants arrived with higher fertility patterns than the native-born white population. But soon after arrival, foreign-born white women began to move quickly toward the native-white woman norms. In a study of native- and foreign-born whites in Chicago from 1920 to 1940, the spread between the native- and foreign-born population in terms of total fertility was constantly decreasing. Moreover, this decline occurred for all income groups and was most rapid for the richest immigrants. In fact, by 1920, these wealthy immigrants had a lower rate of fertility than native-born whites in their same socioeconomic class.[24] The same occurred in Detroit between 1920 and 1930, when the foreign-born women in all age groups lowered their fertility much more rapidly than did the native-born white women, and their experience was the most important factor driving down overall birth rates in the city.[25] In a detailed analysis of the Italian immigrants to the United States in the late 19th and early 20th centuries, Livi Bacci found that immigrant families were quickly adapting to the reduced native-born white birth rates. In fact, he found that younger mothers (under 34 years of age) who had been born in Italy – who had fertility rates almost double that of native-born whites in 1920 – had fertility rates at or below that of the native-born whites by the late 1930s.[26] He also estimated that between 1910 and 1940, the fertility of almost all immigrant groups at all ages (except for the Italians and the Mexicans) fell more rapidly than for native-born white women, although none surpassed the low fertility rate of the native white women. But at the younger ages for these foreign-born women (that is, from 15 to 34 years of age), he estimated that already half of the major immigrant groups in these same thirty years had already achieved lower fertility rates than that obtained by the native-born in this age

[24] Evelyn M. Kitagawa, "Differential Fertility in Chicago, 1920–40," *American Journal of Sociology* 58, no. 5 (March 1953), Table 1, p. 485.

[25] Albert Mayer and Carol Klapprodt, "Fertility Differentials in Detroit, 1920–1950," *Population Studies* 9, no. 2 (November 1955), p. 154.

[26] Massimo Livi Bacci, *L'immigrazione e l'assimilazione degli italiani negli Stati Uniti secondo le statistiche demografiche americane.* (Milano: Giuffrè, 1961), Table 23, p. 68.

category.[27] In fact, in the United States as a whole, it is estimated that of the three basic groups of the population – native-born whites, nonwhites, and foreign-born whites – the latter's rate of fertility decreased at double the rate of the other two groups. Whereas fertility for women 15–44 years of age between 1920 and 1929 for the United States as a whole was estimated to have fallen by 20% for native-born whites, it fell by almost a third for the foreign-born and just 18% for blacks.[28] In another estimate of fertility by origin, it was suggested that the period 1910–1914 showed the largest spread in fertility rates between native-born and foreign-born whites since such data became available from 1875–1879. But it then fell so rapidly that by 1925–1929, the fertility of the foreign-born population was actually below that of the native-born whites for the first time ever (see Graph 5.12).[29] Moreover, this pattern of initially higher fertility rates of the foreign born and their progressive decline to at or below the level of the native born is noted in every study and for every group arriving in the United States in the 19th and 20th centuries, with the possible exception of only the Mexicans in the most recent period. No matter if the immigrants came from Europe in the early 1900s or would come from Latin America or China in the 1980s, the pattern held over time and place.

---

[27] Livi Bacci, *L'immigrazione e l'assimilazione*, Table 19, p. 58.

[28] Warren S. Thompson and P. K. Whelpton, *Population Trends in the United States*. New York: McGraw-Hill, 1933, Table 76, p. 270.

[29] Richard A. Easterlin, "The American Baby Boom in Historical Perspective, *American Economic Review* LI, no. 5 (December 1961), Table A3, p. 906. All major immigrant groups in the 1905–1909 period had achieved native white rates by the second generation, except for the Italians and non-Jewish Polish immigrants. But even these two groups experienced total fertility rate declines, with the Italians of the second generation having 2 children less than their first generation parents (or 4.9 children per completed family) and the Catholic Polish immigrants dropping by half a child less – though they remained unusual in the still very high 6.6 children per completed fertility. For a detailed analysis of the immigrant and native fertility at this time, and the declining fertility rates of second generation immigrants by ethnic groups see S. Philip Morgan, Susan Cotts Watkins and Douglas Ewbank, "Generating Americans: Ethnic Differences in Fertility," in Susan Cotts Watkins, ed., *After Ellis Island: Newcomers and Natives in the 1910 Census* (New York: Russell Sage Foundation. 1994), pp. 83–124.

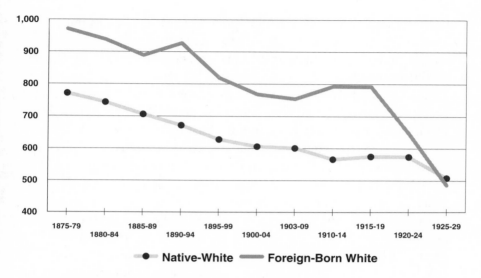

Source: Easterlin, "The American Baby Boom in Historical Perspective," Table A-3.

Graph 5.12: Fertility Ratio for White Population by Origin, 1875–1929 (children under 5 per 1,000 women, 20–44 years).

The volume of immigration to the United States from 1914 to 1945 was also one of great change from previous patterns. Although the early years of the period saw a peak movement of the international migrations to the United States, the postwar period saw long-term trends reversed, by both international and national events. As late as the decade of 1911–1920, when 5.7 million immigrants entered the United States, some three quarters of them came from Europe, and in the census of 1930, some 83% of the foreign born living in the United States listed their origin as European.[30] This meant that changes in the North Atlantic economy and political situation had a dramatic effect on immigration flows. The first change occurred with World War I, which blocked the arrival of Europeans

[30] Campbell J. Gibson and Emily Lennon, "Historical Census Statistics on the Foreign-Born Population of the United States: 1850–1990," Population Division Working Paper No. 29; U.S. Bureau of the Census, Washington, D.C., February 1999, Table 2; and U.S. Immigration and Naturalization Service, *Statistical Yearbook of the Immigration and Naturalization Service, 2000*. Washington, D.C.: GPO, 2002, Table 2, p. 19.

to the United States. This resulted in a dramatic decline in immigration flows. Although the late 1910s began to see a rise again of massive immigration, the Great Depression created another shock, with the crisis in the American labor market seriously affecting the attractiveness of America to European workers. Finally, the United States began to restrict immigration in this period. In 1917, it started by deciding that all illiterates and all Asians were to be excluded. In 1921 came the Immigration Quota Law that limited the number of aliens of any nationality entering the United States to 3% of the foreign-born persons of that nationality who lived in the United States in 1910.[31] Approximately 350,000 such aliens were to be permitted to enter each year – a figure well below the 1 million arrivals per annum reached in almost half the years in the period 1900–1914. Then, in 1922, the U.S. Congress tightened this quota even more, reducing the ratio to 2% per annum and the year used for calculating eligible immigrant origins was now pushed back to 1890. This was an obvious move to reduce the relative importance of the eastern and southern Europeans in any future immigration. By these quota acts, the United States finally and effectively closed its doors to mass legal migration for thirty years, not opening them again until 1952.[32]

The effect of these acts was immediate. Whereas in 1914 some 1.2 million immigrants had arrived, and in the postwar boom annual arrivals reached some 800,000 in the same year as the first Quota Act of 1921, by the late 1920s, the flow had dropped to an average of 300,000 immigrants per annum, and the Great Depression and World War II brought this entire movement to a halt. After 1930, fewer than 100,000 immigrants per year were reaching the United States, with only some 38,000 immigrants arriving in 1945 (see Graph 5.13). In short, an era had ended within American demographic history and the results quickly became apparent. In

---

[31] For a detailed background to the enactment of this act, see John Higham, *Strangers in the Land: Patterns of American Nativism, 1860–1925*. New York: Atheneum Press, 1963, pp. 300–30.

[32] All immigration data taken from U.S. Immigration and Naturalization Service, *Statistical Yearbook . . . 2000*, Table 1, p. 18.

Thousands

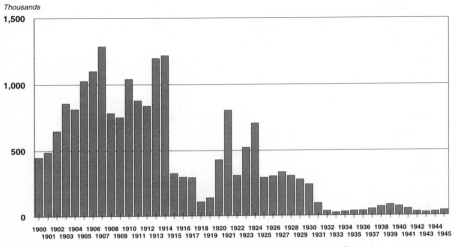

Source: U.S. Immigration and Naturalization Service, Statistical Yearbook of 2000, Table 1.

Graph 5.13: Annual Arrival of Immigrants to the United States, 1900–1945.

each census after 1920, the ratio of foreign born in the total population declined. In 1910, the foreign born made up 14.7% of the population, and by 1940, they had fallen to 8.8% of the population residing in the United States.[33]

In this period, the shift from northern European to southern and eastern European was the major structural change in the origins of the migrants. Whereas in the decade of the 1880s, only 19% of the Europeans came from southern and eastern Europe, by the decade of the 1890s, half of the Europeans came from this region, and this ratio rose to over 70% in the next two decades. In the 1880s, Germany was the leading source of immigrants, followed by the United Kingdom, the two accounting for 2.2 million of the 4.7 million Europeans arriving in this decade. By the 1900s, the Austro-Hungarian empire was sending 2.1 million immigrants, Italy another 2 million, followed by Russia with 1.6 million migrants – this of a total of 8 million migrants arriving in that decade. In the decade of the 1910s, Italy moved into first place as a source of migrants,

[33] Gibson and Lennon, "Historical Statistics on the Foreign-Born," Table 1.

followed by Russia and then the Austro-Hungarian empire, the three accounting for some 2.9 million of the 4.3 million Europeans arriving.[34] The basic causes for this shift in origins were twofold. In the first place, the growth of the economy of northern Europe enabled these regions, by the end of the 19th century, to offer wages competitive to those in the United States as they themselves underwent major urbanization and industrialization. At the same time their own populations were beginning their transition to much lower birth rates in response to the changes in their economies, which raised the cost of children to most couples. These rising costs were due to the increasing limitations of space in the urban area and the need for children to spend more time in education and out of the labor market.[35] In contrast, the southern and eastern Europeans were still in their early stages of very rapid population growth due to the long-term decline in mortality, and their developing economies and urban centers could still not offer enough opportunities to absorb this expanding population. The result was that the wage differential between the United States and Europe remained high for these new European regions of growth, transportation costs continued to decline under the impact of ever-larger steamships crossing the Atlantic, and their respective nations were more than willing to ease the pressures on their own industrial and urban growth by permitting the easy emigration of their populations.[36] The pattern would have been for these flows of migration from the new regions to slow as their own economies took off in the next few decades. But all of this changed with the outbreak

[34] U.S. INS, *Statistical Yearbook . . . 2000*, Table 2, pp. 19–21.

[35] For a discussion of the changing "costs" of childbearing and its influence on fertility, see Richard A. Easterlin, "An Economic Framework for Fertility Analysis," *Studies in Family Planning* 6, no. 3 (March 1975), pp. 54–63; and Richard A. Easterlin, "The Economics and Sociology of Fertility, A Synthesis," in Charles Tilly, ed., *Historical Studies of Changing Fertility*. Princeton: Princeton University Press, 1978, pp. 57–134.

[36] For a discussion of the push–pull factors influencing migration and their relative importance over time, see Timothy J. Hutton and Jeffrey G. Williamson, "What Drove Mass Migrations from Europe in the Late Nineteenth Century," *Population and Development Review* 20, no. 3 (September 1994), pp. 533–59.

of World War I in 1914, which was fought by the very nations that were the major suppliers of immigrants to the United States.

World War I would not only have an impact on international migrations to the United States but it would also have a profound impact on the patterns of internal migration as well. Although the progressive movement to the cities and toward the West for the resident native-born white population continued long-term trends, there was a new internal migration that began in this period that would have a profound impact on the American population for the entire century. The blockage of foreign workers due to the outbreak of war in 1914 and the increasing mobilization of the United States for war created a tremendous demand for labor, especially as conscription began to withdraw ever larger numbers of native-born whites from the labor market. A major untapped labor supply then available, especially for the unskilled and semiskilled jobs, was the black American population. Although a minor migration had begun out of the South by the end of the 19th century, that trickle became a flood after 1910. In 1910, some 89% of the black population in the United States still resided in the South. By 1950, only 68% could be found below the Mason–Dixon line.

Whereas the black population overall grew by 1.1% per annum in the period, the black population in the Northeast and Midwest grew at a rate greater than 3% per annum, which resulted in these two regions having over a quarter of the black population by midcentury. There was even movement of southern blacks to the West, which saw a rate of growth of blacks there double the rate experienced by the northern regions (see Graph 5.14).[37] This migration of blacks out of the South and primarily to the Midwest and Northeastern regions was also a migration from rural to urban areas. Whereas blacks were primarily rural in 1910, by midcentury they were increasingly urban, and by the end of the century they would, in fact, be far more urban and more likely than

---

[37] Frank Hobbs and Nicole Stoops, "Demographic Trends in the 20th Century," U.S. Census Bureau, Census 2000; Special Reports, Series CENSR-4, Washington, D.C.: GPO, 2002, Table 8.

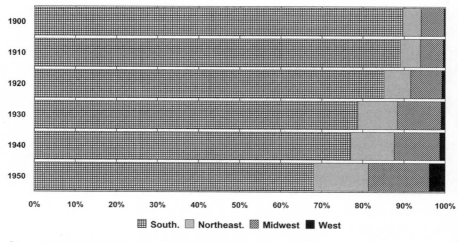

Graph 5.14: Distribution of the Black Population by Region, 1900–1950.

the native-born white population to be residing in metropolitan centers.[38] It has been estimated that the percentage of blacks in central city populations everywhere in the nation moved from 6.5% of that metropolitan population in 1900 to 9.5% by 1940 and continued to grow in every decade after that. Whereas the whites began to slowly move out of the city centers, especially after World War II, the blacks, from the beginning of the great migration, moved primarily to the center of large cities in every region of the country, including the South.[39] Given the patterns of racial prejudice at the time, shared by whites of the North and the South, the black migrants arriving in the large metropolitan cities were forced into well-defined districts within the cities of the North, which quickly became known as ghettos because of their immediate shift to all-black residents. In turn, there began the movement of whites away from the central core districts of these cities to the outer rings of the urban centers or even

[38] Jesse McKinnon and Karen Humes, "The Black Population in the United States: Population Characteristics," U.S. Census Bureau, Current Population Report, March 1999, p. 2.

[39] Irene B. Taeuber and Conrad Taeuber, *People of the United States in the 20th Century*, Washington, D.C.: GPO, 1971, p. 894.

into the nearby suburbs, although this centrifugal movement became intense only in the years just before and after the World War II. Thus began the evolution of Harlem and the Chicago South Side ghettos along with the change in the color composition of every major city, including the District of Columbia, a process that would redefine the urban space in the second half of 20th-century America.

But blacks were not the only resident population on the move. The movement of the rural population to the cities proceeded at the same rapid pace as in previous eras, and the movement of population from the older Eastern Seaboard regions westward continued unabated. But in both cases, the feverish pace of earlier periods was not maintained. In the census of 1910, the national population was still over half rural, but by the census of 1920, urban dwellers finally represented just over half of the national population. The year 1920 also marked another milestone in the urban evolution of the United States. In that census, over half of the urban population of America was now found living in cities of 100,000 or more inhabitants – in fact, a quarter of all Americans now lived in these metropolitan centers. In the next three decades, surprisingly, the urban population grew at a much slower pace, but the great metropolises took an even larger share of the urban population. By 1930, those living in cities of over 100,000 now accounted for over two-thirds of all urban residents and for 30% of the national population, ratios that held steady in the census of 1940 as well.[40] The 1920s and 1930s, however, seem to have been the peak of the growth of such large centers. Although the total urban population began to expand rapidly after 1950, surprisingly, the ratio of those living in urban centers of 100,000 or more persons never went beyond the ratios achieved by 1930, and in fact they actually declined somewhat. Clearly, the movement toward the suburbs and the continuing spread of the population across the continent were factors that influenced the end of the trend toward increasing concentration of the residents in large urban centers for the rest of the 20th century. This is also seen in the actual decline in urbanization in the New England, Middle Atlantic, and East North

[40] U.S. Census Bureau, *Historical Statstics*, Table A 57–72.

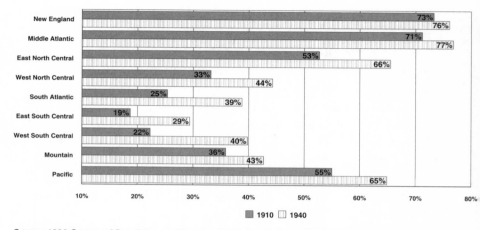

Source: 1990 Census of Population and Housing, "1990 Population and Housing Unit Counts: United States," (CPH-2); and 1980 PC80-1-1.

Graph 5.15: Percentage Urban by Geographic Division, 1910–1940.

Central divisions of the country, as well as in the Pacific area in the period from 1930 to 1940. There was, however, a rise of urbanization in the formerly low urban areas of the South, Great Plains, and Southwest (see Graph 5.15).

The movement of the national population into the West and parts of the South continued at a rapid pace. In the period from 1910 to 1940, the national population grew at an annual rate of 2.2%, whereas the states of California, Florida, and Arizona grew at over double that rate. But although individual states would grow rapidly, the relative share of population by regions changed slowly (see Graph 5.16). The West did increase its share of total national population from 7% to 10% by the end of the period, mostly at the expense of the Midwest. But the Northeast lost ground only after 1930 due to the decline of international migration, and the South actually increased its share of population in this period. In fact, each region had states that grew at rates above the national average, and all regions had a positive growth rate from census to census. Clearly, even the growth of the West was slowing after 1920, and in general migration internally declined in the period from 1920 to the outbreak of World War II.

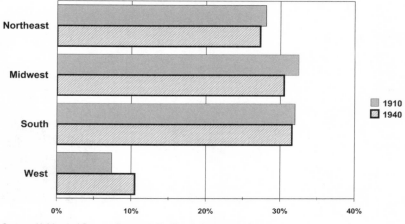

Source: Hobbs and Stoops, *Demographic Trends in the 20th Century*, Table A1.

Graph 5.16: Changes in the Relative Share of the Regions in the Populations of the United States, 1910–1940.

The reason for this slowing of internal migration was clearly due to the economic crisis known as the Great Depression, which affected the United States from the Crash of 1929 to 1940, when the war economy began to have an effect. Per capita gross national product rates peaked in 1929 and did not return to these levels again until 1940. In fact, by 1933 they had dropped by a third from the 1929 level and only slowly recovered in the next few years (see Graph 5.17). As we have seen, the most immediate impact of the depression was on rates of fertility as married couples radically reduced the number of children they were willing to conceive in this period, reaching the lowest levels in American history and in fact levels that would not be passed again until the last decade of the 20th century. But migration movements also slowed as did the rural to urban migrations, as labor markets suffered and economic opportunities became limited everywhere.

Thus the period from 1914 to 1945 was marked by basic changes in mortality as the United States finally moved toward a modern mortality and morbidity structure in which the highest rates of death were due to degenerative diseases rather than infectious diseases,

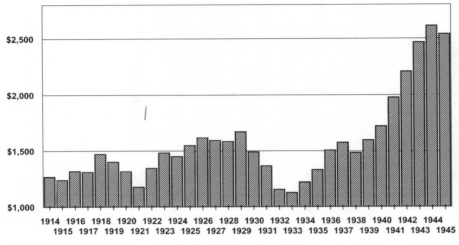

Source: U.S. Bureau of the Census, *Historical Statistics*, Table Series F1–5.

Graph 5.17: Per Capita Gross National Product, 1914–1945 (in 1958 Dollars).

which before the 20th century had been the most important cause of death for most premodern populations, including that of the United States. Fertility, in contrast, saw no fundamental changes in this period. The decline of fertility was relatively constant although it was clearly pushed below trend with the advent of the Great Depression in 1929. By 1936, it reached a level not experienced again until the end of the century. Although all groups participated in the pattern of declining fertility, one group, Native Americans, was slow to respond to this trend and correspondingly did experience increased mortality decline. This created a situation of relatively rapid expansion in this population, which had been moving toward extinction in 1900.

In terms of population movements, this period also saw some profound changes. Internal migration and the steady growth of the western states continued unabated, although the rate of this movement seems to have slowed in this period. But a new migration began that would profoundly reshape national identity and the urban landscape of America in all regions. This, of course, was the "Great Migration" of African Americans from the South to the rest of the nation. There was also a profound change in the origin and flow of immigrations. This was the era that saw both the greatest and the lowest migration flows, as well as the full shift from the old northern European migration to eastern and southern European migration. Also, the increasing hostility toward immigrants, especially those from Italy and eastern Europe, led Congress in 1922 finally to adopt a quota system. As a result of World War I, the post–1922 restrictive legislation, and the Great Depression, the United States moved from being a major importer of foreign workers to a relatively closed society in terms of international migrations. This was reflected in the successive decline of foreign born in each successive census from 1940 onward. This whole process ushered in a new period in American demographic history, one in which immigrants no longer played a significant role in national development. But this era would only last for some thirty years, for by the end of World War II, the United States would again become a major market for foreign immigrants, although this time Europe would no longer play a significant role as a source.

CHAPTER SIX

THE BABY BOOM AND CHANGING FAMILY VALUES, 1945–1980

If the pre–World War II period was one in which major changes in mortality and morbidity were most significant, the major theme in the immediate postwar period was one of significant fluctuations in fertility. In what would prove to be a temporary change in direction but with important long-term implications, the national population reversed its century-and-a-half-long secular decline in fertility and began moving toward higher birth rates. Yet by the end of this period, that trend would be reversed and replaced by startling new trends in both fertility and family organization. There were also changes in the intensity of the decline of mortality and morbidity and some interesting shifts in the ages experiencing declining rates due to the massive introduction of antibiotics. At the beginning of this period, foreign immigration reached its lowest point in over a century and yet, by the end of this era, immigration completely reversed its trend and a whole new chapter in the history of immigration to the United States began with the participation of new peoples populating the nation. This postwar period was also a time when internal patterns of migration began to clearly define some new and rather uniquely American patterns in urban settlement, with the rise of the suburbs and the corresponding changes in the inner cities. Finally, this was a period of the most intense African American migration, when the then-largest minority population in the national population ended its massive migration out of the South.

Unquestionably, the event that most defined this period in the popular perception and even in the historical literature was the sudden postwar shift to higher fertility, which created what has come to

be called the "baby boom." Because this boom in births was immediately followed by a return to low fertility, which some have called
the "baby bust," it has meant that those born in this period were a
well-defined cohort that could be easily identified as they grew older.
The members of this generation have come to be known as the "baby
boomers." The questions that intrigued the demographers at the time
were: Why had this massive shift occurred and was it permanent?
Was the United States, now one of the world's wealthiest societies,
about to enter a new era and create a unique model of high fertility in
an advanced industrial society, something no other comparable society was experiencing in this period? Although everyone expected a
temporary postwar shift in fertility, initially it seemed as if this would
be a permanent change in attitudes toward fertility and family life.
It is now seen that this shift in the direction of fertility was to last
for only some fifteen years, but its impact on the nation was to last
until well into the 21st century as the baby boom generation worked
its way through the labor market and into the retirement ages in the
first decades of the new century.

Numerous reasons have been suggested for this massive shift. First,
the Depression years had driven fertility rates to levels below trend
and clearly reflected economic constraints on what people wanted
in terms of family size. The easing of that economic crisis on the eve
of World War II allowed the fertility rate to start moving slowly up-
ward. This trend was temporary repressed by the withdrawal of so
many men from the marriage market because of national conscription. The return of these men after 1945 then allowed the fertility
rate to rise again. But the fact that it began rising ever faster at the
end of the 1940s and throughout the decade of the 1950s and did
not peak until the early 1960s was the result of a shift in expectations and possibilities on the part of the young women and men who
were then entering into marriage.

The factors that clearly changed traditional family expectations
were the unprecedented postwar economic expansion combined
with rapid socioeconomic mobility. This economy favored young
adults as never before. First, a rapidly expanding postwar labor market was absorbing a generation originating in the low fertility period

of the late 1920s. This would create a tight labor market, which in turn would push up wages. There was also a massive government subsidization for adult education in the immediate postwar years through the GI Bill, which resulted in a major increase in years of schooling for a large share of the population who would never have been able to afford that schooling. These two factors help to explain a major shift of young workers into higher status and better paying jobs. It is now estimated that median male income in the decade from 1947 to 1957 grew at 5% per annum in current dollars.[1] This increasing income and the increasing availability of government housing credit for mortgages also explains an explosion of home ownership, which went from 44% of the total population to 64% between 1940 and 1980.[2]

The demand for children was also strong as millions of returning veterans brought with them a pent up desire to start a family in 1945. New levels of family income, new availability of federal credit to the middle and lower classes for home ownership, the introduction of cheap mass produced tract housing, and increasing economic mobility due to the movement to higher status employment on the part of the younger population all had their impact on temporarily reversing the trends in fertility. The space and income for providing for more children was now available, and Americans responded to these opportunities by lowering the age at which they married, beginning their families at an earlier age, and opting for marriage more frequently, thus increasing their overall fertility (see Graph 6.1).[3] In

---

[1] U.S. Census Bureau, Historical Income Tables, People, Table P-2, based on the Annual Demographic Supplements for Current Population Survey, 30-Sep-2002. The rate of growth in terms of 2001 dollars was 2.7% per annum, the highest rate of growth in median male income recorded for any decade since 1947.

[2] It appears that the growth of income in the bottom and next two lowest quintiles was more rapid than for any groups above these levels between 1935–1936 and 1954, which clearly allowed more individuals to enter the housing market. See Donald J. Bogue, *The Population of the United States*. Glencoe, Ill.: Free Press, 1959, pp. 652–53.

[3] For the standard interpretations of the baby boom and bust phenomena, see Richard A. Easterlin, *Population, Labor Force and Long Swings in Economic Growth. The American Experience*. New York: Columbia University Press, 1968, chapters

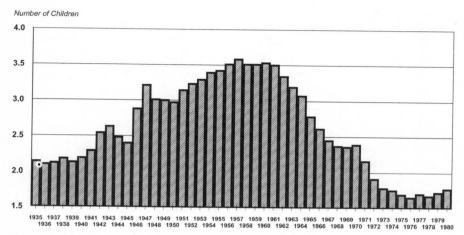

Source: Coale and Zelnik, *New Estimates of Fertility and Population in the United States,* Table 2 and Population Reference Bureau, AmeriStat,"U.S. Fertility Trends: Boom and Bust and Leveling Off," January 2003, found at *http://www.ameristat.org/.*

Graph 6.1: Total Fertility Rate for the U.S. White Population, 1935–1980.

1940, the mean age at marriage for men was 24.3 years and for women it was 21.5 years. By 1956, it had declined to 22.5 years for men and to just 20.1 years for women – the former being probably the lowest age of first marriage ever recorded for men in the United States as a whole, and the latter rate being the lowest age of first marriage ever recorded for women in the 20th century and probably one of the lowest such ages ever experienced by the American population. It was a rate, in fact, that would not be sustained in the following years as age at first marriage would began slowly rising again and would reach 25 years for women by the end of the century.[4] At the same time, the ratio of women 20 to 24 years who were married reached an all time high of 70% in 1960, a rate that would quickly decline again to just 32% by 1990.[5] The number of women who remained

3 and 4; and Peter H. Lindert, *Fertility and Scarcity in America.* Princeton: Princeton University Press, 1978, Chapter 5.

4   U.S. Bureau of the Census, Table MS-2. "Estimated Median Age at First Marriage, by Sex: 1890 to the Present," Internet release date: July 27, 1998.

5   Michael R. Haines, "Long Term Marriage Patterns in the United States from Colonial Times to the Present." Boston: NBER, Working Paper Series, Historical Paper 80, 1996, Table 2.

unmarried throughout their lives dropped considerably in the period of the baby boom and reached the lowest levels in this period. Whereas in 1900, almost a third of the women over 15 years of age were never married, by 1950 the rate had fallen to 18% and to 17% by 1960 – again, rates that would be reversed in the following period.[6] Finally, the median age of first births also dropped to its lowest level in this period. In 1930, women had their first child at 21.3 years, and by 1956, this had declined to its lowest recorded level in the century at just 20.3 years. This too would reverse in the subsequent years, as the median age of mothers having their first child reached 25 years by the end of the century.[7] Finally, the spacing between marriage and first child and then between the first and second children dropped to their lowest levels in the period from 1930 to 1970 in the first half of the 1960s, again beginning a long-term reversal by the second half of that decade.

All of these changes in behavior explain how this new level of fertility was achieved. The total number of children produced by women who had completed their fertility went from a low average of 2.1 children in 1936 to an extraordinarily high average for a modern industrial society of 3.6 children in 1957 – a rate not seen in the United States since 1898.[8] This of course meant that median age of the entire population by 1970 had dropped to 28.1 years, the lowest since 1930 and far below the median of 35 years for all sexes found in the population in the census of 2000.[9] At the same time, the ratio of the economically active population dropped below 60%

[6] U.S. Bureau of the Census; online Table 1418. "Marital Status of the Population, by Sex." Data taken from the census rather than the current population surveys.
[7] For the 2000 numbers, see Centers for Disease Control and Prevention, [CDC], NCHS, *National Vital Statistics Reports* 51 no. 1 (December 11, 2002), Table 1, p. 6. For the earlier periods, see U.S. Bureau of the Census, Table MS-2. "Estimated Median Age at First Marriage, by Sex: 1890 to the Present," Internet release date: July 27, 1998.
[8] Ansley J. Coale and Melvin Zelnik, *New Estimates of Fertility and Population in the United States*. Princeton: Princeton University Press, 1963, Table 2, p. 36.
[9] Frank Hobbs and Nicole Stoops, *Demographic Trends in the 20th Century*. U.S. Census Bureau, Census 2000; Special Reports, Series CENSR-4, Washington, D.C.: GPO, 2002, Table 5.

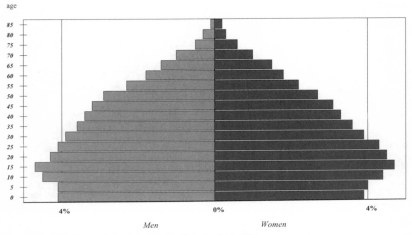

age

Men   Women

Source: Hobbs and Stoops, *Demographic Trends,* Table A5.

Graph 6.2: Age Pyramid of the U.S. Population in 1940.

in 1960 for the first and only time in the 20th century because of the
large jump in births. All this had a direct impact on creating a very
large cohort of population that slowly worked its way through the
population pyramid and became conspicuous as the generations that
followed returned to lower birth rates. These changes can be seen in
age pyramids of the period. In 1940, the low birth rates of the Great
Depression truncated the younger ages of what should have been a
normal pyramid (Graph 6.2). By 1950, a big increase in births was
showing up as a very large increase in the two youngest age groups
below 10 years of age and this child and infant base kept expanding
in the next decade (see Graphs 6.3 and 6.4). Then came the decline
in fertility, and the age pyramid of 1970 began to look again like that
of 1940 in the bottom ages (see Graph 6.5). The big difference from
thirty years earlier, however, was the bulge in the teen and young
adult ages caused by the huge influx of baby boomers working their
way through the age structure. By 1970, this baby group was being
replaced by a smaller birth cohort of 0 to 4 year olds and, in turn,
was bulging out at the ages 5 to 14. It then moved on to expand

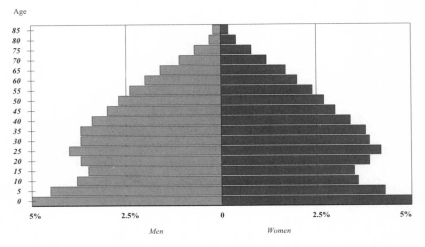

Source: Hobbs and Stoops, *Demographic Tends,* Table A5.

Graph 6.3: Age Pyramid of the U.S. Population in 1950.

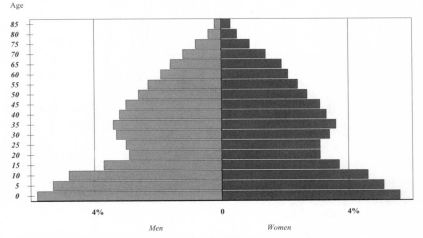

Source: Hobbs and Stoops, *Demographic Trends,* Table A5.

Graph 6.4: Age Pyramid of the U.S. Population in 1960.

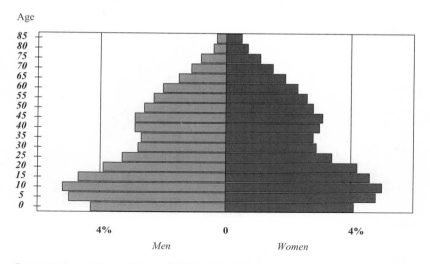

Age

4%   0   4%

Men   Women

Source: Hobbs and Stoops, Demographic Trends, Table A5.

Graph 6.5: Age Pyramid of the U.S. Population in 1970.

ages 15 to 24 in 1980 (see Graph 6.6), moving steadily toward middle age and retirement by the beginning of the 21st century.

But the baby boom was just that, a deviation in long-term trends that was due to a set of unusual factors that all came together at the same time to reverse long-term trends in fertility decline. After just two decades, Americans were back again to marrying later, producing children later, and having fewer children. Whereas Gallop polls found the majority of women wanting four children in 1945, 1957, and 1966, by 1971, women who desired this number of children were in the minority. Equally, attitudes toward sex itself were changing abruptly in this period as those who opposed premarital sex dropped from 68% in 1969 to 48% in 1973 in these same public opinion surveys.[10] Given this sea change in attitudes and the changing economic conditions,[11] each succeeding generation after

[10] Elaine Tyler May, *Homeward Bound. American Families in the Cold War Era*. New York: Basic Books, 1988.
[11] Lindert had argued that although economic growth was higher in the 1960s than in 1950s, the relative shift of incomes between the 1950s and the prewar period

Age

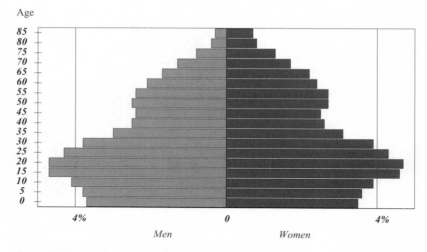

Source: Hobbs and Stoops, Demographic Trends, Table A5.

Graph 6.6: Age Pyramid of the U.S. Population in 1980.

the 1960s reduced their fertility to such an extent that native-born white Americans quickly reached the low fertility norms of the advanced industrial world, and by the last decades of the 20th century they differed little from their peers in Europe. As early as the mid–1970s, the total fertility rate of white non-Hispanic women who had completed their fertility dropped in half to just 1.8 children per woman, a rate that would thereafter never return to even the theoretical replacement level of 2.1 births per women.[12] Moreover, just as the family values and the dominant role of young mothers in the fertility of Americans was having its greatest impact in this period of the baby boom, this was also a time when the American family was beginning to lose its overwhelming importance in society and even in fertility itself. Between rising rates of births outside of marriage

was far greater than from the 1950s to the 1960 and was so perceived by young couples. He argued that "income prospects in the late 1960s were not so greatly improved over the experience of the previous two decades as was the case for the baby-boom cohorts ...." Lindert, *Fertility and Scarcity in America*, p. 169.

[12] Amara Bachu and Martin O'Connell, "Fertility of American Women: June 2000," Current Population Reports, P20-543RV (October 2001), pp. 1, 3.

and divorce, the family began to loose its role as the predominant determinant of fertility and of household organization. Illegitimacy progressively reduced the importance of marital fertility over time, and the rising rate of divorce was one of the key factors favoring the increasing importance of single parent headed households that contained young children. In turn, the increasing reluctance of young women to marry would also influence the rise of single person households throughout America. Thus, as early as the 1970s, the United States was beginning to experience a profound change in its basic social structure. Whereas the ratio of births outside of marriage to total births remained at 10% or below to 1965–69 (its historic rate) by the next quinquennium the ratio was up to 15% of births and by 1975–79 it had reached over a quarter of all births and was still rising. Moreover, these parents of extramarital children now had a greater tendency not to marry before the birth of the child. In the pre-1970 period, half the illegitimately conceived children saw their parents marry; only a third did so in the late 1970s and that rate kept dropping.[13] Equally, divorce rates doubled between 1900 and the 1960s, going from 4 divorces per thousand married women in 1900 to 9 divorces per thousand married women by 1960. Then from 1967 through 1975, no-fault divorce laws were adopted in almost all the states, and the rate in the post–1960 period jumped to an average of 20 per thousand married women at the end of the century. Between 1950 and 1980, the number of divorced persons in the adult population 15 years or older grew at the steady rate of 5% per annum, accounting for over 7% of the total adult female population and 5% of the male population by 1980 (see Graph 6.7). One estimate suggested that half the marriages contracted in 1967 would end in divorce,[14] whereas a more recent estimate gives a slightly lower figure, suggesting that four of ten marriages contracted in the year 2000 will end in divorce. Whatever the actual level, it would seem that

[13] Amara Bachu, "Trends in Premarital Childbearing, 1930–1994," CPS Special Report (October 1999), Table 1.

[14] The 1967 estimate comes from Steven Ruggles, "The Rise of Divorce and Separation in the United States, 1880–1990," Demography 34, no. 4 (November 1997), p. 455.

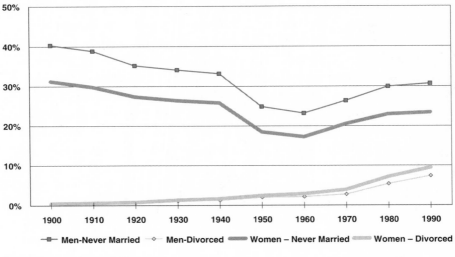

Source: Census of 1990, Table 1418.

Graph 6.7: Marital Status of Persons 15 Years or Older, 1900–1990 Census.

between 40% and 50% of marriages contracted in the past twenty years have ended in divorce and the rate has not fluctuated greatly since the 1980s.[15]

Much of this shift was due to major changes in socioeconomic mobility and the national economy in the post-1960 period and to

[15] The data from 1900 to 1997 and the 2000 estimate are given in Theodore Caplow, Louis Hicks, and Ben J. Wattenberg, *The First Measured Century. An Illustrated Guide to Trends in America, 1900–2000*. Washington, D.C.: The AEI Press, 2001, pp. 78–9. Although Caplow and others gave the divorce rate as per 1,000 married persons in that year, the U.S. Census Bureau uses a divorce rate per 1,000 resident population – the same way they calculate their marriage rate. In 2001, for example, there were 8.4 marriages per 1,000 mid-year resident population and 4.0 divorces registered for the same base population, suggesting that divorce rate was 48% of the marriage rate. The divorce rate was 49% of the marriage rate in 1980, 47% of the marriage rate in 1990, and 49% of the marriage rate in 1995, showing little change over the past few decades. See U.S. Bureau of the Census, *Statistical Abstract of the United States, 2002*. Washington, D.C.: GPO, 2002, Table 111, p. 88. For the 1980 rates, see U.S. Bureau of the Census, *Statistical Abstract of the United States, 1995*. Washington, D.C.: GPO, 1996, Table 149, p. 105.

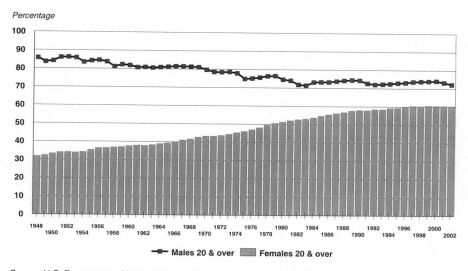

Percentage

● Males 20 & over   ▨ Females 20 & over

Source: U.S. Department of Labor, *Report on the American Workforce, 2001*, Appendix, Table 5.

Graph 6.8: Ratio of Adults in the Labor Force by sex, 1948–2002.

some basic changes in attitudes toward the role of women within society. Female labor force participation rates began to climb in this period, and women began entering professions at a rate never before experienced. Equally, as might be expected after an unusually rapid growth and restructuring of the economy in the immediate postwar period, the secular mobility of these years – when most people increased their status from that of their parents – was now replaced by the more traditional circular mobility, when as many people moved down the socioeconomic ladder as moved up. In 1950, only 34% of adult women were in the labor force. By 1970, it was 43% and by 1978, half the adult women were working, a ratio that kept increasing every year thereafter, reaching over 60% by the end of the century (see Graph 6.8).[16]

[16] U.S. Department of Labor, *Report on the American Workforce, 2001*. Washington D.C., 2001, Appendix, Table 5. "Civilian labor force participation rates for selected demographic groups, annual averages, 1948–2000." For background of this surge in female labor participation, see Alice Kessler-Harris, *Out to Work: A History of Wage-Earning Women in the United States*. New York: Oxford University Press, 1982, Chapter 11.

Although fertility moved back to a long-term trend of decline, a pattern common to all industrial societies as the cost of having children increased due to the increasing urbanization of the population and the increasing costs of education, women's role within the household and in the marketplace now began to change in profound ways never before seen. Women entered universities in ever-larger numbers, thus delaying marriage. In turn, they began to enter professional careers at an unprecedented rate and to keep working at those careers longer than ever before. They also moved into households either alone or with a nonmarried companion with increasing frequency. The cause for this change had much to do with the changes in attitude toward women's place in society that occurred in the 1960s and 1970s, when traditional values were rejected by lead elements in the generation coming of age in this period. The introduction of the birth control pill in the early 1960s was important in this change, giving women complete control over their own fertility.[17] But even more important was a new attitude toward the equality of women in the society as a whole. In this midcentury period, a group of writers from Margaret Mead and Simone de Beauvior to Betty Friedan began rethinking the role of women and sexuality within society, and their works found a ready audience in these increasingly wealthy industrial societies.[18] By the 1960s, there came a spate of legislation against sexual discrimination in the work place by a federal government made aware of this issue as never before.

This evolution of new attitudes toward and by women can be seen demographically in many ways. There was, first of all, a major change in the education of women that became manifest in this period.

[17] For the development and introduction of the oral contraceptive pill, see Linda Gordon, *The Moral Property of Women: A History of Birth Control Politics in America*. Urbana, Ill.: University of Illinois Press, 2002, pp. 286–88. The pill was already in use by the late 1950s for other purposes before it was approved by the FDA for use as an oral contraceptive in 1960.

[18] For a partial chronology of this movement, see Katheen C. Berkeley, *The Women's Liberation Movement in America*. Westport, Conn.: Greenwood Press, 1999. For broader interpretations of this movement and its impact on the family, see Elaine Tyler May, *Homeward Bound: American Families in the Cold War Era*. New York: Basic Books, 1988; and most recently Sara M. Evans, *Tidal Wave: How Women Changed America at Century's End*. New York: Free Press, 2003.

Women had always done well in primary and secondary education. In the mid-19th century, when the first comparable data became available, women already were more likely to be secondary school graduates than men, and for most of the period since then, more women made up the secondary graduating class than men.[19] But it was only in 1980 that women finally became more than half of all college students, and it was only in 1984 that they finally represented the majority in graduate school enrollment as well.[20] Even so, the progress in this area has been much slower and they have yet to pass men in enrollments in postcollege professional education.[21] They also began to move into the labor market in ever higher numbers and to remain in the labor market at higher rates than ever before. At the end of the 19th century, less than a fifth of all women were in the salaried labor force; by the 1980s, the figure had risen to 60%. But this was not a linear trend. In fact, female participation rates and the ratio of single and married women in the labor force probably dropped to their lowest point in the 1920s and only reversed that trend in a significant way with World War II. Both the rates of older women returning to work and younger ones entering the market increased dramatically in the 1960s and were one of the forces behind the equal pay movement. Whereas in 1940 among adult women only 14% of those who were married and 46% of those who were single were in the workforce, by 1980 half the married women were working and almost two-thirds of the single women were earning their living. But discriminatory wage policies were still the norm and the slogan "59 cents to the dollar" became a major issue in legal challenges as it was estimated that as late as the 1960s, women earned only 60% of male wages earned for comparable labor.[22]

[19] U.S. Department of Education, National Center of Educational Statistics, *The Digest of Educational Statistics 2001*, Table 103.
[20] U.S. Department of Education, National Center of Educational Statistics, *The Digest of Educational Statistics 2001*, Tables 174 and 189.
[21] U.S. Department of Education, National Center of Educational Statistics, *The Digest of Educational Statistics 2001*, Table 190.
[22] Claudia Goldin, *Understanding the Gender Gap. An Economic History of American Women*. New York: Oxford University Press, 1990, especially Chapters 1 and 2 and Table 2.1, p. 17.

There was also a major change in mortality in the post-1940 period associated with the mass introduction of the first antibiotics in history: first came the sulfonamide drugs and then penicillin. Whereas most of the mortality decline in the first half of the 20th century had been through the decline of communicable diseases among infants and children, the post-1940 mortality declines were beginning to affect other age groups as well. In the earlier period, sanitation, clean drinking water, and better quantity and quality of food supplies had a major impact on reducing disease and death in the North American population. In this new era of antibiotic medicine, communicable diseases, which affected all age groups, began to decline quite dramatically. In the late 1930s appeared the first sulfonamides from Europe. This was followed a few years later by the introduction of penicillin, which began to be widely used by the early 1940s. Although the properties of penicillin were discovered in 1928, it took over a decade to create a viable product that could be used to fight infection and thus it did not come into wide usage until the mid 1940s.[23] The impact of this chemical–medical revolution, which included ever more vaccination therapies and the massive use of antibiotics on the world's population in the second half of the 20th century, was profound. Its impact on the United States can be seen in the extraordinarily rapid fall of the death rate for all groups from the late 1930s to the early 1950s. It has been estimated that between 1938 and 1952, the decline in mortality from nine major infectious diseases was on the order of 8.2% per annum compared to rates of decline of only 2% per annum in the periods before and after that.[24] Also, there were significant benefits for adults as well. For nine major infectious diseases, it has been estimated that the mortality rate of those from 15 to 24 years of age fell by an extraordinary 13% per annum in the period 1935 to 1955, and all age groups from 5 to

[23] Henry F. Dowling, *Fighting Infection. Conquests of the Twentieth Century.* Boston: Harvard University Press, 1977, Chapters 8 and 9.
[24] Gregory L. Armstrong, Laura A. Conn, and Robert W. Pinner, "Trends in Infectious Disease Mortality in the United States During the 20th Century," *Journal of the American Medical Association* 281, no. 1 (January 6, 1999), pp. 61–6.

Thousands deaths per 100,000 population

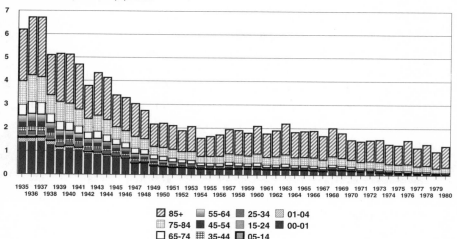

85+	55-64	25-34	01-04
75-84	45-54	15-24	00-01
65-74	35-44	05-14	

Source: Data provided by Gregory J. Armstrong of the CDC, also see Armstrong, Conn, and Pinner, "Trends in Infectious Disease Mortality".

Graph 6.9: Mortality from Nine Infectious Diseases by Age Groups, 1935–1980.

45 years of age most benefitted from this change. There was nothing like this rapid a decline either before or after this period (Graph 6.9).[25] It has been estimated that infectious diseases accounted for 32% of all deaths in 1900, but by 1960 they accounted for 5% of all deaths.[26] The maternal death rate, also much influenced by infections, declined as dramatically, falling by 13% per annum in the same period.[27] Such classic infectious killers as pneumonia and influenza, which had rates of over 100 per 100,000 resident population

[25] Whereas the mortality of the elderly declined by only 0.3% per annum from 1900 to 1940, from 1940 to 1960 it declined at 1.1% per annum. Young adult (15–44 years of age) mortality, which fell at a rate of 2.1% from 1900 to 1940, declined at 3.1% per annum from 1940 to 1960. See David M. Cutler and Ellen Meara, "Changes in the Age Distribution of Mortality Over the 20th Century" Cambridge, Mass.: National Bureau of Economic Research, Working Paper No. 8556, October 2001, Table 2.

[26] Culter and Mera, "Changes in Age Distribution of Mortality," Table 3.

[27] CDC, NCHS, *Vital Statistics of the United States, 1992*, vol. II (Mortality), part A, Tables 1–16, p. 69.

in the 1930s, fell to below 50 per 100,000 by the 1950s.[28] The increasing use of antibiotics was also helping to prolong life at all ages, and this was seen in life expectancy not only at birth, which rose by 9.1 years for men and 12.3 years for women between 1929–1931 and 1959–1961, but also for those over 65 years of age (1.3 years for men and 3.0 years for women) in this same period.[29]

Probably the most profound geographic changes that occurred within American society in this period were those related to the physical redistribution of population in terms of urban settlement and the relative shift in populations by region. The 1950s and 1960s saw a series of developments that would profoundly reshape the national landscape. To begin with there was the so-called Great Migration of rural blacks out of the South. Whereas a steady stream of southern blacks had been leaving the region from the end of the last century, this suddenly became a flood in the 1940s to 1960s. Between tight labor markets in the South and mechanization of the cotton crop, which progressively destroyed the old sharecropping system, the push factors were profound. The pull factors were related to the decline of the foreign immigration flows from the 1920s onward, which opened up the northern labor markets for semiskilled and unskilled positions for black southern migrants. Whereas in the 1910s, some 454,000 southern blacks left the region and another 800,000 left in the 1920s, this movement was halved during the depression years of the 1930s. But in the 1940s, 1950s, and 1960s, over a million southern blacks were on the move northward in each decade. Moreover, their moves were toward the traditional northern industrial states and above all to their cities.[30] As a result of the

---

[28] CDC, NCHS, *Health, US, 2002*. Hyattsville, MD, 2002, Table 30, p. 119.

[29] CDC, NCHS, *Health, US, 2002*. Hyattsville, MD, 2002, Data used for figure 18, p. 64.

[30] For the most detailed demographic surveys of this migration, see Daniel M. Johnson and Rex R. Campbell, *Black Migration in America: A Socio-Demographic History*. Durham, N.C.: Duke University Press, 1981; and Neil Fligstein, *Going North. Migration of Blacks and Whites from the South, 1900–1950*. New York: Academic Press, 1981. The estimates of the net migration will be found in U.S. Bureau of the Census, *The Social and Economic Status of the Black Population in*

migration, African Americans, who had accounted for the greatest number of rural residents of the national population until 1950, now surpassed whites as the most urban part of the native-born population, reaching 85% urban by 1980.[31] They were also no longer confined to the South, and by 1970 some 47% of African Americans were residing in the northern and western states.[32]

In turn, there were fundamental transformations going on in the cities, which in many ways were tied to this southern black migration. The first was the rise of the suburbs and with it the phenomenon of suburban sprawl. Although urbanization had increased steadily for most of the century, and rising from just over half the population to almost two-thirds by 1960, and again climbed to almost four-fifths by 1970, growth then slowed in the following decades. Moreover, the concentration of that urban population in cities of 100,000 or more persons not only slowed, but in fact the ratio of the urban population in these large centers actually declined from the 1940s onward. This paradoxical change was due to the massive movement of population out of the central metropolitan areas – the so-called core centers or central cities – and into new white middle and working class suburban areas in what had been farmlands. Thus began the so-called suburban revolution, which changed the landscape of urban America. Small suburban towns grew ever larger and the central cities of the metropolitan areas either lost population or stagnated as these peripheral areas grew.

This profound change – fairly unique to the United States in this period – was due to many factors. Government policy was clearly a prime factor in this transformation. First came the creation of a

the United States, 1790–1978: An Historical View. Current Population Reports, P-23, No. 80; Washington, D.C.: GPO, 1978, Table 8, p. 15.

[31] U.S. Bureau of the Census, The Social and Economic Status of the Black Population in the United States, 1790–1978: An Historical View. Current Population Reports, P-23, no. 80; Washington, D.C.: GPO, 1978, Table 6, p. 14; and U.S. Census of 1980, Summary Volumes, vol. 1 (pc80-1-B1), Table 43, p. 27ff.

[32] Frank Hobbs and Nicole Stoops, Demographic Trends in the 20th Century. U.S. Census Bureau, Census 2000; Special Reports, Series CENSR-4; Washington, D.C.: GPO, 2002, Table 8.

vast housing credit market from the late 1930s onward with the establishment of the Federal Housing Administration, which financed the massive move of white Americans into the status of homeowners in the postwar period. The next was the postwar construction of a modern highway system, which began with the 1956 federal gas tax establishing funds to pay for new highway construction. The result of this new funding was the creation of the interstate turnpikes and four-lane divided highways across America and stretching from the towns into the rural hinterlands everywhere. This new system of transport permitted industry and services to move outside the central cities, which in turn promoted a series of major new institutions developed by the market in response to these changes. In 1947, Levitt and Sons, a real estate developer, began the construction of Levittown tract housing on Long Island. From 1947 to 1951, some 17,000 standardized homes were built by the company, and this became the model for all the massive cheaply constructed tract housing that permitted the suburbanization of America. This was followed by the first enclosed shopping mall, built in a Minnesotan suburb in 1956, and of course malls and strip malls moved the downtown shops to the suburbs to accommodate the out-migration of the working and middle classes.

But not everyone moved to the suburbs. Whereas over half of the urban whites eventually moved to the suburbs, some three quarters of the urban blacks remained in the central cities by 1980.[33] Although the black ghetto is thought to have first appeared in Norfolk, Virginia, in 1890, the intensity of ghettoization increased with the migration of the rural blacks to the northern cities in this period. By 1940, some 55 cities had black ghettos and by 1980, the figure had risen to 179 metropolitan areas.[34] Of the 43 urban

---

[33] *U.S. Census of 1980*, Summary Volumes, vol. 1, (pc80-1-B1), Table 43, p. 27ff.

[34] I have calculated this number from U.S. Census Bureau material using the "index of dissimilarity," which measures the share of the black population that would be needed to change for the races to be distributed evenly in the city. A ratio over 0.6 is considered to define a ghetto. See David M. Cutler, Edward L. Glaeser, and Jacob L. Vigdor, "The Rise and Decline of the American Ghetto," *Journal of Political Economy* 107, no. 3 (1999), p. 456. Some 157 metropolitan statistical areas qualified for this definition in the census of 1980. Calculated

centers with more than 100,000 persons that contained more than 3% (or 20,000) blacks, all but 3 contained what has been defined as ghettos. The worst were traditional cities such as Chicago, New York, Philadelphia, Detroit, and Boston, but also in this worst category situation were such new Sun Belt cities as Dallas, Los Angeles, Miami, and Oakland.[35] In 1890, the average urban black lived in a community that was about a quarter black; by 1970 they were likely to live in a neighborhood that was over two-thirds black.[36] In 1980, three quarters of urban blacks lived in the central core of the big cities as compared to only 41% of the urban whites, the majority of whom now lived in the suburbs. Even the new Asian and Hispanic immigrants were not as concentrated in the center of the big cities as were the African Americans. Deliberate racist policies and attitudes prevented blacks from entering this new home buying market and blocked their movements to the suburbs. At the same time, there was a massive assault on the cities, which furthered their decline. In 1949, the government adopted a landmark housing act that permitted the massive destruction of downtowns through "urban

from data made available by the U.S. Bureau of the Census in November 2002 and used in John Iceland, Daniel H. Weinberg, and Erika Steinmetz, *Racial and Ethnic Residential Segregation in the United States: 1980–2000.* U.S. Census Bureau, Series CENSR-3, Washington, D.C.: GPO, 2002. Culter, Glaeser, and Vidgor suggested that the average score for American cities, weighted by black population, went from a dissimilarity index of 0.71 in 1940 to 0.79 in 1970, the highest ever recorded. By 1990, it had dropped down to 0.66. Cutler, et al., "The Rise and Decline of the American Ghetto," p. 464.

[35] Here, I am using the 0.6 dissimilarity index to suggest the presence of a ghetto. This has been calculated from table 5-4 found in John Iceland, Daniel H. Weinberg, and Erika Steinmetz, *Racial and Ethnic Residential Segregation in the United States: 1980–2000.* U.S. Census Bureau, Series CENSR-3, Washington, D.C.: GPO, 2002, p. 69.

[36] David M. Cutler, Edward L. Glaeser, and Jacob L. Vigdor, "The Rise and Decline of the American Ghetto," *Journal of Political Economy* 107, no. 3 (1999), p. 456. For a detailed analysis of the evolution of northern metropolitan black ghettos, see Douglas S. Massey and Nancy A. Denton, *American Apartheid: Segregation and the Making of the Underclass.* Cambridge, Mass.: Harvard University Press, 1993. The status of blacks in the middle decades of the 20th century was analyzed in Irene B. Taeuber and Conrad Taeuber, *People of the United States in the 20th Century.* Washington, D.C.: U.S. Bureau of the Census, GPO, 1971, pp. 895–902.

renewal," which was often marked by urban destruction. The 3 million African Americans who now moved into the central cities abandoned by the native-born and foreign-born whites found themselves with far fewer job opportunities than the previous residents as the industries followed the workers to the suburbs. Deteriorating schools and "redlining" of home loans to prevent blacks from obtaining mortgages for home ownership played their part in reshaping the core areas of the great metropolises. The decline of the central cities was defined by the abandonment of the downtown stores and by urban renewal, which often destroyed stable historic neighborhoods and replaced them with highways or public housing of poor quality. Housing prices fell, the quality of the housing stock fell dramatically, and the neighborhoods became increasingly all black. All these changes took their toll on African Americans, and the population became increasing segregated by race. By the late 1960s, this led to major urban riots, which began in the Watts district of Los Angeles in 1965 and continued on and off until the massive uprising that erupted after the assassination of Martin Luther King, Jr. in 1968. By 1980, urban blacks were far more likely to live in the core central city zone of the large metropolitan areas than were whites. In that year, roughly two out of three urban African Americans lived in the center city, compared to just two out of seven whites. Thus was born the modern American ghettos, which so profoundly influenced American urban life in the second half of the 20th century.[37]

The 1945–1980 era also saw the return to major internal migration after a period of relatively low migrations and changes in regional significance within the nation. The century-long process of movement to the West, which maintained itself even in this period of relatively low geographic mobility, was soon complemented by a late starting shift of national population toward the southern regions. By the 1970s, a new migration to the "sun belt" began to

---

[37] As Massey and Denton point out, all this occurred despite the enactment of the Fair Housing Act of 1968, which banned racial discrimination in mortgages, rentals, and housing sales for all private and public housing in the nation. See Massey and Denton, *American Apartheid*, Chapter 7.

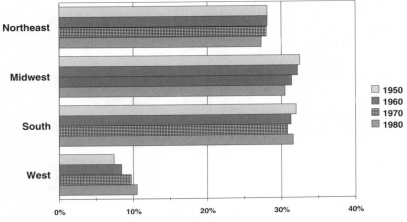

Source: Hobbs and Stoops, *Demographic Trends,* Table A1.

Graph 6.10: Changes in the Relative Share of Populations by regions of the United States, 1940–1980.

occur, primarily fueled by the massive introduction of air conditioning in the 1950s and 1960s. Although migration to the West was
not as dependent on this new technology, migration to the South
and Southwest totally depended on the universal introduction of
cheap air conditioning. This explains why the massive growth of
southern migration did not take off until the 1970s. Between 1970
and 1980, Americans began escaping the harsh northern winters for
Florida, the Southwest, and California. Although all regions lost
shares of population to the West in the 1950–1970 period, in the
1970–1980 decade, the South reversed this trend and began its spec-
tacular growth along with the West – draining population out of
the Northeastern and Midwestern regions (Graph 6.10; Maps 6.1
through 6.3).

But the loss of native-born populations in the older regions
was somewhat compensated for by the beginnings of a new age of
international migration. Very quickly, in the older states and cities
the departing native-born whites were replaced by foreign-born immigrants. This trend would increase over time, so that the states with

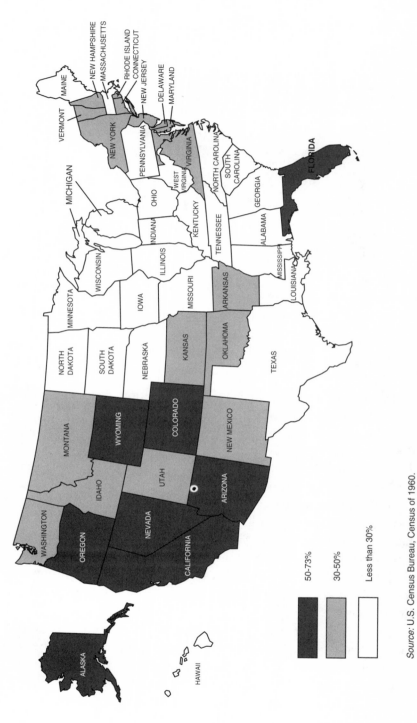

Source: U.S. Census Bureau, Census of 1960.

Map 6.1: Ratio of Resident State Population Born in Another State, 1960.

50-73%

30-50%

Less than 30%

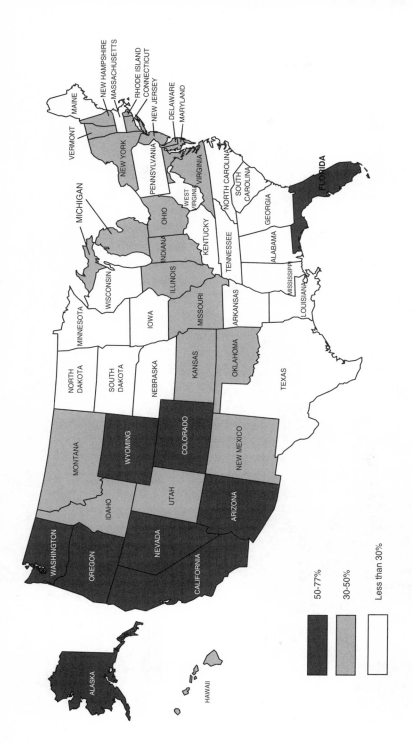

50-77%

30-50%

Less than 30%

Source: U.S. Census Bureau, Census of 1970.

Map 6.2: Ratio of Resident State Population Born in Another State, 1970.

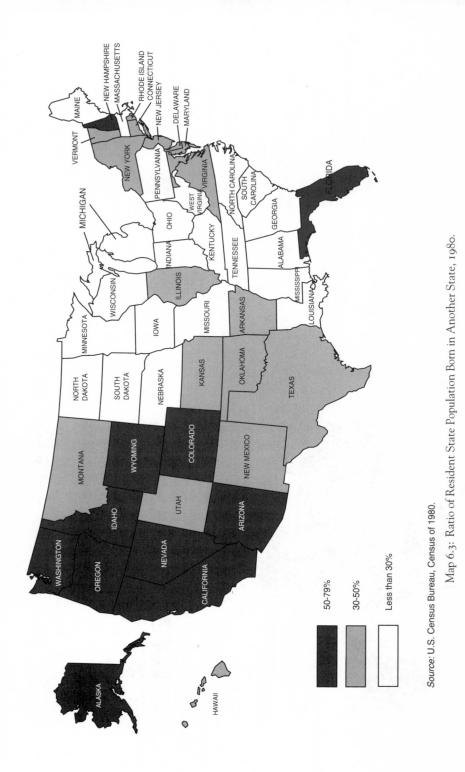

NEW HAMPSHIRE
MASSACHUSETTS
RHODE ISLAND
CONNECTICUT
NEW JERSEY
DELAWARE
MARYLAND

MAINE

VERMONT

NEW YORK

PENNSYLVANIA

VIRGINIA

WEST
VIRGINIA

NORTH CAROLINA

SOUTH
CAROLINA

FLORIDA

MICHIGAN

OHIO

KENTUCKY

GEORGIA

INDIANA

TENNESSEE

ALABAMA

ILLINOIS

MISSISSIPPI

WISCONSIN

MISSOURI

ARKANSAS

LOUISIANA

MINNESOTA

IOWA

IOWA

NORTH
DAKOTA

SOUTH
DAKOTA

NEBRASKA

KANSAS

OKLAHOMA

TEXAS

MONTANA

WYOMING

COLORADO

NEW MEXICO

IDAHO

UTAH

ARIZONA

WASHINGTON

NEVADA

OREGON

CALIFORNIA

ALASKA

HAWAII

50-79%

30-50%

Less than 30%

Source: U.S. Census Bureau, Census of 1980.

Map 6.3: Ratio of Resident State Population Born in Another State, 1980.

the highest ratio of foreign born were usually the states with the lowest or negative levels of net internal migration. By the last quarter of the 20th century, even California was sustaining itself by foreign immigration rather than the traditional internal migration, which had fallen dramatically in this period. In contrast, the states of the South and Southwest thrived on this internal migration and consistently had the highest net migrations of any states in the Union. At the same time, except for Florida, they obtained few of the new immigrants (Map 6.4).

There was also considerable movement in this period within regions. Connecticut and New Jersey, for example, continued to increase their population at the expense of other states in the Northeast region as part of the movement of population to the suburbs, which were growing rapidly at this time – more rapidly than the central cities. At the same time, the West, which had been a primarily rural area, showed a major growth of urban centers for every census in this period, becoming the second most urbanized region of the country after the Northeast. Even the South continued to urbanize in this period (Graph 6.11). What is impressive is that of the ten largest cities in the United States in 1980, five of them were in the West or Southwest. To New York, Chicago, Philadelphia, Detroit and Baltimore were now added Los Angeles, Houston, Dallas, Phoenix, and San Diego. The five traditional cities of the Northeast and North Central regions had a combined population of 13.7 million, and those of the Southwest and Far West had 7 million and these were already growing more rapidly than the traditional Eastern and Midwestern centers. It was also in 1980 that, for the first time, the South and West together accounted for over half the metropolitan populations of America, a ratio that increased with time.[38]

Not only were Americans on the move within the country, but also foreigners were on the move to the United States. Even in the period of low international migration in the 1950s and early 1960s,

---

[38] Hobbs and Stoops, *Demographic Trends in the 20th Century*, Appendix Tables 3 and 4.

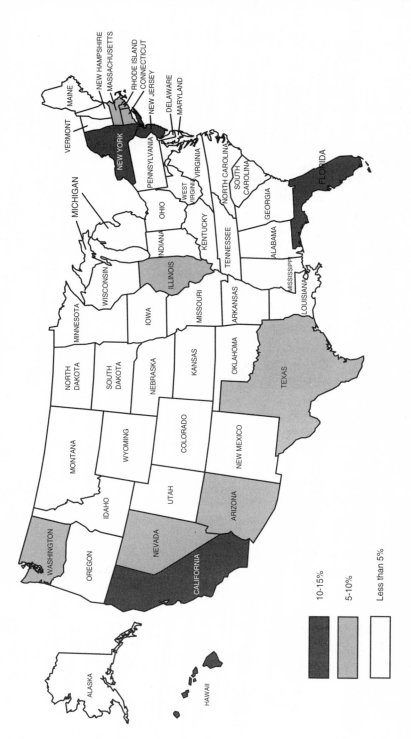

Source: Gibson and Lennon, *Historical Census Statistics on the Foreign-Born Population of the United States: 1850–1990*, USBC, Pop Division Working Papers, 29, Table 13.

Map 6.4: Ratio of Foreign Born by State, 1980.

10-15%

5-10%

Less than 5%

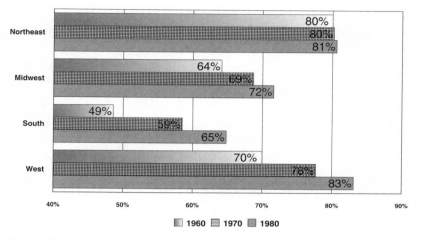

Source: 1990 Census of Population and Housing, "1990 Population and Housing Unit Counts: United States," (CPH-2); and 1980 PC80-1-1.

Graph 6.11: Percentage of Urban Population by Region, 1950–1980.

noncontinental migrants began arriving to the cities. This was the period of peak migration of Puerto Ricans – United States citizens since 1916 – to the mainland. In the 1940s, some 151,000 arrived, most to the northeastern metropolitan centers, followed by an impressive 470,000 in the 1950s and another 214,000 in the 1960s.[39] By this last decade, there was also a major reversal of trends in terms of foreign immigration to the United States. From the quota laws of the 1920s to the end of World War II, foreign immigration to the United States had been progressively declining. The low point was reached during the early 1940s, when only some 23,000 immigrants arrived to the United States. The immediate postwar period saw the expected rise in immigration, which soon ran into the quota limits imposed in the 1920s. The first breach in the wall was the Immigration Act of 1952, which moved the quota base from the 1880s arrivals breakdown to the 1920s resident foreign-born population, which eliminated the bias toward the old northern European

---

[39] José L. Vázquez Calzada, *La población de Puerto Rico y su trayectoria histórica*. Rio Piedras: Raga Printing, 1988, p. 286.

immigration. In October 1965, Congress finally abolished the quota system and allowed anyone to apply for admission, although it placed the first restrictions ever on Western Hemisphere immigration.[40] By this and subsequent congressional acts, the United States opened itself up to new waves of foreign immigration and from regions other than the traditional European sources. Whereas in the 1940s, immigrants from Europe still made up 60% of the arriving aliens, by the 1970s they accounted for only 18% of them. Two new major movements were now emerging, that from Latin America and a second wave from Asia. In the 1940s, Latin Americans already accounted for over a third of the immigrants, but Asians were still a small group, accounting for just 4% of the total. By the 1970s, Asians were up to 35% and Latin Americans accounted for 44% and were the largest single group entering the United States. In the 1970s, Mexicans represented 14% of all immigrants and made up a third of all those coming from the Western Hemisphere. The 640,000 Mexicans who legally entered the country in the 1970s were the largest single national contingent arriving in that decade, followed by 355,000 people who came from the Philippines.[41]

Thus, as early as the 1970s, the "new-new" immigration had emerged, which is the one that continued to dominate American immigration throughout the rest of the century. Immigration was now growing at some 7% per annum from 1945 to 1980, and the

[40] The entire set of immigration laws from the earliest to the most recent is found in the website http://www.immigration.gov/graphics/shared/aboutus/statistics/legishist/index.htm, which is maintained by the new U.S. Bureau of Citizenship and Immigration. For the general impact of the 1965 act in its early years, see Richard Polenberg, *One Nation Divisible: Class, Race and Ethnicity in the United States Since 1938.* New York: Viking Press, 1980, pp. 281–92. But for the first time in immigration history, the 1965 act also placed a limit on Western Hemisphere migration. For the negative consequences of this decision on the pattern of Mexican legal and illegal migration, see Douglas S. Massey, Jorge Durand, and Nolan J. Malone, *Beyond Smoke and Mirrors: Mexican Immigration in an Era of Economic Integration.* New York: Russell Sage Foundation, 1992.

[41] U.S. Immigration and Naturalization Service, *Statistical Yearbook of the Immigration and Naturalization Service, 2000.* Washington, D.C.: GPO, 2002, Tables 1 and 2, pp. 18–21.

nature of the immigration was now dramatically shifting and with it the nature of the foreign-born population in the United States. In terms of volume, the average annual immigrant flow went steadily from 180,000 in the late 1940s to 434,000 in the 1970s (the highest average movement since the 1920s) and was on the road to becoming the largest ever flow of migrants to America. In terms of origins, of course, came the shift from Europe to Latin America and Asia. This major structural change in the source and volume of immigration were well reflected in the census of 1980, when, for the first time ever, residents of European birth were no longer the majority of the foreign-born population. From 62% in the census of 1970, European-born residents declined to 39% of the foreign born in 1980 and Latin Americans now accounted for a third of the foreign born, up from 19% ten years earlier. Asians were 19% in 1980, up from just 9% in the previous census. This, of course, was an underestimate of the Latin influence in American immigration, because Puerto Ricans were considered American citizens and were not listed as immigrants. If the estimated Puerto Rican migration to the mainland is added to that of the Latin Americans in the 1960s and 1970s, these Spanish-speaking migrants made up one-half to two-thirds of all foreign immigrants in these two decades, accounting for 1.3 and 2.2 million persons coming to the mainland in these two decades. Moreover, these trends accelerated even more in the post–1980 period as Latin Americans became the largest group of the foreign born.[42]

As had occurred with all the other post–1880 immigrations, the majority of the new foreign-born arrivals headed for the cities. In fact, most moved to a relatively few cities. It is estimated that in 1980, four out of ten new immigrants lived in either the Los Angeles or New York City area.[43] Only the Mexican agricultural migrants

---

[42] Campbell J. Gibson and Emily Lennon, "Historical Census Statistics on the Foreign-Born Population of the United States: 1850–1990." Population Division Working Paper No. 29; Washington, D.C.: U.S. Bureau of the Census, Population Division (February 1999), Table 2 (updated 2001).

[43] Roger Waldinger, "From Ellis Island to LAX: Immigrant Prospects in the American City," International Migration Review 30, no. 4 (Winter 1996), p. 1078.

headed to the rural areas, and a large share of these were temporary workers and illegals. Thus, the ratio of Latin Americans and Asians in the cities was higher than any of the native-born populations. In the census of 1980, Asians and Latins were more urban than any native-born group – reaching 90% or more – although they were far less concentrated in the center cities than were the blacks.[44]

All of this new immigration also reversed the relative importance of the foreign born within the national population. From the 1920s to the 1950s, the foreign born became an ever smaller share of the national population. By 1940, they had already fallen below the 10% mark achieved in 1850, and by the census of 1970, they fell below even that rate to just 4.7% of the resident national population – the lowest ratio in the century.[45] But in the 1970s, not only was this decline reversed but also in every subsequent census the foreign-born ratio within the national population has been on the increase as foreign immigration has intensified decade after decade. By 2000, they were back up to 11.1% of the national total, a level not seen since 1930.[46]

Now almost as urban as the foreign immigrants and even more concentrated in the core central city ghettos, the black population seemed to be heading in a different direction than the rest of American society in the period after World War II. Although their rates of mortality, disease, and fertility paralleled the changes that were occurring for the white majority, their rates never seem to converge. They still were as far from the white population at the end of this period as they were at the beginning, always having the higher mortality and lower life expectancy. But at the same time, the black population was now beginning to differ in important ways from the white society. Not only were blacks far more urban and far more

[44] U.S. Census of 1980, Summary Volumes, Vol. 1 (pc80-1-B1), Table 43, p. 27ff.

[45] Campbell J. Gibson and Emily Lennon, "Historical Census Statistics on the Foreign-Born Population of the United States: 1850–1990." Population Division Working Paper No. 29; U.S. Bureau of the Census, Washington, D.C. (February 1999), Table 1.

[46] U.S. Bureau of the Census, Vital Statistics of the US 2002, part 1, Table 41.

concentrated in isolated central city districts – especially in the North – but there also appeared tendencies that seemed to suggest that this significant minority was deviating from the white majority in relation to traditional family values. The earlier signs of the decline in the importance of the traditional family in the black community were quite evident by 1980. The births outside of marriage by 1980 had now become common; teenage pregnancies were on the rise, and the number of mothers living alone with their children was becoming a much more prominent part of the social organization of the black community. The black illegitimacy rate, which had always been higher than that of the whites, now seemed to be heading in a different direction from that of the whites as births out of wedlock almost doubled between 1960–1964 and 1965–1969, reaching an extraordinary 54% of all black births. In this same period, the white illegitimate rate was only 9% of all white births.[47] In 1970, the black teenage (15–18 years of age) birth rates reached 101 births per 1,000 teenagers and almost two-thirds of these were illegitimate, compared to white teenagers, whose birth rate was just 29 such births per 1,000 teenagers; moreover, only 17% of these white teenage births were illegitimate. Although black teenage birth rates began to drop by a quarter in the next decade, the illegitimacy rate would eventually reach 86% of births by black teenagers by the end of the century.[48] Equally, there was a steady rise among blacks of female-headed households that contained children under 18 years of age, which accounted for 24% of all black households by 1980, compared to just 5% among white households.[49] This suggested to researchers at the time and later that the black family was in transition to a new

[47] Amara Bachu, *Trends in Premarital Childbearing, 1930–1994*, CPS, Special Report (October 1999), Table 1.

[48] Population Research Bureau, AmeriStat staff, "Declining Fertility Among Teenagers," Table 1. Found at http://www.prb.org.

[49] Taken from "AmeriStat" and based on an analysis of data taken from the 1970–2002 Current Population Survey (March supplement). See Population Research Bureau, "Diversity, Poverty Characterize Female-Headed Households" (AmeriStat, March 2003).

form of matriarchal family, distinct from the dominant white society. Many thought that this was a deviant pattern of behavior and was due to either their previous condition of slavery or was a result of the migration of southern rural blacks into the seemingly disorganized world of the modern urban slum. But all thought of these changes as distinct from the norm of the majority society.

CHAPTER SEVEN

A Modern Industrial Society,

1980–2003

The patterns that had been evolving in the late 1960s and early 1980s came fully to fruition in the post–1980 period. Fertility and mortality – with some exceptions – continued to decline at the same rate as in the 1980s and the immigration movement increased in tempo, with the new immigration from Latin America and Asia continuing to dominate the flow. But there also began to appear in this period significant and unexpected changes in the traditional household and family organization. The trends of increasing illegitimate births, increasing importance of female-headed households, and higher ratios of adults living alone, which had previously appeared as the deviant behavior of the black minority, now began to appear with increasing frequency in the white majority. Although the reasons may have been different for these changes, the resulting trends and changes in household and marriage organization looked quite similar. For example, for all ethnic groups and races, ratios of birth outside marriage began to climb, female-headed households with children increased with each census and survey, and the number of persons living alone in single person households was on the increase. In fact, these patterns were to appear in all advanced industrial societies at this time and probably emerged in the United States for the same reasons. Changing roles for women in society, especially their advancement into high-status professional jobs as well as entrance into the workforce, the high cost of having children, and basic changes in ideas about contraception and premarital sex all led to a fundamental shift in opinions and then in performance. Whereas the black family structure may have emerged from dire poverty, the white family patterns had their origins in affluence. What is apparent is that these demographic trends in family organization and fertility were soon quite common to all groups and were converging, and in this the United States seemed to be in step with western Europe.

But some long-term trends also slowed in this period and new patterns began to emerge. The shifts of population from urban centers to suburbs – one of the most prominent features in the previous period – continued in the post–1980 period but at a slower pace as the suburban populations stabilized and the central cities in turn became more attractive living spaces for the white native- and foreign-born populations. In turn, the flow of immigration, clearly continuing post–1960 trends, began to have a profound impact in changing the ethnicity of American society in new ways. The post–1980 period was one in which large-scale international migration of both a legal and an illegal kind (the so-called undocumented workers) once again became a prominent feature of population growth in the United States. The result of this new immigration was a major shift in ethnicity and race, as persons of Hispanic origin finally became the largest minority population in the United States in the census of 2000, surpassing the African American population for the first time in history. This new immigration also transformed previously traditional Anglo-Saxon-dominated states into multiethnic societies. The archetypical case of all this change was California, where non-Hispanic whites finally dropped below half the state's population in 1999, where 40% of the population did not speak English at home in 2000, and where just under half the births in the state were to Hispanic mothers – a ratio that was rising.[1]

At the same time, the rates of change in mortality slowed as degenerative diseases replaced infectious diseases as the major killers. There was also a temporary reversal of trends as a new infectious diseases suddenly erupted in the young adult population. Although the trend in mortality was dropping for all ages, the sudden onslaught of HIV/AIDS temporarily raised mortality rates in the younger adult

---

[1] Statistics generated from the database of RAND California at http:// ca.rand.org/stats/statistics.html.

age categories, although it had relatively little impact on overall mortality trends.

If one were to define the most original demographic feature in this post–1980 period, it would be the changes that were occurring in both families and households for all sections of the national population. The traditional American family was undergoing profound changes for all ages, all races, and all ethnic groups. Every aspect of the American family was experiencing changes: the number of adults who married, the age at which both men and women married, the number of households that were formed by married people, the number of children they were producing, and even the role of marriage in influencing total fertility was in profound transformation.

Ever since the late 1960s, the age of persons contracting marriage was on the rise. From 1980 to 2000, the median age at first marriage rose three years for women and two years for men, so that by the end of the century, men were marrying at 26.8 years of age and women were marrying at 25.1 years. The rise since the midcentury baby boom period was even more impressive, on the order of 4.8 years for women.[2] Americans not only were marrying later but also were not marrying as much as they had in previous eras. Among all races and sexes, for persons over 15 years of age, the ratio who had never married was slowly rising, reaching a third of the men and a quarter of women by the end of the century. Broken down by race, the changes among the whites was occurring at a slower pace than among the blacks, although both saw unmarried rates rising. By century's end, some 22% of adult white women had never married, compared to 42% of adult black women.[3]

All of this, of course, was having its impact on the structure of households and the relationship between families and households. Nonfamily households had always existed as a small share of the total households in the United States, usually made up of elderly

[2] U.S. Census Bureau, "Estimated Median Age at First Marriage, by Sex: 1890 to the Present," Table MS-2. Internet release date: June 29, 2001.

[3] U.S. Census Bureau, "Marital Status of the Population 15 Years Old and Over, by Sex and Race: 1950 to Present," Table MS-1. Internet release date: June 29, 2001.

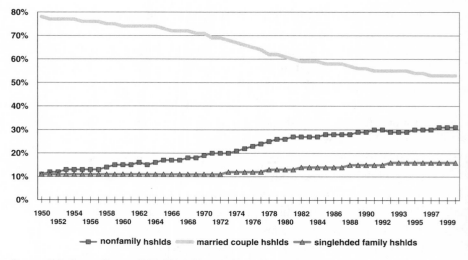

Source: U.S. Census Bureau, Table HH-1. "Households, by Type: 1940 to Present," Internet release date: June 29, 2001.

Graph 7.1: Changing Nature of Households, 1950–2000.

persons with no families left. But now they were being formed by young adults, many of whom never married. Moreover, the ratio of two-parent households even in family households with children was on the decline, as the ratio of single-parent-plus-children households was on the rise. The rapidity of this change is evident when one looks beyond this period. As late as 1960, at the height of the baby boom, married families made up 74% of all households, whereas by the census of 2000, they accounted for just a bit over half (53%) and were on a long-term trend of decline (see Graph 7.1). In turn, non-family households now accounted for 31% of all households, having risen from just 11% of all households at midcentury.[4]

Married couples were also no longer the norm, even for households with children. Households with children under 18 years of age probably experienced the most change in the second half of the 20th century. The number of two-parent families that made up such households with children was steadily on the decline, falling by 20%

[4] U.S. Census Bureau, "Households, by Type: 1940 to Present," Table HH-1. Internet release date: June 29, 2001.

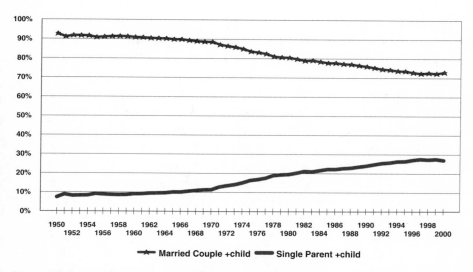

Source: U.S. Census Bureau, FM-1. Families, by Presence of Own Children Under 18: 1950 to Present Internet release date: June 29, 2001.

Graph 7.2: Changing Nature of Families with Children, 1950–2000.

from 1950 to 2000, and accounted for just under four fifths of such households in the census of 2000. At the same time, the number of families headed by a single parent had climbed in the opposite direction, reaching 27% of all families with children under 18 years. Although the trend for all groups was the same, the black population experienced the fastest decline of dual parent family households, by the end of the century, married couples with children accounted for only 39% of all black family households with children.[5] But as the general figures indicate, no group was immune to this fundamental shift of declining two-parent households (Graph 7.2).

There was also a profound change in living arrangements among older persons. Declining mortality and morbidity, the development of social security and other retirement benefits all meant that older persons could financially live alone and were generally healthier and lived longer than in earlier periods. Finally a change in cultural

[5] U.S. Census Bureau, "Families, by Presence of Own Children Under 18: 1950 to Present," Table FM-1. Internet release date: June 29, 2001.

values during the second half of the 20th century seems to have increased the value of privacy among older adults. In 1910, for example, only 12% of widows 65 years of age and older lived alone. Typically they lived with their married children in extended households. By 1990 almost 70% of such widows were living alone.[6] There was also a major rise of "empty nest" households with elderly couples no longer having resident children of any age. By 2000 a surprisingly high 55% of adults over 65 who resided in independent households lived with their spouses.[7] In 1880 extended households, here defined as having kin other than the spouse and children in common residence, represented a fifth of all white households, but by 1980 the figure had declined to 7% of all households. A decline had occurred among black households as well, but not at the rate of the white decline. As of 1980 some 17% of black households still had such kin resident in extended households.[8] It has been suggested in some of the recent literature that there has been a crossover in patterns of residence between blacks and whites in the course of the 20th century. Whereas in 1900 blacks were supposedly more likely to live in simple family households, white families were more likely to reside with older adults in the same household. By the second half of the 20th century the roles were reversed. Blacks tended more than whites to live in extended family arrangements, especially with female-dominated extended households. This "crossover" position is still a controversial one, but there is no question that currently whites are far less likely to live in extended households than blacks. Moreover, there is little question that there has been a profound change among the elderly, with privacy being more highly desired today than in 1900. With better health and more income, more

---

[6] Ellen A. Kramarow, "The Elderly Who Live Alone in the United States: Historical Perspectives on Household Change," *Demography*, Vol. 32, no. 3 (August, 1995), p. 335.

[7] Jason Fields and Lynne M. Casper, *America's Families and Living Arrangements: Population Characteristics* (Washington, DC, US Census Bureau, Current Population Reports, P20-537. June 2001), p. 12. The ratio among men was 73% of all such households and among women only 41%.

[8] Steven Ruggles, "The Tranformation of American Family Structure," *American Historical Review*, Vol. 99, no. 1 (Feb., 1994), p. 107, table 1.

elderly persons clearly had the ability and the desire to "buy" their privacy as never before.[9]

Not only were married families and families in general on the decline but also there was important accompanying shifts in fertility. Although the extremely low total fertility rates of the mid–1970s were somewhat reversed in the 1980s and 1990s, the total fertility rates barely reached replacement and fluctuated between 2.0 and 2.1 children per women who had completed their fertility by the end of the century. In fact, this overall national rate masked a continuing low total fertility rate of non-Hispanic white women, who by 2000 were averaging just 1.8 children – comparable to the rates they had from the mid–1970s. Among all groups, it was only the Hispanic women – who ended their fertility with 2.5 children – who were above the bare replacement level (Graph 7.3).[10] Even among the Hispanic women, it was essentially the Mexican women, the largest single group, that maintained very high fertility rates. Cuban American women were close to the non-Hispanic whites and the Puerto Rican women were closer to the patterns of fertility practiced by non-Hispanic black women (see Graph 7.4).

There was also the beginning of a profound change in the role of marriage in fertility. This was made evident by the rise in births outside of marriage, which guaranteed that married women no longer remained the exclusive arbiters of fertility in the United States. Whereas at midcentury, births out of wedlock were an insignificant phenomenon accounting for only 4% of all births and were still below 10% until 1968, by the end of the century, they amounted to a third of all births and their ratio of total births were steadily rising. Although all groups experienced this growth, non-Hispanic whites experienced a slower rise than all other groups, but even they had illegitimacy rates of 28% by 2000. What is impressive is that these were probably the highest recorded rates for any period in American

[9] Frances K. Goldscheider and Regina M. Bures, "The Racial Crossover in Family Complexity in the United States," *Demography*, vol. 40 no. 3 (August 2003), pp. 569–587.
[10] Amara Bachu and Martin O'Connell, "Fertility of American Women: June 2000," Current Population Reports, P20-543RV (October 2001), p. 3.

Total Number of Children per Mother who have completed their fertility

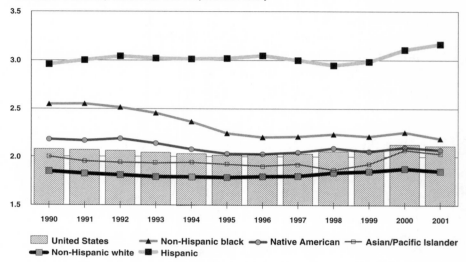

Source: CDC, NCHS, "Births: Final Data for 1997," National Vital Statistics Report 47, no.18 (1999). NCHS, "Births: Final Data for 2001," National Vital Statistics Report 51, no. 2 (2002).

Graph 7.3: Total Fertility by Race and Ethnicity, 1990–2001.

history, and despite all the talk of these rates declining, the increasing illegitimacy rates in Europe suggest that North America is following European trends. Although initially illegitimacy appeared among the poorest elements in the society, the fact that wealthier groups also began to experience these rising trends in births outside of wedlock when the economy was stable if not growing suggests that by the late 20th century this trend was due to changes in cultural norms and attitudes and the changing role of women in society. This can be seen in the shift in the relative rates of illegitimate births by age. In the 1970s, when the issue began to be perceived by the public as one of major concern, it was teenagers who had the highest rates of births outside of marriage, and these births seemed to be rising at the time. But by the end of the century, it was older women whose rate of illegitimacy was highest and rising, whereas that for teenagers was falling (see Graph 7.5).

That this increase of births outside of marriage was not due to poverty per se can be seen in the fact that the United States was not

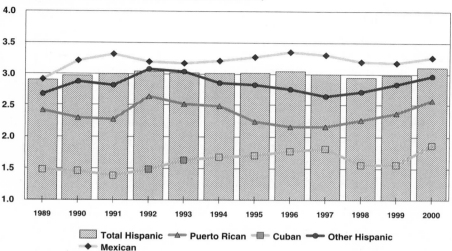

Graph 7.4: Total Fertility among Hispanics, 1989–2000.

Source: NCHS, National Vital Statistics Reports 51, no. 2, (December 18, 2002), Table 9, and NCHS, "Births: Final Data for 2001," National Vital Statistics Report 51, no. 2 (2002).

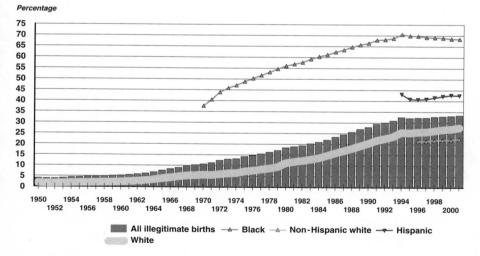

Source: Population Reference Bureau, AmeriStat, "Births to Unmarried Women — End of the Increase?" http://www.ameristat.org/.

Graph 7.5: Ratio of Illegitimate Births to All Births by Race, 1950–2000.

unique in this new pattern of births and the declining importance of traditional marriage. Other wealthy countries, such as Sweden, also experienced this trend. Although Sweden at midcentury still had a low rate of just 10% illegitimate births, by the end of the century its rate of nonmarital births had reached 53% of all births. By 1996, even Catholic countries such as Spain and Portugal had arrived at 16% and 22% illegitimacy rates respectively and France was up to 38% illegitimate births. Although Italy was still quite low, almost all western European advanced industrial countries were experiencing a steady and unabated rise in illegitimate births in this period.[11] Thus, the belief that this was a temporary or uniquely North American development does not appear to be the case. The factors influencing these trends everywhere in the modern industrial world seem to be the same – late marriages, women's increasing participation in the workforce resulting in higher incomes for women, and changing beliefs in the importance and necessity of marriage. These were beliefs and changes that seem to be general phenomena affecting all of Europe and North America at approximately the same time.

In fact even among dual-parent households with children, the traditional family with a single male breadwinner working alone to sustain the family was no longer the norm. By the end of the century, only one in five married couples had just a single male breadwinner working outside the home. Nor was the traditional family model of the stay-at-home mother the norm for families with children. Although the ratio of families with the fathers working and mothers staying at home was higher among these families, even in this subsection of married couples the traditional model no longer accounted for the majority of such families. Among married couples with children, 28% had just a father in the workforce, and in families with children under 6 years of age, only 36% had the mother staying at home with the children and not working. That this pattern is not to be reversed anytime soon is indicated by the fact that the trend of male breadwinners as the only support of the family was down for all

[11] Data taken from the world demographic databank maintained by the Institut National d'Etudes Démographique, http://www.ined.fr/bdd/demogr/.

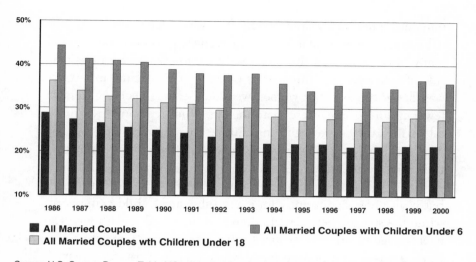

■ All Married Couples
☐ All Married Couples wth Children Under 18
■ All Married Couples with Children Under 6

Source: U.S. Census Bureau, Table MC1, "Married Couples by Labor Force Status of Spouses: 1986 to Present." Internet release date: June 29, 2001.

Graph 7.6: Ratio of Married Couples with Husband-Only Working by Age of Children, 1986–2000.

of this period, and these rates were the lowest recorded in the last part of the century (Graph 7.6). Not only were more women in the workforce – a ratio that was constantly on the rise through the second half of the century – but also the vast majority of married mothers with young children were working outside the home by 2000. Even for women who had given birth to a child during the previous year, the majority at the end of the year were found to be working outside the home – a rate of 55% of them in 2000 compared to just 31% in 1967.[12]

All of these changes had their impact on fertility. Formal marriage was no longer the exclusive arbiter of fertility, and more and more women were reducing the number of children they did have. This was not due to women foregoing children. In fact, there was little change in the number of women going childless, which has

[12] U.S. Census Bureau, "Women 15 to 44 Years Old Who Have Had a Child in the Last Year and Their Percentage in the Labor Force: Selected Years, June 1976 to Present," Table H5. Internet release date: October 18, 2001.

remained quite steady since 1960.[13] Nor was it due to declining sex-ual activity, since sexual activity of teenagers was on the rise and many more women in the 1990s were having sexual relations out-side of marriage than thirty years earlier.[14] This decline in fertility was due to the fact that women were deliberately deciding to have fewer children. They were marrying later, thus reducing their mari-tal fertility; they were beginning childbearing at ever later ages, they were spacing their children farther apart, and they were terminating their fertility at earlier ages. Not only did the average age of moth-ers having their first children rise by 2.7 years from 1960 to 1999, but it also rose significantly for every subsequent child being born, while the spacing between children also increased.[15] Although the average age of mothers at first birth for the entire population was now 24.9 years, for non-Hispanic white women it was 25.9 years.[16] From 1950 to 2000, the number of live births for each age cate-gory declined by over half, with the biggest decline occurring in the 25–39 age group.[17] As was to be expected from the fertility de-clines, the size of families with children was declining as well. The

[13] The rate has stayed relatively steady since 1960 at roughly 15% to 16% for women who have reached 44 years of age. See National Center for Health Statis-tics, *Health, United States, 2001*. Hyattsville, Md.: 2001, Table 4.

[14] As the 1995 health survey carried out by the CDC concluded, "Among ever-married women 15–44 years of age, 82 percent had first intercourse before they were married. About 69 percent of those first married in 1965–74 had their first intercourse before marriage compared with 89 percent of those first married in the 1990's. Only 2 percent of those first married in 1965–74 had their first inter-course 5 years or more before marriage compared with 56 percent of those first married in the 1990," see J. Abma, A. Chandra, W. Mosher, L. Peterson, and L. Piccinino, *Fertility, Family Planning, and Women's Health: New Data from the 1995 National Survey of Family Growth*, Vital Health Statistics 23, no. 19. Wash-ington, D.C. National Center for Health Statistics, 1997, p. 5

[15] CDC, NCHS, Data Warehouse, "Median Age of Mother by Live-Birth Order, According to Race and Hispanic Origin: United States, Selected Years 1940–99." Table 1–5.

[16] T. J. Mathews and Brady E. Hamilton, "Mean Age of Mother, 1970–2000," *Na-tional Vital Statistics Reports* 51, no. 1 (December 11, 2002), Tables 1–2, pp. 6–7.

[17] CDC, *Health, United States, 2002*, Table 3. There was also a steady decline in the median age of mothers at the birth of their last child – dropping by three years from 1915 to 1955. Paul C. Glick and Robert Parke, Jr, " New Approaches in Studying the Life Cycle of the Family," *Demography*, vol. 2 (1965), p. 191.

average number of children in families that included children went from 2.4 children in 1965 at the height of the baby boom to just 1.9 children in 2000.[18]

Women were carrying out these changes in their fertility through a variety of methods. They were making more systematic use of contraceptives and legal abortions.[19] It is estimated that by the end of the century, almost two-thirds of all women ages 15–44 used some form of contraception. Although only a third of the teenagers used some method of birth control, by the time women were reaching the crucial fertility years (after 24 years of age), over 70% of them were using contraceptives. This pattern of rising contraceptive use over time was common to all racial and ethnic groups. Although legal abortion rates rose rapidly initially and reached as much as 43% of the total of live births in the mid-1980s, by the late 1990s they were down to 34% of all births and falling. For the whites, the fall was quite dramatic, reaching just a quarter of white births at the end of the century. Abortion rates among black women, however, once rising to the 65% to 70% range in the earlier years, did not decline and remained steady throughout the period (see Graph 7.7).[20]

Although the impact of legal abortion may have repressed the birth rate somewhat in the early years, the decline of abortions at the end of the century has not reversed fertility rates. These have continued to decline from the 1960s onward. From 1980 to 2000, the crude birth rate dropped from 24 per thousand resident population to just 15 per thousand. Although almost all groups experienced this decline, it was in fact the non-Hispanic whites who experienced the lowest birth rate for any group in the population, reaching just 12.2 births per thousand non-Hispanic white residents. Blacks and American Indians were among the highest fertility groups and

[18] U.S. Census Bureau, "Average Number of Own Children Under 18 per Family, by Type of Family: 1955 to Present," Table FM-3. Internet release date: June 29, 2001.

[19] Contraceptive use went from 56% of all women 15 to 44 in 1982 to 64% in 1995, and although highest for non-Hispanic white women (66%) was on the increase for all groups, including Hispanics.

[20] National Center for Health Statistics, *Health, United States, 2002*. Hyattsville, Md.: 2002, Table 16, p. 100

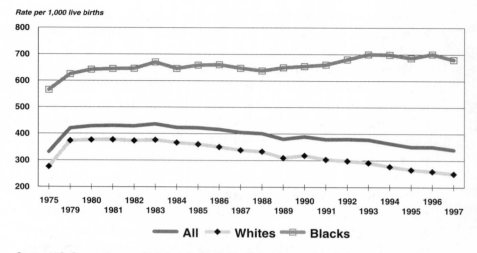

Rate per 1,000 live births

Source: U.S. Census Bureau, *Statistical Abstract of the United States: 2002*, Table 88.

Graph 7.7: Abortion Rate by Race, 1975–1997.

experienced similar declines. The one group that stands out against the trend is Hispanics, whose rate actually increased to 25.1 births per thousand residents of this group in the national population.[21] Although Cuban and other non-Mexican Hispanics tended to have low birth rates, this was compensated for by the Mexicans, who were both the single most important part of the Hispanic population[22] and had overwhelmingly the highest birth rates of any group in the country. Thus in certain urban regions and in the coastal and frontier states, the importance of the Mexicans compensated for the declining fertility rates of the native-born populations.

The levels of mortality in the period since 1980 have tended to be somewhat erratic, although the long-term trend remained one of decline. Overall, the age-adjusted mortality rate from 1980 to 2000

[21] National Center for Health Statistics. *Health, United States, 2002*. Hyattsville, Md.: 2002, Table 3, pp. 83–4.

[22] Births to Mexican mothers accounted for 71% of all Hispanic births in the United States in 2000. They produced almost as many children as black mothers, and these births made up 15% of the over 4 million births that occurred. National Center for Health Statistics, *Health, United States, 2002*. Hyattsville, Md.: 2002, Table 5, pp. 86.

declined by 16%, and the tendency of male mortality to decline faster than female mortality meant that the ratio of male-to-female age-adjusted rates in 2000 was only 1.4 times greater than female rates, as opposed to 1.6 times greater than those rates in 1980.[23] Although the HIV/AIDS epidemic had an impact on mortality of adult men aged 25–44 years in the early 1990s, this impact peaked in 1995 with the introduction of new antiviral treatments that brought the death rate for these men back toward the declining trend in the second half of the decade.[24] Thus, the convergence of death rates between men and women resulted in the reversal of the long-term trend in sexual differences in life expectancy, as males began to converge toward female levels of life expectancy at birth. That divergence had peaked in the 1960s at close to 8 years' difference of life. After the 1970s, the trend reversed itself. Although there were still 7.4 years of difference between men and women in 1980, by 2000 this had been reduced to just 5.4 years.[25]

There was also a marked decline in the infant mortality and maternal mortality death rates due to better medical attention at birth. The infant mortality rate continued its long-term pattern of secular decline, going from 29 deaths per 1,000 lives births at midcentury to 13 deaths in 1980 and 9 deaths in 2001.[26] In this it was similar to all of the advanced industrial societies of the world and in fact was somewhat behind international rates. The western European countries had mostly reached the rate of 5 deaths or less per thousand

---

[23] CDC, NCHS, *National Vital Statistics Report* 50, no. 15 (September 16, 2002), Table 1, p. 19. These rates are age adjusted to the age distribution of the population in 2000.

[24] See National Center for Health Statistics, *Health, United States, 2002.* Hyattsville, Md.: 2002, Table 43, p. 159, for HIV death rates by age and sex, 1987–1999. For overall death rates by age to 1999, see Table 36, pp. 137–40. For the rates after 1999, see CDC, NCHS, *National Vital Statistics Reports* 51, no. 5, March 14, 2003, Table 1, p. 7.

[25] CDC, NCHS, Data Warehouse, "Life Expectancy at Birth, at 65 Years of Age, and at 75 Years of Age, According to Race and Sex: United States, Selected Years," Table 28.

[26] U.S. Bureau of the Census, *Statistical Abstract of the United States, 2002*, Table 66, p. 59.

births by 2000.[27] The maternal death rate, calculated as the number of mothers dying at birth to 100,000 births, declined by over a third from 1980 to the end of the century. In 1998, the rate was calculated at 8.3 deaths per 100,000 live births, which also was a rate higher than comparable rates in Europe.[28]

But there was little change in the leading causes of death from 1980 to 2000. In the former period, as in the latter, it was diseases of the heart, cancers, and strokes that were the three major killers, in that order, with only Alzheimer's disease becoming a new major killer in the top ten list as the elderly population increased.[29] Although these degenerative diseases continued to influence the aging national population, there was, in fact, an improvement in both health and life expectancy among the aged in this period. It has been estimated that over the course of the 20th century the incidence of physical limitations among the elderly, from difficulty walking to paralysis, blindness, and deafness, has consistently declined among those over 50 and over 60 years, on average about 0.7% to 0.9% per annum. In 1900 samples of men over 60 years of age, it was found that over a third of them had difficulty walking; from comparable groups examined in the early 1990s, these rates had fallen to under 14%.[30] Not only was old age less fraught with limitations, but even life expectancy at 65 years of age now rose 3.3 years for men and 4.1 years for women in the half century between 1950 and 1999.[31]

---

[27] J. P Sardon, ODE, "Recent Demographic Trends in Developed Countries" (January 2002), from the website of INED-FRANCE http://www.ined.fr//; also see Jacques Vallin, France Meslé, and Tapani Valkonen, *Trend in Mortality and Differential mortality* (Population Studies, no. 36, Strasbourg: Council of Europe, 2001), Table 3, pp. 61–3.

[28] For European rates, see World Health Organization, WHO Statistics, "Maternal Mortality, 1995 Country Estimates." Accessed at http://www3.who.int/. The American rates were earlier based on a different calculation, that was changed in 1999. For this reason, the pre-1999 rates are noncomparable to those offered by the CDC in that year. See National Center for Health Statistics. *Health, United States, 2002.* Hyattsville, Md.: 2002, Table 44, p. 161.

[29] CDC, *Health, United States, 2002.* Washington, D.C., 2002, Table 32, pp. 21–4.

[30] Dora L. Costa, "Changing Chronic Disease Rates and Long Term Decline in Functional Limitation Among Elderly Men," *Demography* 39, no. 1 (February 2002), Table 3, p. 125.

[31] CDC, *Health, United States, 2002.* Washington, D.C., 2002, Table 28, p. 116.

By this later year older persons in this age group were living an additional 16.1 and 19.2 years respectively. Although this was still below the Japanese rates – now the highest in the world – they were only off by 1.2 years for white men and 2.7 years for white women. In fact, they were now at the survival rates of Spain and Austria. The rates for black men and women in the late 1990s were comparable to those for the elderly men and women of eastern Europe.[32]

As was historically the case, mortality rates in this period as well were not equal for all groups within society. The sharp differences that have always existed between black and white mortality changed little during the last part of the 20th century. Black rates of mortality dropped in this period for all types of death, but there was no convergence on white rates, which declined as fast or faster. At the end of the century, blacks had over double the mortality rate of whites in virtually every category, from neonatal, infant, and maternal mortality to age-specific rates and on average lived 6 years less than whites. Black males even had an HIV/AIDS death rate in the early 1990s one and a half times greater than that of white males in their age category.[33] Moreover, migration to the northern central cities did not lead to better health. In 1990, it was estimated that African Americans in poor southern rural counties had a higher life expectancy than black men and women living in Harlem, Central City Detroit, the South Side of Chicago, and the Watts district in Los Angeles.[34]

[32] CDC, *Health, United States, 2002*. Washington, D.C., 2002, Table 27, p. 115.

[33] Aside from the above cited materials, see Michael R. Haines, "Ethnic Differences in Demographic Behavior in the United States: Has There Been Convergence?" Working Paper no. 9042, National Bureau of Economic Research, July 2002. A CDC survey in 1988 found that even within the groups above and below the poverty line, there was a sharp difference by race with poor blacks suffering almost 7 more deaths per 100,000 live births than poor whites and the ratio among non-poverty being two times as great, with white non-poor suffering just 7.6 deaths per 100,000 live births. "Poverty and Infant Mortality," *Monthly Morbidity and Mortality Weekly Report* 44, no. 49 (December 15, 1995), Table 2, p. 927.

[34] Arline T. Geronimus, John Bound, Timothy A. Waidmann, Cynthia G. Colen, and Dianne Steffick, "Inequality in Life Expectancy, Functional Status, and Active Life Expectancy Across Selected Black and White Populations in the United States," *Demography* 38, no. 2 (May 2001), Table 3, p. 243.

These differences in rates not only reflected the continuing influence of racial prejudice but also, by the end of the century, were clearly marking fundamental class differences in the access to health resources for all types of poor persons, white and nonwhite, in the United States. When death rates are broken down by education completed, a good proxy for class, the difference in rates is impressive. The death rate for persons with less than 12 years of schooling was 2.6 times greater per 100,0000 population in 1999 than for those completing 13 or more years of schooling, and this difference held for sex as well.[35] Although since early in the 20th century living in the cities no longer creates a "mortality penalty" and the rural mortality rates are now in fact higher than those in the urbanized counties, the concentration of poor in the inner cities has meant that mortality rates in the inner city have been higher than mortality rates for the urban population in general and higher than that of the wealthier suburbs.[36] This mortality difference by class and race is clearly related to access to health care, which is unequally given to persons on the basis of wealth.[37] This sharp difference among the populations in the United States in access to health care and in the quality of health care received helps to explain why, at the end of the 20th century, all rates of mortality tend to be higher and life expectancy tends to be lower than those of comparable advanced industrial societies in Europe and Asia.[38] Moreover, all estimates of future rates indicate that

---

[35] National Center for Health Statistics, *Health, United States, 2002*. Hyattsville, Md.: 2002, Table 35, p. 136.

[36] National Center for Health Statistics, *Health, United States, 2002*. Hyattsville, Md.: 2002, Table 34, pp. 133–5

[37] In 1999, it was estimated that 17% of the population younger than 65 years of age did not have health insurance and the same ratio of pregnant women did not receive prenatal care in the first trimester. National Center for Health Statistics, *Health, United States, 2002*. Hyattsville, Md.: 2002, Table 52, pp. 179–80.

[38] U.S. Bureau of the Census, *Statistical Abstract of the United States, 2002*. Washington D.C.: GPO, 2002, Table 1312, p. 829. Average life expectancy at birth in the year 2001 was an extraordinary 3.5 years greater in Japan than the United States, a level that the United States is not expected to reach until well into the 21st century. The infant mortality rate was 43% higher in the United States than in Japan in this same year, with the United States unable to reach even the 2001 Japanese rate by 2010.

the United States will not achieve the current rates of the advanced European and Asian countries until well into the 21st century. Yet this disparity occurs despite the fact that the United States spends a much higher ratio of its gross national product on health care than any other advanced industrial country.[39] Clearly, the spending of this money is unequally distributed, with the result that a large share of the American population has health standards more common to less developed countries than to the advanced industrial world.

If the health of the United States population falls short of international standards, its wealth per capita is among the highest in the world, and it has thus become a magnet for international migrations as never before in its history. Ever since the revision of the immigration laws in the late 1970s, the flow of immigration has increased steadily. The average annual arrivals, which were on the order of 321,000 per annum in the 1960s and 434,000 in the 1970s, reached 633,000 per annum in the 1980s and 978,000 per annum in the 1990s.[40] From 1980 to 2000, some 17 million legal immigrants arrived to the United States (see Graph 7.8). As was apparent from the 1960s onward, the origin of that immigration had shifted to a domination of Latin American and Asian migrants, with Mexico outdistancing all other nations as a source of migrants to the United States. In the 1980s, Mexicans already made up 23% of all immigrants, and this rose to 25% in the 1990s.[41] By the census of 2000, it was estimated that there were 7.8 million Mexicans legally residing in the United States. Moreover, there was not only a legal migration of Mexicans, but given the length of their common border and the great disparity in their wages and income, there was also a massive illegal migration as well. The latest calculations done by the

39 U.S. Bureau of the Census, *Statistical Abstract of the United States, 2002*. Washington, D.C.: GPO, 2002, Table 1313, p. 830.

40 U.S. Immigration and Naturalization Service, *Statistical Yearbook of the Immigration and Naturalization Service, 2000*. Washington, D.C.: GPO, 2002, Table 1, p. 18.

41 U.S. Immigration and Naturalization Service, *Statistical Yearbook of the Immigration and Naturalization Service, 2000*. Washington, D.C.: GPO, 2002, Table 2, p. 19.

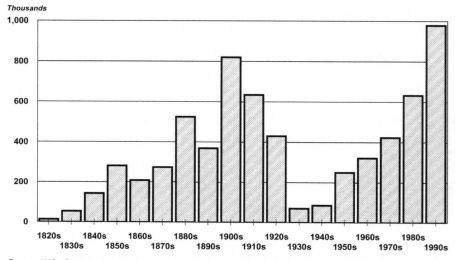

Source: INS, *Statistical Yearbook of the Immigration and Naturalization Service, 2000*, Table 1.

Graph 7.8: Average Annual Immigration to the United States by Decade, 1820–2000.

Census Bureau estimate that in the census of 2000, there were 10.2 million foreign-born undocumented immigrants in the country – a majority of whom were Mexicans – and these illegal immigrants made up close to a third of the permanently residing foreign-born population.[42]

All this has meant that the foreign-born population by the end of the century was again approaching the levels of importance that they had at the beginning of the 20th century, and their total numbers, of course, were the largest ever in American history. These foreign-born migrants, by 2000, accounted for some 31 million of the resident population, up from 14 million in 1980.[43] Most of these foreign born were recent immigrants, with four out of ten arriving in the 1990s

---

[42] Kevin E. Deardorff and Lisa M. Blumerman, "Evaluating Components of International Migration: Estimates of the Foreign-Born Population by Migrant Status in 2000," Population Division, Working Paper Series No. 58; U.S. Bureau of the Census, December 2001, Table 2.

[43] U.S. Census Bureau, *Statistical Abstract of the United States: 2002*, Table 41, p. 45.

and almost seven out of ten coming since 1980.[44] It is evident that Latin Americans or Hispanics, as they were now called by the Bureau of the Census, made up a very high ratio of the foreign born – over half in 2000 – with Asians coming next at just over a quarter of the total.[45] Including those who migrated from Puerto Rico and illegal immigrants, especially important in the Mexican migration, it is estimated that in 2000 there were 32.8 million Hispanics of foreign birth or second generation children born to Hispanic parents and they alone represented 12% of the population.[46] All together the "foreign stock," defined as those born outside the United States and their immediate offspring (the so-called second generation), was estimated at 55.9 million and accounted for a fifth of the total population.[47]

The foreign-born population, especially the 32 million described as Hispanics, were not evenly spread across the entire nation. Foreign migration in general was primarily coastal and urban, although there was no state that did not obtain foreign immigrants in the post-1980 period (see Map 7.1). As for the Hispanics, each subgroup was concentrated in a different region of the country, although few lived in the Midwestern states. Of the 22 million estimated Mexican population in 2000, 57% lived in the Western region; of the 3 million Puerto Ricans, 64% resided in the Northeast and 80% of the 1.3 million Cubans resided in the South.[48] More urban than the population as a whole and more than non-Hispanic whites, Hispanics also tended to live in the central cities of the great metropolitan areas more than any other group in the population except for blacks.

---

[44] U.S. Census Bureau, "Current Population Survey, March 2000," Table 1-6, Internet release date: January 3, 2001.

[45] Lisa Lollock, "The Foreign Born Population in the United States: March 2000," *Current Population Reports*, P20–534, Washington, D.C.: U.S. Census Bureau, 2001, p. 1.

[46] U.S. Census Bureau, "Census 2000 Redistricting Data (P.L. 94–171), Summary File for States and Census 2000 Redistricting Summary File for Puerto Rico," Tables PL1 and PL2. Internet release date: April 2, 2001.

[47] U.S. Census Bureau, *Statistical Abstract of the United States: 2002*, Table 42, p. 45.

[48] U.S. Census Bureau, "Current Population Survey, March 2000, Ethnic and Hispanic Statistics Branch, Population Division," Table 18.1. Internet release date: March 6, 2001.

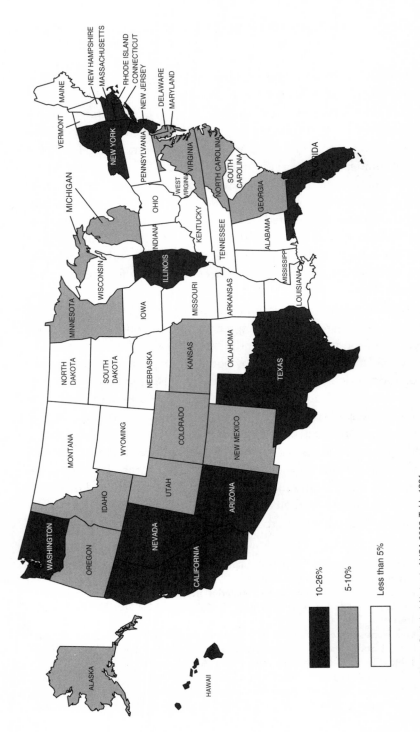

Map 7.1: Ratio of Foreign Born by State, 2000.

Source: Statistical Abstract of USA 2002, Table 1381.

10-26%

5-10%

Less than 5%

Even so, although half the African Americans resided in such central cities, Hispanics were not far behind with 46% residing in these areas. Every Hispanic group, except for Cubans, had a higher ratio than the national average residing in central cities. The most concentrated were Puerto Ricans; some 61% of whom resided in central cities.[49] At 44% resident in the central cities by 2002, even the Asian population, although slightly less concentrated in central cities than Hispanics, were still above the national norm.[50] Moreover, these great metropolitan areas were being sustained by foreign immigration, as the native-born population continued to have a net-negative migration flow from these cities. Even the states in general that were high immigrant states were net-negative states in terms of the internal migration of the native-born population (see Map 7.2). Thus, the population of the foreign stock tended to compensate for the declines in the states and cities that were losing native-born population at the end of the 20th century.[51]

That foreign migrants were crucial for metropolitan growth can be seen in the role they played in bringing positive growth rates to all metropolitan areas between 1998 and 2001 (see Graphs 7.9 and 7.10) and in cutting down the losses for the central cities. They also increasingly migrated to the suburbs, but their weight there was counterbalanced by the continual flow of native-born populations out of the central cities and to the suburbs, which did not change direction in this period although the flow appears to have lessened at the beginning of the 21st century. Given their urban orientation, these foreign-born immigrants had little impact on the rural areas, which continued to have negative population flows for all groups in this period.

[49] U.S. Census Bureau, "Current Population Survey, March 2000, Ethnic and Hispanic Statistics Branch, Population Division," Table 20.1. Internet release date: March 6, 2001.

[50] U.S. Census Bureau, "Current Population Survey, March 2002, Ethnic and Hispanic Statistics Branch, Population Division," Table 3.15. Internet release date: March 10, 2003.

[51] See William H. Frey, "Immigration, Domestic Migration and Demographic Balkanization in America: New Evidence for the 1990s," *Population and Development Review* 22, no. 4 (December 1996), pp. 741–63.

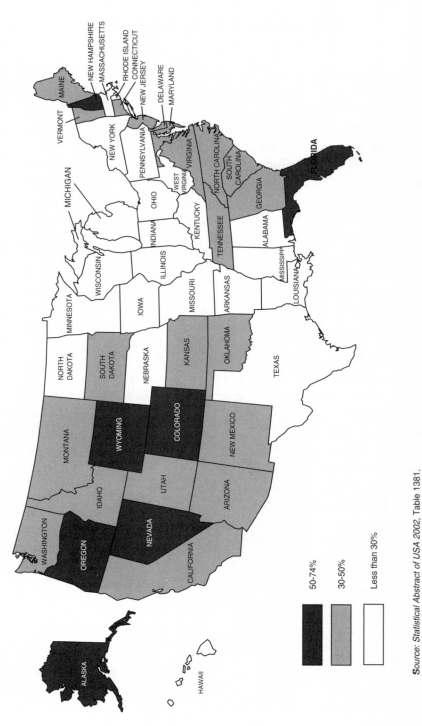

Source: Statistical Abstract of USA 2002, Table 1381.

Map 7.2: Ratio of Native-Born Resident State Population Born in Another State, 2000.

Legend:
- 50-74%
- 30-50%
- Less than 30%

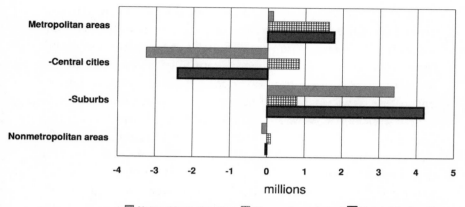

Source: U.S. Census Bureau, Table A-3. "Inmigration, Outmigration, and Net Migration for Metropolitan Areas: 1985–2001," Internet release date: July 12, 2000. Last revised: March 31, 2003.

Graph 7.9: Population Change for Metropolitan Areas and Their Subdivisions between 1999 and 2000.

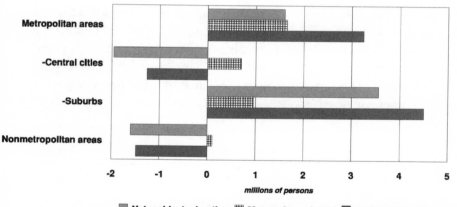

Source: U.S. Census Bureau, Table A-3. "Inmigration, Outmigration, and Net Migration for Metropolitan Areas: 1985–2001," Internet release date: July 12, 2000. Last revised: March 31, 2003.

Graph 7.10: Population Change for Metropolitan Areas and Their Subdivisions between 2000 and 2001.

Despite some slowing of the trends, the suburbs continued to gain population at the cost of the central cities and even at the increasing cost of the nonmetropolitan areas. Equally, the disparities in wealth between central cities and suburbs continued to grow in the last decades of the 20th century. By 2000, the poverty rate in the central cities was twice as high as in the suburbs and income was twice as high in the suburbs. As was to be expected, central cities had a higher unemployment rate and as has been seen, higher mortality rates. The ratio of vacant houses, of home ownership, of professional workers, and even of education level of the population all tended to worsen in the decade between 1990 and 2000. There were some regional differences that showed that the western and eastern cities experienced decreasing spreads between core and suburbs, but the difference increased in the Northeast and Midwest.[52] The only significant change in this period was a modest decline in all metropolitan area housing segregation indices for blacks, in contrast to the rise in segregation indices for Asians and Hispanics. The latter group, in fact, increased its isolation from both whites and blacks with each census.[53]

The high ratio of recent immigrant arrivals among the foreign born, the high ratio speaking the dominant immigrant language [a ratio far higher than the principal language (Italian) had been a century before], and their increasing concentration in densely populated immigrant regions (again at rates far higher than the New Immigrants of the 1880 to 1914 era) resulted in a far higher retention of foreign language among the new arrivals than in earlier periods.[54]

---

[52] John R. Logan, "The Suburban Advantage: New Census Data Show Unyielding City–Suburb Economic Gap, and Surprising Shifts in Some Places." Albany, N.Y.: Lewis Mumford Center for Comparative Urban and Regional Research, SUNY Albany, June 24, 2002, Table 1.

[53] John Iceland, Daniel H. Weinberg, and Erika Steinmetz, *Racial and Ethnic Residential Segregation in the United States: 1980–2000*, U.S. Census Bureau, Series CENSR-3. Washington, D.C.: GPO, 2002, Tables 4.2, 5.2, and 6.2, pp. 43, 64, and 84. Also see John R. Logan, *Hispanic Populations and Their Residential Patterns in the Metropolis*. Albany, N.Y.: Lewis Mumford Center for Comparative Urban and Regional Research, SUNY Albany, May 8, 2002, Table 3.

[54] It has been argued that native language retention will be higher and last longer than in any previous generation of migrants and that there is a potential for the nation to become truly bilingual if this pattern of migration continues. See

It was estimated in the census of 2000 that 47 million (or 18%) of the 262 million persons who were over the age of 5 years did not speak English at home, of whom 60% (or 28 million) were Spanish speakers. The states with the highest ratio of non-English speakers were the expected coastal states, the southern frontier states, and Hawaii. In California an extraordinary 40% of the population did not speak English at home.[55] Given these patterns, Spanish speakers, unlike earlier migration streams, tended to retain their native language over several more generations than was common for earlier immigrant groups.[56]

In the context of the declining birth rates of the native-born non-Hispanic whites, the net arrival of foreign born accounted for 39% of the natural growth of the American population in this and subsequent years.[57] Yet this input, although maintaining the positive growth of the national population, only slowed somewhat the aging of the American population, which was a process occurring in all the advanced industrial societies. Given the low fertility rates of the dominant non-Hispanic white population, the aged were becoming an ever more important element in the society. Together with a rising life expectancy, the fertility and mortality trends at the end of the 20th century were transforming the age structure of the national population in profound ways. First, the mean age of the population was progressively rising along with the share of the population of persons in the older age groups. In the last twenty years of the century, the median age of the national population rose 5.3 years to reach 35.3 years of age. As can seen in the age pyramids for the three decades, the shape of age distribution was becoming ever heavier on

Douglas S. Massey, "The New Immigration and Ethnicity in the United States," *Population and Development Review* 21, no. 3 (September 1995), pp. 646–47.

[55] U.S. "Census Bureau, Census 2000," Summary File 3, Tables P19, PCT13, and PCT14. Internet release data: February 25, 2003.

[56] Richard Alba, John Logan, Amy Lutz, and Brian Stults, "Only English by the Third Generation? Loss and Preservation of the Mother Tongue Among the Grandchildren of Contemporary Immigrants," *Demography* 39, no. 3 (August 2002), pp. 467–84.

[57] U.S. Census Bureau, "Components of Change for the Total Resident Population: Middle Series, 1999 to 2100," Table NP-T6-A. Internet release date: January 13, 2000.

the top and smaller at the younger ages – moving from the classic pyramid to a more jarlike shape (see Graph 7.10 earlier and Graphs 7.11 and 7.12). At the same time, there was a steady growth of the ratio of the population over 65 years of age, which went from 11.3% of the population in 1980 to 12.4% in the latest census.[58] Although this was still slightly behind the European rate of 15.5% at the end of the century, it is projected that the United States will reach that rate by 2010 and that the elderly will make up 20% of the population as early as 2030.[59]

All this demographic change was beginning to have a profound and increasing impact on the labor market as over the next few generations fewer workers would be supporting more nonworkers. The so-called dependency or support ratio, which is the ratio of workers to nonworkers, will be progressively increasing with each census, with all its consequent impact both here and in other advanced industrial societies. In 2000, some 41% of the population was elderly or younger than 20 years of age and thus being supported by 59% of the people who were in the workforce. Given the fact that the baby boomers in 2000 were still in the workforce, the ratio of working population from the 1970s to 2000 actually increased. Before baby boomers entered the workforce, the ratio of 20- to 64-year-olds to total population was 52.2% (1970) and then rose to 56.7% in 1980 when they entered the workforce and reached a new high at the end of the century. But as the baby boomers enter retirement age in 2010 and are replaced by children coming from low fertility cohorts, the ratio of working aged persons will be reversed and begin its long-term decline and the United States will look more and more like the aging European populations.[60]

[58] All age data comes from Frank Hobbs and Nicole Stoops, "Demographic Trends in the 20th Century," U.S. Census Bureau, Census 2000, Special Reports, Series CENSR-4. Washington, D.C.: GPO, 2002, Table 5.

[59] Kevin Kinsella and Victoria A. Velkoff, An Aging World: 2001, U.S. Census Bureau, Series P95/01–1. Washington, D.C.: GPO, 2001, p. 9.

[60] For a discussion of the relative impact of these changes both in future projections and in historical perspective, see Richard A. Easterlin, "Twentieth-Century American Population Growth," in Stanley L. Engerman and Robert E. Gallman, The Cambridge Economic History of the United States, 3 vols. Cambridge: Cambridge University Press, 1996–2000, vol. III, pp. 544–47.

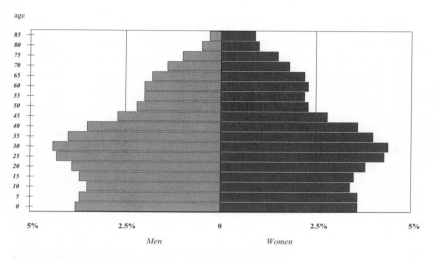

Source: Hobbs and Stoops, *Demographic Trends*, 2002, Table A5.

Graph 7.11: Age Pyramid of the U.S. Population in 1990.

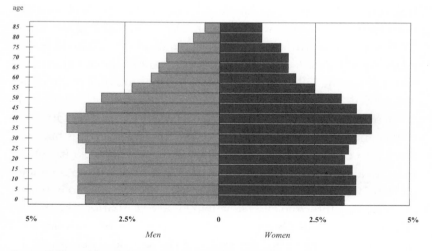

Source: Hobbs and Stoops, *Demographic Trends*, 2002, Table A5.

Graph 7.12: Age Pyramid of the U.S. Population in 2000.

At the same time, as the elderly become a larger share of the population, their impact on family structure and kinship is becoming more pronounced. It has been estimated that in 1940, only one in three women 50 years old had living mothers, whereas by 1980 the proportion had doubled to two in three women aged 50.[61] More and more people in their 40s and 50s, the so-called sandwich generation, will have surviving parents or relatives for whom they may have to provide care and will also most likely still be providing care for their children, who had been born when they themselves were in their late 20s and early 30s. By the 21st century, three to four surviving generations will be the norm. Questions of costs and benefits of the elderly, from their increasing needs for health care, housing, and maintenance to their role as child care providers for working mothers, are becoming major concerns of public policy, as the never-ending debate over the financial viability of the Social Security system indicates.

By the first decade of the 21st century America looked like most of the advanced industrial nations of the world. Its native-born non-Hispanic white population had fertility rates equal to the lowest in the advanced industrial world, but thanks to immigrants, the total fertility rate was still at the replacement level of 2.1 children. Its mortality schedule looked like a classic advanced industrial society with the leading killers being the same as those in European and industrialized Asian countries and its mortality rates at the high end of these advanced countries. In the trends in fertility, illegitimate births, and abortion rates, not only was the United States moving more into conformity with the rest of the world but also its internally divided population was also converging toward these common patterns, whether whites, blacks, Asians, or Hispanics. Also in terms of family structures and changing household organization, the trends evident in the United States tended to be common for all groups and in turn are paralleling the experience in the advanced European nations. The decline of the dual-parent family, the rise of cohabiting unmarried adult households, the increasing importance of fertility

[61] Kinsella and Velkoff, *An Aging World*, p. 79.

outside of marriage, and the growing influence of multigenerational families and the elderly are all patterns as common to Europe as they are to the United States.[62]

But the United States also exhibited patterns unique to its own historical evolution. In terms of health care delivery and mortality by class, race, and ethnic group, the United States stands apart with wider spreads of mortality rates among its population and poorer results for a minority of the population than found elsewhere among the developed nations. Moreover, there is still no convergence between the black and white populations in terms of morbidity and mortality, something that has not changed since the 19th century. The United States is also unusual in the increasing intensity of its international immigration – the highest in volume in its history. Moreover, this migration is more concentrated than at any previous period in only a few states and metropolitan areas, leading to dense concentrations of native-speaking groups, with Spanish becoming a second lingua franca of the nation. In this, the United States seems to be able to handle and absorb such immigration with relatively less conflict than most other societies – even in periods of economic stagnation, as well as periods of economic growth.

The advance of suburbanization, more pronounced in the United States than in most other countries, slowed but did not stop as the country entered the 21st century. The very sharp racial housing and residential segregation has slowly reversed itself as more blacks move to the suburbs and more affluent whites move back into the central cities along with the new immigrants. The elimination of the legal institutions that helped maintain racial segregation and the rapid advance of blacks into skilled and professional occupations after the civil rights movement opened up the workplace for African Americans and have contributed to that decline of segregation and

---

[62] For comparable European data, see Antonella Pinnelli, Hans Joachim Hoffman-Nowotny, and Beat Fux, *Fertility and New Types of Household and Family Formation in Europe*, Population Studies, no. 35. Strasbourg: Council of Europe, 2001; and Jacques Vallin, France Meslé, and Tapani Valkonen, *Trend in Mortality and Differential Mortality*, Population Studies, no. 36. Strasbourg: Council of Europe, 2001.

isolation that had been entrenched in the northern cities at the beginning of the 20th century and was slowly coming to an end in the new century. The quality of life in the central cities also seems to be moving toward convergence with the suburban populations, currently the longest lived and healthiest people in the nation. The level of urbanization, however, has changed little in the past several decades, and it is evident that the great metropolitan areas have reached their maximum level of importance and that most of the change will now occur between the fringe and core areas of the large population concentrations, with little shift between the metropolitan and nonmetropolitan areas.

That demographic issues have became major issues in the current political environment has a great deal to do with these changing aspects of the national society. As the only advanced industrial society without a national health plan, it is evident that the rates of disease and death will remain high as long as a large share of the population does not have adequate access to health care. Every study shows that poverty and lack of health care insurance are major factors influencing these rates. Equally, the increasing importance of the elderly and the increasing size of a population that needs to be supported by a shrinking workforce means that issues of government support for pensions and medicare are becoming ever more critical. Almost all of the advanced world, which already has the majority of the world's elderly population,[63] must face the question of the costs of maintaining that population. In the United States, this question is made even more complex by a system in which private as well as public investments are of crucial importance and where there still remain major political debates about the role of the government in these areas – debates that have long been settled in most of the developed nations of the world.

[63] It was estimated that in 2000, the advanced countries of the world held 59% of the world's elderly, and this will rise to 71% by 2030. Kinsella and Velkoff, An Aging World, p. 1.

Appendix Tables, Graphs, and Maps

Table A.1: Population of the United States by Region, Division, and State, 1790–2000.

Region/Division STATE	2000	1990	1980	1970	1960	1950	1940	1930	1920	1910
United States	281,421,906	248,709,873	226,542,199	203,302,031	179,323,175	151,325,798	132,164,569	123,202,624	106,021,537	92,228,496
NORTHEAST	53,594,378	50,809,229	49,136,816	49,060,514	44,677,819	39,477,986	35,976,777	34,427,091	29,662,053	25,868,573
New England	13,922,517	13,206,943	12,348,920	11,847,245	10,509,367	9,314,453	8,437,290	8,166,341	7,400,909	6,552,681
Maine	1,274,923	1,227,928	1,125,043	993,722	969,265	913,774	847,226	797,423	768,014	742,371
New Hampshire	1,235,786	1,109,252	920,610	737,681	606,921	533,242	491,524	465,293	443,083	430,572
Vermont	608,827	562,758	511,456	444,732	389,881	377,747	359,231	359,611	352,428	355,956
Massachusetts	6,349,097	6,016,425	5,737,093	5,689,170	5,148,578	4,690,514	4,316,721	4,249,614	3,852,356	3,366,416
Rhode Island	1,048,319	1,003,464	947,154	949,723	859,488	791,896	713,346	687,497	604,397	542,610
Connecticut	3,405,565	3,287,116	3,107,564	3,032,217	2,535,234	2,007,280	1,709,242	1,606,903	1,380,631	1,114,756
Middle Atlantic	39,671,861	37,602,286	36,787,896	37,213,269	34,168,452	30,163,533	27,539,487	26,260,750	22,261,144	19,315,892
New York	18,976,457	17,990,455	17,558,165	18,241,391	16,782,304	14,830,192	13,479,142	12,588,066	10,385,227	9,113,614
New Jersey	8,414,350	7,730,188	7,365,011	7,171,112	6,066,782	4,835,329	4,160,165	4,041,334	3,155,900	2,537,167
Pennsylvania	12,281,054	11,881,643	11,864,720	11,800,766	11,319,366	10,498,012	9,900,180	9,631,350	8,720,017	7,665,111

MIDWEST									
64,392,776	59,668,632	58,866,998	56,890,294	51,619,139	44,460,762	40,143,332	38,594,100	34,019,792	29,888,542
East North Central									
45,155,037	42,008,942	41,682,908	40,262,747	36,225,024	30,399,368	26,626,342	25,297,185	21,475,543	18,250,621
Ohio 11,353,140	10,847,115	10,797,603	10,657,423	9,706,397	7,946,627	6,907,612	6,646,697	5,759,394	4,767,121
Indiana 6,080,485	5,544,159	5,490,210	5,195,392	4,662,498	3,934,224	3,427,796	3,238,503	2,930,390	2,700,876
Illinois 12,419,293	11,430,602	11,427,409	11,110,285	10,081,158	8,712,176	7,897,241	7,630,654	6,485,280	5,638,591
Michigan 9,938,444	9,295,297	9,262,044	8,881,826	7,823,194	6,371,766	5,256,106	4,842,325	3,668,412	2,810,173
Wisconsin 5,363,675	4,891,769	4,705,642	4,417,821	3,951,777	3,434,575	3,137,587	2,939,006	2,632,067	2,333,860
West North Central									
19,237,739	17,659,690	17,184,090	16,327,547	15,394,115	14,061,394	13,516,990	13,296,915	12,544,249	11,637,921
Minnesota 4,919,479	4,375,099	4,075,970	3,806,103	3,413,864	2,982,483	2,792,300	2,563,953	2,387,125	2,075,708
Iowa 2,926,324	2,776,755	2,913,808	2,825,368	2,757,537	2,621,073	2,538,268	2,470,939	2,404,021	2,224,771
Missouri 5,595,211	5,117,073	4,916,766	4,677,623	4,319,813	3,954,653	3,784,664	3,629,367	3,404,055	3,293,335
North Dakota 642,200	638,800	652,717	617,792	632,446	619,636	641,935	680,845	646,872	577,056
South Dakota 754,844	696,004	690,768	666,257	680,514	652,740	642,961	692,849	636,547	583,888
Nebraska 1,711,263	1,578,385	1,569,825	1,485,333	1,411,330	1,325,510	1,315,834	1,377,963	1,296,372	1,192,214
Kansas 2,688,418	2,477,574	2,364,236	2,249,071	2,178,611	1,905,299	1,801,028	1,880,999	1,769,257	1,690,949
SOUTH									
100,236,820	85,445,930	75,367,068	62,812,980	54,973,113	47,197,088	41,665,901	37,857,633	33,125,803	29,389,330
South Atlantic									
51,769,160	43,566,853	36,957,453	30,678,826	25,971,732	21,182,335	17,823,151	15,793,589	13,990,272	12,194,895
Delaware 783,600	666,168	594,338	548,104	446,292	318,085	266,505	230,380	223,003	202,322
Maryland 5,296,486	4,781,468	4,216,933	3,923,897	3,100,689	2,343,001	1,821,244	1,631,526	1,499,661	1,295,346

(continued)

Table A.1: (continued)

Region/Division STATE	1910	1920	1930	1940	1950	1960	1970	1980	1990	2000
District of Columbia	331,069	437,571	486,869	663,091	802,178	763,956	756,668	638,432	606,900	572,059
Virginia	2,061,612	2,309,187	2,421,851	2,677,773	3,318,680	3,966,949	4,651,448	5,346,797	6,187,358	7,078,515
West Virginia	1,221,119	1,463,701	1,729,205	1,901,974	2,005,552	1,860,421	1,744,237	1,950,186	1,793,477	1,868,344
North Carolina	2,206,287	2,559,123	3,170,276	3,571,623	4,061,929	4,556,155	5,084,411	5,880,095	6,628,637	8,049,313
South Carolina	1,515,400	1,683,724	1,738,765	1,899,804	2,117,027	2,382,594	2,590,713	3,120,729	3,486,703	4,012,012
Georgia	2,609,121	2,895,832	2,908,506	3,123,723	3,444,578	3,943,116	4,587,930	5,462,982	6,478,216	8,186,453
Florida	752,619	968,470	1,468,211	1,897,414	2,771,305	4,951,560	6,791,418	9,746,961	12,937,926	15,982,378
East South Central	**8,409,901**	**8,893,307**	**9,887,214**	**10,778,225**	**11,477,181**	**12,050,126**	**12,808,077**	**14,666,142**	**15,176,284**	**17,022,810**
Kentucky	2,289,905	2,416,630	2,614,589	2,845,627	2,944,806	3,038,156	3,220,711	3,660,324	3,685,296	4,041,769
Tennessee	2,184,789	2,337,885	2,616,556	2,915,841	3,291,718	3,567,089	3,926,018	4,591,023	4,877,185	5,689,283
Alabama	2,138,093	2,348,174	2,646,248	2,832,961	3,061,743	3,266,740	3,444,354	3,894,025	4,040,587	4,447,100
Mississippi	1,797,114	1,790,618	2,009,821	2,183,796	2,178,914	2,178,141	2,216,994	2,520,770	2,573,216	2,844,658
West South Central	**8,784,534**	**10,242,224**	**12,176,830**	**13,064,525**	**14,537,572**	**16,951,255**	**19,326,077**	**23,743,473**	**26,702,793**	**31,444,850**
Arkansas	1,574,449	1,752,204	1,854,482	1,949,387	1,909,511	1,786,272	1,923,322	2,286,357	2,350,725	2,673,400
Louisiana	1,656,388	1,798,509	2,101,593	2,363,880	2,683,516	3,257,022	3,644,637	4,206,116	4,219,973	4,468,976
Oklahoma	1,657,155	2,028,283	2,396,040	2,336,434	2,233,351	2,328,284	2,559,463	3,025,487	3,145,585	3,450,654
Texas	3,896,542	4,663,228	5,824,715	6,414,824	7,711,194	9,579,677	11,198,655	14,225,513	16,986,510	20,851,820
WEST	**7,082,051**	**9,213,889**	**12,323,800**	**14,378,559**	**20,189,962**	**28,053,104**	**34,838,243**	**43,171,317**	**52,786,082**	**63,197,932**
Mountain	**2,633,517**	**3,336,101**	**3,701,789**	**4,150,003**	**5,074,998**	**6,855,060**	**8,289,901**	**11,371,502**	**13,658,776**	**18,172,295**
Montana	376,053	548,889	537,606	559,456	591,024	674,767	694,409	786,690	799,065	902,195
Idaho	325,594	431,866	445,032	524,873	588,637	667,191	713,015	944,127	1,006,749	1,293,953

242

Wyoming	493,782	453,588	469,557	332,416	330,066	290,529	250,742	225,565	194,402	145,965
Colorado	4,301,261	3,294,394	2,889,735	2,209,596	1,753,947	1,325,089	1,123,296	1,035,791	939,629	799,024
New Mexico	1,819,046	1,515,069	1,303,302	1,017,055	951,023	681,187	531,818	423,317	360,350	327,301
Arizona	5,130,632	3,665,228	2,716,546	1,775,399	1,302,161	749,587	499,261	435,573	334,162	204,354
Utah	2,233,169	1,722,850	1,461,037	1,059,273	890,627	688,862	550,310	507,847	449,396	373,351
Nevada	1,998,257	1,201,833	800,508	488,738	285,278	160,083	110,247	91,058	77,407	81,875
Pacific	*45,025,637*	*39,127,306*	*31,799,815*	*26,548,342*	*21,198,044*	*15,114,964*	*10,228,556*	*8,622,011*	*5,877,788*	*4,448,534*
Washington	5,894,121	4,866,692	4,132,353	3,413,244	2,853,214	2,378,963	1,736,191	1,563,396	1,356,621	1,141,990
Oregon	3,421,399	2,842,321	2,633,156	2,091,533	1,768,687	1,521,341	1,089,684	953,786	783,389	672,765
California	33,871,648	29,760,021	23,667,764	19,971,069	15,717,204	10,586,223	6,907,387	5,677,251	3,426,861	2,377,549
Alaska	626,932	550,043	401,851	302,853	226,167	128,643	72,524	59,278	55,036	64,356
Hawaii	1,211,537	1,108,229	964,691	769,913	632,772	499,794	422,770	368,300	225,881	191,874

(continued)

Table A.1: (continued)

Region/Division STATE	1900	1890	1880	1870	1860	1850	1840	1830	1820	1810	1800	1790
United States	76,212,168	62,979,766	50,189,209	38,558,371	31,443,321	23,191,876	17,063,353	12,860,702	9,638,453	7,239,881	5,308,483	3,929,214
NORTHEAST	21,046,695	17,406,969	14,507,407	12,298,730	10,594,268	8,626,851	6,761,082	5,542,381	4,359,916	3,486,675	2,635,576	1,968,040
New England	5,592,017	4,700,749	4,010,529	3,487,924	3,135,283	2,728,116	2,234,822	1,954,717	1,660,071	1,471,973	1,233,011	1,009,408
Maine	694,466	661,086	648,936	626,915	628,279	583,169	501,793	399,455	298,335	228,705	151,719	96,540
New Hampshire	411,588	376,530	346,991	318,300	326,073	317,976	284,574	269,328	244,161	214,460	183,858	141,885
Vermont	343,641	332,422	332,286	330,551	315,098	314,120	291,948	280,652	235,981	217,895	154,465	85,425
Massachusetts	2,805,346	2,238,947	1,783,085	1,457,351	1,231,066	994,514	737,699	610,408	523,287	472,040	422,845	378,787
Rhode Island	428,556	345,506	276,531	217,353	174,620	147,545	108,830	97,199	83,059	76,931	69,122	68,825
Connecticut	908,420	746,258	622,700	537,454	460,147	370,792	309,978	297,675	275,248	261,942	251,002	237,946
Middle Atlantic	15,454,678	12,706,220	10,496,878	8,810,806	7,458,985	5,898,735	4,526,260	3,587,664	2,699,845	2,014,702	1,402,565	958,632
New York	7,268,894	6,003,174	5,082,871	4,382,759	3,880,735	3,097,394	2,428,921	1,918,608	1,372,812	959,049	589,051	340,120
New Jersey	1,883,669	1,444,933	1,131,116	906,096	672,035	489,555	373,306	320,823	277,575	245,562	211,149	184,139
Pennsylvania	6,302,115	5,258,113	4,282,891	3,521,951	2,906,215	2,311,786	1,724,033	1,348,233	1,049,458	810,091	602,365	434,373
MIDWEST	26,333,004	22,410,417	17,364,111	12,981,111	9,096,716	5,403,595	3,351,542	1,610,473	859,305	292,107	51,006	...
East North Central	15,985,581	13,478,305	11,206,668	9,124,517	6,926,884	4,523,260	2,924,728	1,470,018	792,719	272,324	51,006	...
Ohio	4,157,545	3,672,329	3,198,062	2,665,260	2,339,511	1,980,329	1,519,467	937,903	581,434	230,760	45,365	...
Indiana	2,516,462	2,192,404	1,978,301	1,680,637	1,350,428	988,416	685,866	343,031	147,178	24,520	5,641	...
Illinois	4,821,550	3,826,352	3,077,871	2,539,891	1,711,951	851,470	476,183	157,445	55,211	12,282	...	...
Michigan	2,420,982	2,093,890	1,636,937	1,184,059	749,113	397,654	212,267	31,639	8,896	4,762	...	...
Wisconsin	2,069,042	1,693,330	1,315,497	1,054,670	775,881	305,391	30,945	...	...	...	...	...

West North

Central	**10,347,423**	**8,932,112**	**6,157,443**	**3,856,594**	**2,169,832**	**880,335**	**426,814**	**140,455**	**66,586**	**19,783**	...	...
Minnesota	1,751,394	1,310,283	780,773	439,706	172,023	6,077	...	...	...	...	...	...
Iowa	2,231,853	1,912,297	1,624,615	1,194,020	674,913	192,914	43,112	...	...	...	...	...
Missouri	3,106,665	2,679,185	2,168,380	1,721,295	1,182,012	682,044	383,702	140,455	66,586	19,783	...	...
North Dakota	319,146	190,983	36,909	2,405	...	...	...	...	...	...	...	...
South Dakota	401,570	348,600	98,268	11,776	4,837	...	...	...	...	...	...	...
Nebraska	1,066,300	1,062,656	452,402	122,993	28,841	...	...	...	...	...	...	...
Kansas	1,470,495	1,428,108	996,096	364,399	107,206	...	...	...	...	...	...	...
SOUTH	**24,523,527**	**20,028,059**	**16,516,568**	**12,288,020**	**11,133,361**	**8,982,612**	**6,950,729**	**5,707,848**	**4,419,232**	**3,461,099**	**2,621,901**	**1,961,174**
South Atlantic	*10,443,480*	*8,857,922*	*7,597,197*	*5,853,610*	*11,133,361*	*4,679,090*	*3,925,299*	*3,645,752*	*3,061,063*	*2,674,881*	*2,286,494*	*1,851,866*
Delaware	184,735	168,493	146,608	125,015	112,216	91,532	78,085	76,748	72,749	72,674	64,273	59,096
Maryland	1,188,044	1,042,390	934,943	780,894	687,049	583,034	470,019	447,040	407,350	380,546	341,548	319,728
District of Columbia	278,718	230,392	177,624	131,700	75,080	51,687	33,745	30,261	23,336	15,471	8,144	...
Virginia	1,854,184	1,655,980	1,512,565	1,225,163	1,219,630	1,119,348	1,025,227	1,044,054	938,261	877,683	807,557	691,737
West Virginia	958,800	762,794	618,457	442,014	376,688	302,313	224,537	176,924	136,808	105,469	78,592	55,873
North Carolina	1,893,810	1,617,949	1,399,750	1,071,361	992,622	869,039	753,419	737,987	638,829	555,500	478,103	393,751
South Carolina	1,340,316	1,151,149	995,577	795,606	703,708	668,507	594,398	581,185	502,741	415,115	345,591	249,073
Georgia	2,216,331	1,837,353	1,542,180	1,184,109	1,057,286	906,185	691,392	516,823	340,989	252,433	162,686	82,548
Florida	528,542	391,422	269,493	187,748	140,424	87,445	54,477	34,730	...	...	...	...
East South												
Central	**7,547,757**	**6,429,154**	**5,585,151**	**4,404,445**	**4,020,991**	**3,363,271**	**2,575,445**	**1,815,969**	**1,190,489**	**708,590**	**335,407**	**109,368**
Kentucky	2,147,174	1,858,635	1,648,690	1,321,011	1,155,684	982,405	779,828	687,917	564,317	406,511	220,955	73,677
Tennessee	2,020,616	1,767,518	1,542,359	1,258,520	1,109,801	1,002,717	829,210	681,904	422,823	261,727	105,662	35,691

(continued)

245

Table A.1: (continued)

Region/Division STATE	1900	1890	1880	1870	1860	1850	1840	1830	1820	1810	1800	1790
Alabama	1,828,697	1,513,401	1,262,505	996,992	964,201	771,623	590,756	309,527	127,901	9,046	1,250	...
Mississippi	1,551,270	1,289,600	1,131,597	827,922	791,305	606,526	375,651	136,621	75,448	31,306	7,600	...
West South Central	**6,532,290**	**4,740,983**	**3,334,220**	**2,029,965**	**1,747,667**	**940,251**	**449,985**	**246,127**	**167,680**	**77,618**	...	...
Arkansas	1,311,564	1,128,211	802,525	484,471	435,450	209,897	97,574	30,388	14,273	1,062	...	...
Louisiana	1,381,625	1,118,588	939,946	726,915	708,002	517,762	352,411	215,739	153,407	76,556	...	...
Oklahoma	790,391	258,657	...	...	...	...	...	...	...	...	...	...
Texas	3,048,710	2,235,527	1,591,749	818,579	604,215	212,592	...	...	...	...	...	...
WEST	**4,308,942**	**3,134,321**	**1,801,123**	**990,510**	**618,976**	**178,818**	...	...	...	...	...	...
Mountain	**1,674,657**	**1,213,935**	**653,119**	**315,385**	**174,923**	**72,927**	...	...	...	...	...	...
Montana	243,329	142,924	39,159	20,595	...	...	...	...	...	...	...	...
Idaho	161,772	88,548	32,610	14,999	...	...	...	...	...	...	...	...
Wyoming	92,531	62,555	20,789	9,118	...	...	...	...	...	...	...	...
Colorado	539,700	413,249	194,327	39,864	34,277	...	...	...	...	...	...	...
New Mexico	195,310	160,282	119,565	91,874	93,516	61,547	...	...	...	...	...	...
Arizona	122,931	88,243	40,440	9,658	...	...	...	...	...	...	...	...
Utah	276,749	210,779	143,963	86,786	40,273	11,380	...	...	...	...	...	...
Nevada	42,335	47,355	62,266	42,491	6,857	...	...	...	...	...	...	...
Pacific	**2,634,285**	**1,920,386**	**1,148,004**	**675,125**	**444,053**	**105,891**	...	...	...	...	...	...
Washington	518,103	357,232	75,116	23,955	11,594	1,201	...	...	...	...	...	...
Oregon	413,536	317,704	174,768	90,923	52,465	12,093	...	...	...	...	...	...
California	1,485,053	1,213,398	864,694	560,247	379,994	92,597	...	...	...	...	...	...
Alaska	63,592	32,052	33,426	...	...	...	...	...	...	...	...	...
Hawaii	154,001	...	...	...	...	...	...	...	...	...	...	...

Source: *1990 Census of Population and Housing*, "1990 Population and Housing Unit Counts: United States," (CPH-2); and U.S. Census 2000.

Table A.2: Race and Hispanic Origin in the United States, 1790–2000.

| Census Year | Total Population | Race | | | | | Hispanic Origin (of Any Race) | White, Not of Hispanic Origin |
		White	Black	American Indian, Eskimo, and Aleut	Asian and Pacific Islander	Other Race		
NUMBER								
2000	281,421,906	211,460,626	34,658,190	2,475,956	10,242,998	15,359,073	35,505,818	194,552,774
1990	248,709,873	199,686,070	29,986,060	1,959,234	7,273,662	9,804,847	22,354,059	188,128,296
1980	226,545,805	188,371,622	26,495,025	1,420,400	3,500,439	6,758,319	14,608,673	180,256,366
1970	203,211,926	177,748,975	22,580,289	827,255	1,538,721	516,686	(NA)	(NA)
1960	179,323,175	158,831,732	18,871,831	551,669	980,337	87,606	(NA)	(NA)
1950	150,697,361	134,942,028	15,042,286	343,410	321,033	48,604	(NA)	(NA)
1940	131,669,275	118,214,870	12,865,518	333,969	254,918	(X)	1,858,024	(NA)
1930	122,775,046	110,286,740	11,891,143	332,397	264,766	(X)	(NA)	(NA)
1920	105,710,620	94,820,915	10,463,131	244,437	182,137	(X)	(NA)	(NA)
1910	91,972,266	81,731,957	9,827,763	265,683	146,863	(X)	(NA)	(NA)
1900	75,994,575	66,809,196	8,833,994	237,196	114,189	(X)	(NA)	(NA)
1890	62,947,714	55,101,258	7,488,676	248,253	109,527	(X)	(NA)	(NA)

(*continued*)

Table A.2: (continued)

Census Year	Total Population	Race					Hispanic Origin (of Any Race)	Black			White, Not of Hispanic Origin
		White	Black	American Indian, Eskimo, and Aleut	Asian and Pacific Islander	Other Race		Total	Free	Slave	
1880	50,155,783	43,402,970	6,580,793	66,407	105,613						
1870	38,558,371	33,589,377	4,880,009	25,731	63,254						
1860	31,443,321	26,922,537	4,441,830	44,021	34,933			4,441,830	488,070	3,953,760	
1850	23,191,876	19,553,068	3,638,808	(NA)	(NA)			3,638,808	434,495	3,204,313	
1840	17,063,353	14,189,705	2,873,648	(NA)	(NA)			2,873,648	386,293	2,487,355	
1830	12,860,702	10,532,060	2,328,642	(NA)	(NA)			2,328,642	319,599	2,009,043	
1820	9,638,453	7,866,797	1,771,656	(NA)	(NA)			1,771,656	233,634	1,538,022	
1810	7,239,881	5,862,073	1,377,808	(NA)	(NA)			1,377,808	186,446	1,191,362	
1800	5,308,483	4,306,446	1,002,037	(NA)	(NA)			1,002,037	108,435	893,602	
1790	3,929,214	3,172,006	757,208	(NA)	(NA)			757,208	59,527	697,681	

Notes: (X) Not applicable. (NA) Not available. 1960 includes Alaska and Hawaii.
1940 Hispanic origin based on the white population of Spanish mother tongue.
1890 Includes Indian Territory and Indian reservations.
Source: U.S. Census Bureau
Internet Release Date: September 13, 2002
Cambell Gibson and Kay Jung, Historical Census Statistics on Population Totals by Race, 1790 to 1990, and by Hispanic Origin, 1970 to 1990, for the United States Regions, Divisions, and States (U. S. Census Bureau, Population Division, Working Paper Series No. 56; Washington, D.C., September 2002), table1. and Census of 2000.

Table A.3: Population by Race and Hispanic or Latino Origin for the United States (Regions, Divisons, and States) and for Puerto Rico, 2000.

| United States Region Division State Puerto Rico | Total Population | Race | | | | | | | Hispanic or Latino (of Any Race) | White Alone, Not Hispanic or Latino |
| | | One race | | | | | | Two or More Races | | |
		White	Black or African American	American Indian and Alaska Native	Asian	Native Hawaiian and Other Pacific Islander	Some Other Race			
United States	281,421,906	211,460,626	34,658,190	2,475,956	10,242,998	398,835	15,359,073	6,826,228	35,305,818	194,552,774
NORTHEAST	53,594,378	41,533,502	6,099,881	162,558	2,119,526	20,880	2,429,670	1,228,461	5,254,087	39,327,262
New England	13,922,517	12,050,905	719,063	42,257	374,361	5,316	448,315	282,300	875,225	11,686,617
Maine	1,274,923	1,236,014	6,760	7,098	9,111	382	2,911	12,647	9,360	1,230,297
New Hampshire	1,235,786	1,186,851	9,035	2,964	15,931	371	7,420	13,214	20,489	1,175,252
Vermont	608,827	589,208	3,063	2,420	5,217	141	1,443	7,335	5,504	585,431
Massachusetts	6,349,097	5,367,286	343,454	15,015	238,124	2,489	236,724	146,005	428,729	5,198,359
Rhode Island	1,048,319	891,191	46,908	5,121	23,665	567	52,616	28,251	90,820	858,433
Connecticut	3,405,565	2,780,355	309,843	9,639	82,313	1,366	147,201	74,848	320,323	2,638,845
Middle Atlantic	39,671,861	29,482,597	5,380,818	120,301	1,745,065	15,564	1,981,355	946,161	4,378,862	27,640,645
New York	18,976,457	12,893,689	3,014,385	82,461	1,044,976	8,818	1,341,946	590,182	2,867,583	11,760,981
New Jersey	8,414,350	6,104,705	1,141,821	19,492	480,276	3,329	450,972	213,755	1,117,191	5,557,209
Pennsylvania	12,281,054	10,484,203	1,224,612	18,348	219,813	3,417	188,437	142,224	394,088	10,322,455

(continued)

Table A.3: (continued)

United States Region Division State Puerto Rico	Total Population	Race						Two or More Races	Hispanic or Latino (of Any Race)	White Alone, not Hispanic or Latino
		One race								
		White	Black or African American	American Indian and Alaska Native	Asian	Native Hawaiian and Other Pacific Islander	Some Other Race			
MIDWEST	64,392,776	53,833,651	6,499,733	399,490	1,197,554	22,492	1,417,388	1,022,468	3,124,532	52,386,131
East North Central	45,155,037	36,826,856	5,405,418	177,014	880,635	13,686	1,123,544	727,884	2,476,719	35,669,945
Ohio	11,353,140	9,645,453	1,301,307	24,486	132,633	2,749	88,627	157,885	217,123	9,538,111
Indiana	6,080,485	5,320,022	510,034	15,815	59,126	2,005	97,811	75,672	214,536	5,219,373
Illinois	12,419,293	9,125,471	1,876,875	31,006	423,603	4,610	722,712	235,016	1,530,262	8,424,140
Michigan	9,938,444	7,966,053	1,412,742	58,479	176,510	2,692	129,552	192,416	323,877	7,806,691
Wisconsin	5,363,675	4,769,857	304,460	47,228	88,763	1,630	84,842	66,895	192,921	4,681,630
West North Central	19,237,739	17,006,795	1,094,315	222,476	316,919	8,806	293,844	294,584	645,813	16,716,186
Minnesota	4,919,479	4,400,282	171,731	54,967	141,968	1,979	65,810	82,742	143,382	4,337,143
Iowa	2,926,324	2,748,640	61,853	8,989	36,635	1,009	37,420	31,778	82,473	2,710,344
Missouri	5,595,211	4,748,083	629,391	25,076	61,595	3,178	45,827	82,061	118,592	4,686,474
North Dakota	642,200	593,181	3,916	31,329	3,666	230	2,540	7,398	7,786	589,149
South Dakota	754,844	669,404	4,685	62,283	4,378	261	3,677	10,156	10,903	664,585
Nebraska	1,711,263	1,533,261	68,541	14,896	21,931	836	47,845	23,953	94,425	1,494,494
Kansas	2,688,418	2,313,944	154,198	24,936	46,806	1,313	90,725	56,496	188,252	2,233,997

SOUTH	100,236,820	72,819,399	18,981,692	725,919	1,922,407	51,217	3,889,171	1,847,015	11,586,696	65,927,794	
South Atlantic	51,769,160	37,283,595	11,026,722	233,192	1,101,965	25,762	1,175,288	922,636	4,243,946	34,575,917	
Delaware	783,600	584,773	150,666	2,731	16,259	283	15,855	13,033	37,277	567,973	
Maryland	5,296,486	3,391,308	1,477,411	15,423	210,929	2,303	95,525	103,567	227,916	3,286,547	
District of Columbia	572,059	176,101	343,312	1,713	15,189	348	21,950	13,446	44,953	159,178	
Virginia	7,078,515	5,120,110	1,390,293	21,172	261,025	3,946	138,900	143,069	329,540	4,965,637	
West Virginia	1,808,344	1,718,777	57,232	3,606	9,434	400	3,107	15,788	12,279	1,709,966	
North Carolina	8,049,313	5,804,856	1,737,545	99,551	113,689	3,983	186,629	103,260	378,963	5,647,155	
South Carolina	4,012,012	2,695,560	1,185,216	12,718	36,014	1,628	39,926	39,950	95,076	2,652,291	
Georgia	8,186,453	5,327,281	2,349,542	21,737	173,170	4,246	196,289	114,188	435,227	5,128,661	
Florida	15,982,378	12,465,029	2,335,505	53,541	266,256	8,825	477,107	376,315	2,682,715	10,458,509	
East South Central	17,022,810	13,113,106	3,418,542	57,850	136,378	5,741	121,441	169,752	299,176	12,067,670	
Kentucky	4,041,769	3,640,889	295,994	8,616	29,744	1,460	22,623	42,443	59,939	3,608,013	
Tennessee	5,689,283	4,563,310	932,809	15,152	56,662	2,205	56,036	63,109	123,838	4,505,930	
Alabama	4,447,100	3,162,808	1,155,930	22,430	31,346	1,409	28,998	44,179	75,830	3,125,819	
Mississippi	2,844,658	1,746,099	1,033,809	11,652	18,626	667	13,784	20,021	39,569	1,727,908	
West South Central	31,444,850	22,422,698	4,536,428	434,877	684,064	19,714	2,592,442	754,627	7,043,574	18,384,207	
Arkansas	2,673,400	2,138,598	418,950	17,808	20,220	1,668	40,412	35,744	86,866	2,100,135	
Louisiana	4,468,976	2,856,161	1,451,944	25,477	54,758	1,240	31,131	48,265	107,738	2,794,391	
Oklahoma	3,450,654	2,628,434	266,968	273,230	46,767	2,372	82,898	155,985	179,304	2,556,368	
Texas	20,851,820	14,799,505	2,404,566	118,362	562,319	14,434	2,438,001	514,633	6,669,666	10,933,313	
WEST	63,197,932	43,274,074	3,076,884	1,187,989	5,003,611	304,246	7,622,844	2,728,284	15,340,503	36,911,587	
Mountain	18,172,295	14,591,933	523,283	614,553	353,429	38,508	1,541,704	508,885	3,543,573	12,883,812	
Montana	902,195	817,229	2,692	56,068	4,691	470	5,315	15,730	18,081	807,823	
Idaho	1,293,953	1,177,304	5,456	17,645	11,889	1,308	54,742	25,609	101,690	1,139,291	

(continued)

Table A.3: (*continued*)

| United States Region Division State / Puerto Rico | Total Population | One race | | | | | | Two or More Races | Hispanic or Latino (of Any Race) | White Alone, not Hispanic or Latino |
		White	Black or African American	American Indian and Alaska Native	Asian	Native Hawaiian and Other Pacific Islander	Some Other Race			
Wyoming	493,782	454,670	3,722	11,133	2,771	302	12,301	8,883	31,669	438,799
Colorado	4,301,261	3,560,005	165,063	44,241	95,213	4,621	309,931	122,187	735,601	3,202,880
New Mexico	1,819,046	1,214,253	34,343	173,483	19,255	1,503	309,882	66,327	765,386	813,495
Arizona	5,130,632	3,873,611	158,873	255,879	92,236	6,733	596,774	146,526	1,295,617	3,274,258
Utah	2,233,169	1,992,975	17,657	29,684	37,108	15,145	93,405	47,195	201,559	1,904,265
Nevada	1,998,257	1,501,886	135,477	26,420	90,266	8,426	159,354	76,428	393,970	1,303,001
Pacific	45,025,637	28,682,141	2,553,601	573,436	4,650,182	265,738	6,081,140	2,219,399	11,796,930	24,027,775
Washington	5,894,121	4,821,823	190,267	93,301	322,335	23,953	228,923	213,519	441,509	4,652,490
Oregon	3,421,399	2,961,623	55,662	45,211	101,350	7,976	144,832	104,745	275,314	2,857,616
California	33,871,648	20,170,059	2,263,882	333,346	3,697,513	116,961	5,682,241	1,607,646	10,966,556	15,816,790
Alaska	626,932	434,534	21,787	98,043	25,116	3,309	9,997	34,146	25,852	423,788
Hawaii	1,211,537	294,102	22,003	3,535	503,868	113,539	15,147	259,343	87,699	277,091
Puerto Rico	3,808,610	3,064,862	302,933	13,336	7,960	1,093	260,011	158,415	3,762,746	33,966

Source: U.S. Census Bureau, Census 2000 Redistricting Data (P.L. 94–171) Summary File for States and Census 2000 Redistricting Summary File for Puerto Rico, Tables PL1 and PL2.
Internet Release date: April 2, 2001

Table A.4: Census Bureau Projections of Total Population and Net Change for States, 1995–2025 Thousands, Resident Population.

| Region, Division, and State | Projections for July 1 | | | | | Components of Change | | | Net Migration | |
	2005	2010	2015	2020	2025	Net Change	Births	Deaths	Interstate Migration	International Immigration
United States	285,981	297,716	310,133	322,742	335,050	72,294	126,986	84,633		24,666
NORTHEAST	52,767	53,692	54,836	56,103	57,392	5,927	21,585	16,537	−7,168	6,830
New England	13,843	14,172	14,546	14,938	15,321	2,009	5,448	4,096	−1,041	1,338
Maine	1,285	1,323	1,362	1,396	1,423	181	437	402	86	20
New Hampshire	1,281	1,329	1,372	1,410	1,439	291	481	344	84	31
Vermont	638	651	662	671	678	94	221	180	26	7
Massachusetts	6,310	6,431	6,574	6,734	6,902	828	2,520	1,860	−815	831
Rhode Island	1,012	1,038	1,070	1,105	1,141	151	423	318	−94	113
Connecticut	3,317	3,400	3,506	3,621	3,739	464	1,368	992	−329	337
Middle Atlantic	38,923	39,520	40,289	41,164	42,071	3,918	16,136	12,441	−6,127	5,492
New York	18,250	18,530	18,916	19,359	19,830	1,694	8,117	5,598	−5,038	3,886
New Jersey	8,392	8,638	8,924	9,238	9,558	1,613	3,535	2,542	−747	1,201
Pennsylvania	12,281	12,352	12,449	12,567	12,683	611	4,484	4,301	−342	405
MIDWEST	64,825	65,915	67,024	68,114	69,109	7,305	26,334	19,534	−3,541	2,365
East North Central	45,151	45,764	46,410	47,063	47,675	4,219	18,512	13,557	−3,653	1,839
Ohio	11,428	11,505	11,588	11,671	11,744	594	4,417	3,626	−758	247
Indiana	6,215	6,318	6,404	6,481	6,546	742	2,377	1,879	−35	110
Illinois	12,226	12,515	12,808	13,121	13,440	1,610	5,672	3,582	−1,699	1,037
Michigan	9,763	9,836	9,917	10,002	10,078	528	3,965	2,874	−1,122	310
Wisconsin	5,479	5,590	5,693	5,788	5,867	744	2,081	1,596	−39	134

(continued)

Table A.4: (continued)

Region, Division, and State	Projections for July 1					Components of Change			Net Migration	
	2005	2010	2015	2020	2025	Net Change	Births	Deaths	Interstate Migration	International Immigration
West North Central	**19,673**	**20,151**	**20,615**	**21,051**	**21,434**	**3,086**	**7,822**	**5,978**	**112**	**526**
Minnesota	5,005	5,147	5,283	5,406	5,510	900	1,993	1,349	−89	190
Iowa	2,941	2,968	2,994	3,019	3,040	198	1,073	958	−97	83
Missouri	5,718	5,864	6,005	6,137	6,250	927	2,260	1,858	255	105
North Dakota	677	690	704	717	729	88	270	214	6	13
South Dakota	810	826	840	853	866	137	341	246	6	6
Nebraska	1,761	1,806	1,850	1,892	1,930	293	718	543	35	29
Kansas	2,761	2,849	2,939	3,026	3,108	543	1,167	810	7	102
SOUTH	**102,788**	**107,597**	**112,384**	**117,060**	**121,448**	**29,588**	**43,142**	**32,054**	**11,067**	**5,273**
South Atlantic	**52,921**	**55,457**	**57,966**	**60,411**	**62,675**	**15,680**	**20,682**	**16,883**	**6,707**	**3,790**
Delaware	800	817	832	847	861	144	313	249	35	24
Maryland	5,467	5,657	5,862	6,071	6,274	1,232	2,295	1,537	−251	593
District of Columbia	529	560	594	625	655	101	334	213	−156	135
Virginia	7,324	7,627	7,921	8,204	8,466	1,848	2,839	2,074	299	605
West Virginia	1,849	1,851	1,851	1,850	1,845	17	555	715	105	14
North Carolina	8,227	8,552	8,840	9,111	9,349	2,154	3,039	2,612	1,295	199
South Carolina	4,033	4,205	4,369	4,517	4,645	972	1,566	1,313	546	58
Georgia	8,413	8,824	9,200	9,552	9,869	2,669	3,571	2,340	953	306
Florida	16,279	17,363	18,497	19,634	20,710	6,544	6,169	5,829	3,879	1,856
East South Central	**17,604**	**18,122**	**18,586**	**19,002**	**19,345**	**3,279**	**6,593**	**5,791**	**1,737**	**262**
Kentucky	4,098	4,170	4,231	4,281	4,314	454	1,439	1,344	175	67
Tennessee	5,966	6,180	6,365	6,529	6,665	1,409	2,217	1,909	845	97

Alabama	4,631	4,798	4,956	5,100	5,224	971	1,759	1,563	577	71
Mississippi	2,908	2,974	3,035	3,093	3,142	445	1,179	975	140	27
West South Central	**32,263**	**34,019**	**35,832**	**37,647**	**39,427**	**10,599**	**15,867**	**9,380**	**2,624**	**1,222**
Arkansas	2,750	2,840	2,922	2,997	3,055	572	1,000	979	436	31
Louisiana	4,535	4,683	4,840	4,991	5,133	790	2,054	1,501	45	90
Oklahoma	3,491	3,639	3,789	3,930	4,057	779	1,411	1,224	412	92
Texas	21,487	22,857	24,280	25,729	27,183	8,459	11,403	5,676	1,730	1,008
WEST	**65,603**	**70,512**	**75,889**	**81,465**	**87,101**	**29,505**	**35,925**	**16,508**	**−358**	**10,198**
Mountain	*19,249*	*20,221*	*21,122*	*22,049*	*22,962*	*7,317*	*8,794*	*4,938*	*2,490*	*646*
Montana	1,006	1,040	1,069	1,097	1,121	251	374	316	143	13
Idaho	1,480	1,557	1,622	1,683	1,739	576	627	379	257	33
Wyoming	568	607	641	670	694	214	244	160	111	2
Colorado	4,468	4,658	4,833	5,012	5,188	1,442	1,855	1,122	504	123
New Mexico	2,016	2,155	2,300	2,454	2,612	927	1,030	526	403	12
Arizona	5,230	5,532	5,868	6,111	6,412	2,195	2,542	1,434	753	276
Utah	2,411	2,551	2,670	2,781	2,883	931	1,310	486	−31	80
Nevada	2,070	2,179	2,241	2,312		782	813	516	351	106
Pacific	*46,354*	*50,291*	*54,768*	*59,416*	*64,139*	*22,188*	*27,130*	*11,570*	*−2,848*	*9,553*
Washington	6,258	6,658	7,058	7,446	7,808	2,377	2,600	1,708	931	394
Oregon	3,613	3,803	3,992	4,177	4,349	1,209	1,364	1,169	712	197
California	34,441	37,644	41,373	45,278	49,285	17,696	22,035	8,248	−4,429	8,725
Alaska	700	745	791	838	885	281	422	105	−84	28
Hawaii	1,342	1,440	1,553	1,677	1,812	625	709	339	21	209

Source: Paul Campbell, *Population Projections: States, 1995–2025*, Current Population Reports, P25–1131, May 1997, p. 3, table 1

Table A.5: Percentage Distribution of Projected Households by Type, 2001–2010, Series 1, 2, and 3 (Reference date is July 1).

Series and Year	All Households	Family Households				Nonfamily Households		
		Total	Married Couple	Other Family Female Householder	Male Householder	Total	Female Householder	Male Householder
Series 1								
2001	100	69.3	53.6	11.9	3.8	30.7	16.6	14.1
2002	100	69.1	53.4	11.9	3.8	30.9	16.6	14.2
2003	100	69.0	53.1	12.0	3.9	31.0	16.7	14.3
2004	100	68.8	52.9	12.0	3.9	31.2	16.8	14.4
2005	100	68.7	52.7	12.0	3.9	31.3	16.8	14.5
2006	100	68.5	52.5	12.0	4.0	31.5	16.9	14.6
2007	100	68.4	52.3	12.1	4.0	31.6	16.9	14.7
2008	100	68.2	52.1	12.1	4.0	31.8	17.0	14.8
2009	100	68.0	51.9	12.1	4.0	32.0	17.1	14.9
2010	100	67.8	51.7	12.1	4.1	32.2	17.2	15.0
Series 2								
2001	100	70.5	55.7	11.2	3.6	29.5	16.2	13.3
2002	100	70.4	55.7	11.2	3.6	29.6	16.2	13.4
2003	100	70.4	55.7	11.2	3.6	29.6	16.2	13.4
2004	100	70.3	55.6	11.1	3.6	29.7	16.2	13.4
2005	100	70.3	55.6	11.1	3.6	29.7	16.3	13.5
2006	100	70.3	55.6	11.0	3.6	29.7	16.3	13.5
2007	100	70.2	55.6	11.0	3.6	29.8	16.3	13.5
2008	100	70.2	55.6	11.0	3.6	29.8	16.3	13.5
2009	100	70.1	55.6	10.9	3.6	29.9	16.4	13.5
2010	100	70.0	55.6	10.9	3.6	30.0	16.4	13.6

Series 3

2001	100	70.7	55.4	11.6	3.7	29.3	16.0	13.3
2002	100	70.7	55.4	11.6	3.7	29.3	16.0	13.3
2003	100	70.7	55.3	11.6	3.7	29.3	16.0	13.3
2004	100	70.7	55.3	11.6	3.7	29.3	16.0	13.4
2005	100	70.7	55.3	11.6	3.8	29.3	16.0	13.4
2006	100	70.6	55.3	11.6	3.8	29.4	16.0	13.4
2007	100	70.6	55.2	11.6	3.8	29.4	16.0	13.4
2008	100	70.6	55.2	11.6	3.8	29.4	16.0	13.4
2009	100	70.5	55.1	11.6	3.8	29.5	16.0	13.5
2010	100	70.5	55.1	11.6	3.8	29.5	16	13.5

Projections of the Number of Households and Families in the United States: 1995 to 2010.

Source: U.S. Bureau of the Census.

Release date: May 1996.

Notes: Series 1, based on a time series model, is the preferred projection in light of past and possible future trends in household change.

Series 2 reflects the consequences of projected change in the age/sex structure of the population only; that is, assuming no change from the composition in 1990 of the proportion maintaining households for specific types by age and sex. This series provides a basis for evaluating the implications of alternative assumptions in other series.

Series 3 reflects the consequences of projected change in both the age/sex structure and race/origin composition of the population; again this assumes no change in the composition in 1990 proportions maintaining specific types of households by age and sex, also projected separately by race and Hispanic origin.

Number of Children

Source: Coale and Zelnik, *New Estimates of Fertility and Population*, Table 2 and Population Reference Bureau, AmeriStat, "U.S. Fertility Trends: Boom and Bust and Leveling Off," January 2003.

Graph A.1: Total Fertility Rate for the U.S. White Population, 1800–1998.

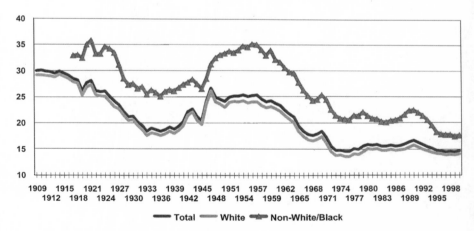

Source: CDC, NCHS, Vital Statistics of the United States, 1997 I "Natality," Table 1.1; and *National Vital Statistics Report* 50, no. 5 (February 12, 2002), p. 27 [To 1964-non-white/from 1964 black rate]

Graph A.2: Crude Birth Rate by Race, 1909–2000 (Births per 1,000 Resident Population).

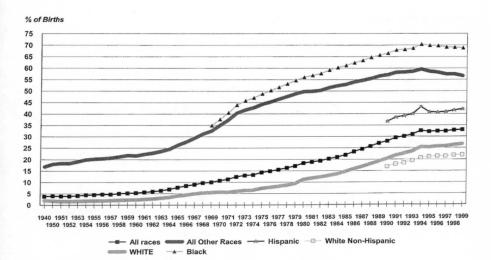

Source: CDC, National Vital Statistics Reports 48, no. 16 (October 18, 2000), Table 4.

Graph A.3: Percentage of Births to Unmarried Women by Race and Ethnicity, 1940–2000.

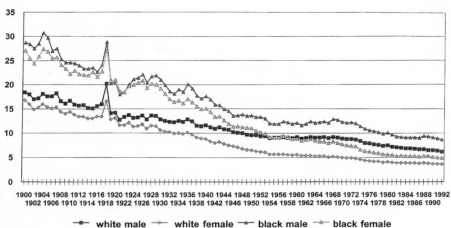

Source: CDC, NCHS, "Vital Statistics of the United States, 1992," Mortality, II, A Table 1–3.

Graph A.4: Age-Adjusted Mortality Rate by Sex and Race, 1900–1992 (Rate of Deaths per 1,000 Resident Population).

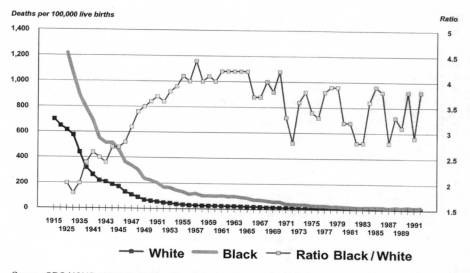

Source: CDC,NCHS, "Vital Statistics of the United States, 1992," Mortality, II, A Table 1–16.

Graph A.5: Maternal Mortality by Race, 1915–1992.

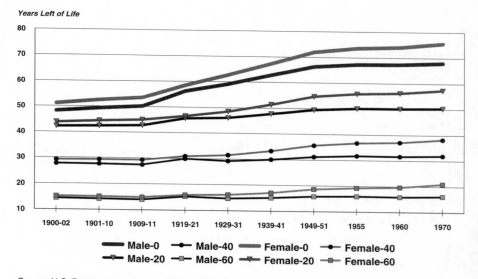

Source: U.S. Bureau of the Census *Historical Statistics*, Table 'Series B 116–125.

Graph A.6: Life Expectancy of White Population at Selected Ages, 1900–1970.

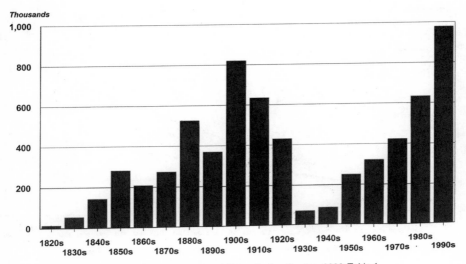

Source: Statistical Yearbook of the Immigration and Naturalization Service, 2000, Table 1.

Graph A.7: Average Annual Immigration to the United States by Decade, 1820–2000.

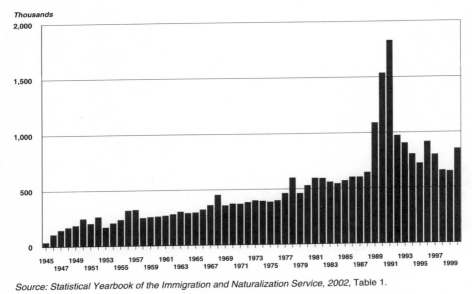

Source: Statistical Yearbook of the Immigration and Naturalization Service, 2002, Table 1.

Graph A.8: Legal Immigration Arrivals to the United States, 1945–2000.

Millions of Persons

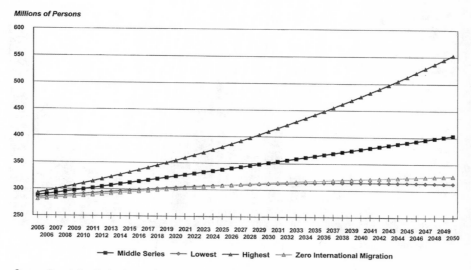

Source: Population Projections Program, Population Division, U.S. Census Bureau. Internet release date: January 13, 2000.

Graph A.9: Projections of Population Growth of United States, 2005–2050.

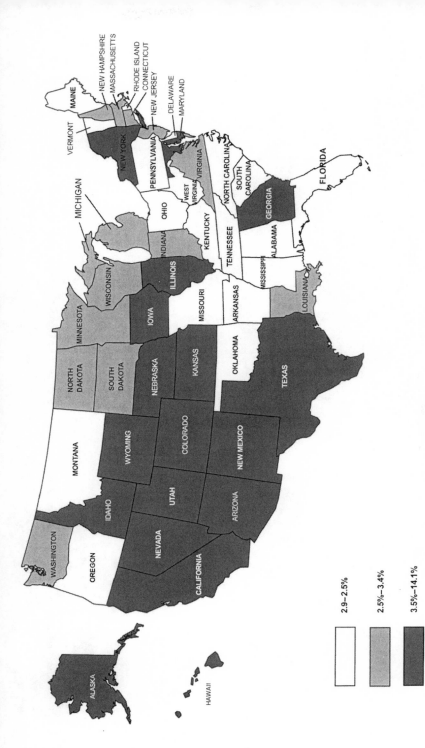

Source: Paul Campbell, *Population Projections: States, 1995–2025* (U.S. Bureau of the Census, Current Population Reports, P25–1131, Issued May 1997, p. 2.

Map A.1: Projected Annual Rate of Natural Increase per 1,000 Population 1995–2025.

2.9–2.5%

2.5%–3.4%

3.5%–14.1%

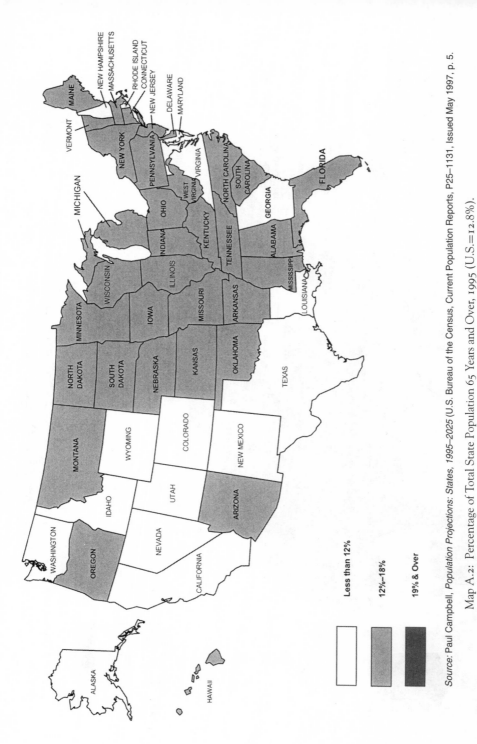

Map A.2: Percentage of Total State Population 65 Years and Over, 1995 (U.S.=12.8%).

Source: Paul Campbell, *Population Projections: States, 1995–2025* (U.S. Bureau of the Census, Current Population Reports, P25–1131, Issued May 1997, p. 5.

Less than 12%

12%–18%

19% & Over

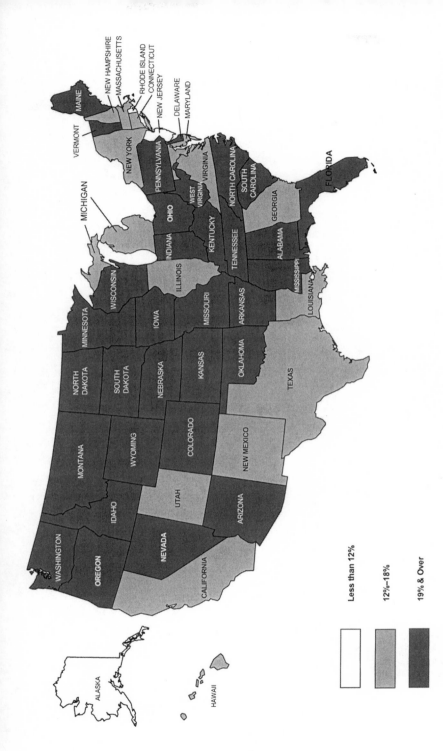

Less than 12%

12%–18%

19% & Over

Source: Paul Campbell, *Population Projections: States, 1995–2025* (U.S. Bureau of the Census, Current Population Reports, P25–1131, Issued May 1997, p. 5.

Map A.3: Percentage of Total State Population 65 Years and Over, 2025 (US=12.8%).

265

BIBLIOGRAPHY

Abma Joyce, A. Chandra, W. Mosher, L. Peterson, and L. Piccinino, *Fertility, Family Planning, and Women's Health: New data from the 1995 National Survey of Family Growth.* Vital and Health Statistics, Series 23, No. 19; Washington, D.C.: National Center for Health Statistics, 1997.

Alba, Richard, John Logan, Amy Lutz, and Brian Stults, "Only English by the Third Generation? Loss and Preservation of the Mother Tongue Among the Grandchildren of Contemporary Immigrants," *Demography* 39, no. 3 (August 2002), pp. 467–84.

Alter, George, "Infant and Child Mortality in the United States and Canada," in Alan Bideau, Bertrand Desjardins and Héctor Pérez Brignoli, eds., *Infant and Child Mortality in the Past.* Oxford: Clarendon Press, 1997.

Anderson, David G., and J. Christoper Gillam, "Paleoindian Colonization of the Americas: Implications from an Examination of the Physiography, Demography and Artifact Distribution," *American Antiquity* 65, no. 1 (2000), pp. 43–66.

Anderson, Margo J., *The American Census: A Social History.* New Haven: Yale University Press, 1988.

Anderton, Douglas, L. Lee, and L. Bean, "Birth Spacing and Fertility Limitation: A Behavioral Analysis of a Nineteenth Century Frontier Population," *Demography* 22, no. 2 (May 1985), pp. 169–83.

Appleby, Andrew B., "Grain Prices and Subsistence Crises in England and France, 1590–1740," *The Journal of Economic History* 39, no. 4 (December 1979), pp. 865–87.

"Epidemics and Famine in the Little Ice Age," *Journal of Interdisciplinary History* 10, no. 4 (Spring 1980), pp. 643–63.

"The Disappearance of Plague: A Continuing Puzzle," *The Economic History Review*, New Series, 33, no. 2. (May 1980), pp. 161–73.

Archer, Richard, "New England Mosaic: A Demographic Analysis for the Seventeenth Century," *William and Mary Quarterly*, 3d ser., 47, no. 4 (October 1990), pp. 477–502.

Armstrong, Gregory L., Laura A. Conn, and Robert W. Pinner, "Trends in Infectious Disease Mortality in the United States during the 20th Century," *Journal of the American Medical Association* 281, no. 1 (January 6, 1999), pp. 61–6.

Bachu, Amara, *Trends in Premarital Childbearing, 1930–1994*, Current Population Report P23, Special Studies no. 197, issued October 1999.

Bachu, Amara, and Martin O'Connell, *Fertility of American Women: June 2000*, Current Population Reports, P20–543RV, issued October 2001.

Bairoch, Paul, Jean Batou, and Pierre Chèvre, *La population des villes européennes de 800 à 1850*. Geneve: Droz, 1988.

Bardet, Jean-Pierre, and Jacques Dupâquier, eds., *Histoire des populations de l'Europe*, 3 vols. Paris: Fayard, 1998.

Berkeley, Katheen C., *The Women's Liberation Movement in America*, Westport, Conn.: Greenwood Press, 1999.

Biraben, J-N, "An essay concerning Mankind's Evolution," *Population* 4 (1980), pp. 1–13.

Bogue, Donald J., *The Population of the United States*. Glencoe, Ill.: Free Press, 1959.

Burnard, T. G., "'Prodigious riches': The Wealth of Jamaica before the American Revolution," *Economic History Review* 54, no. 3 (2001), pp. 506–24.

Cassedy, James H., *Demography in Early America. Beginnings of the Statistical Mind, 1600–1800*. Cambridge, Mass.: Harvard University Press, 1969.

Caplow, Theodore, Louis Hicks, and Ben J. Wattenberg, *The First Measured Century. An Illustrated Guide to Trends in America, 1900–2000*. Washington, D.C.: The AEI Press, 2001.

Cavalli-Sforza, L. Luca, Paolo Menozzi, and Alberto Piazza, *The History and Geography of Human Genes*. Princeton: Princeton University Press, 1994.

Centers for Disease Control and Prevention, National Center for Health Statistics, *Vital Statistics of the United States, 1992*, Volume II—"Mortality" Part A.

"Poverty and Infant Mortality," *Monthly Morbidity and Mortality Weekly Report*, 44, no. 49 (December 15, 1995), pp. 922–7.

Vital Statistics of the United States, 1997, vol. I (Natality) Table 1.1.

Health, United States, 2001. Hyattsville, Md., 2001.

Health, United States, 2002. Hyattsville, Md., 2002.

National Vital Statistics Report 50, no. 6 (March 21, 2002).

Chesnais, Jean-Claude, *The Demographic Transition....1720–1984*. Oxford: Clarendon Press, 1992.

Clark, Colin, *Population Growth and Land Use* 2nd ed. London: MacMillan Press, 1977.

Coale, Ansley J., and Melvin Zelnik, *New Estimates of Fertility and Population in the United States*. Princeton: Princeton University Press, 1963.

Condran, Gretchin A., and Rose A. Cheney, "Mortality Trends in Philadelphia: Age- and Cause-Specific Death Rates 1870–1930," *Demography* 19, no. 1 (February 1982), pp. 97–123.

Costa, Dora L., "Changing Chronic Disease Rates and Long Term Decline in Functional Limitation among Elderly Men," *Demography* 39, no. 1 (February 2002), pp. 119–37.

Crawford, Michael H., *The Origins of Native Americans: Evidence from Anthropological Genetics*. Cambridge: Cambridge University Press, 1998.

Cutler, David M., Edward L. Glaeser, and Jacob L. Vigdor, "The Rise and Decline of the American Ghetto," *Journal of Political Economy* 107, no. 3 (1999), pp. 455–506.

David, Paul A.; and Warren C. Sanderson, "The Emergence of a Two-Child Norm among American Birth-Controllers," *Population and Development Review* 13, no. 1 (March 1987), pp. 1–41.

David, Paul A., Thomas A. Mroz, Warren C. Sanderson, Kenneth W. Wachter, and David R. Weir, "Cohort Parity Analysis: Statistical Estimates of the Extent of Fertility Control," *Demography* 25, no. 2 (May 1988), pp. 163–88.

Deardorff, Kevin E., and Lisa M. Blumerman, *Evaluating Components of International Migration: Estimates of the Foreign-Born Population by Migrant Status in 2000*, Population Division, Working Paper Series No. 58; U.S. Bureau of the Census, December 2001.

Demos, John, "Notes on Life in Plymouth Colony," *William and Mary Quarterly*, 3d ser., 22, no. 2 (April 1965), pp. 264–86.

"Families in Colonial Bristol, Rhode Island: An Exercise in Historical Demography," *William and Mary Quarterly*, 3d ser., 25, no. 1 (January 1968), pp. 40–57.

A Little Commonwealth: Family Life in Plymouth Colony. New York: Oxford University Press, 1970.

Denevan, William, "Native American Population in 1492: Recent Research and a Revised Hemispheric Estimate," in William M. Denevan, ed., *The Native Population of the Americas in 1492*. 2d ed; Madison, Wisc.: University of Wisconsin Press, 1992, pp. xviii–xxxvii.

Dillehay, Thomas D., *The Settlement of the Americas: A New Prehistory*. New York: Basic Books, 2000.

Dowling, Henry F., *Fighting Infection. Conquests of the Twentieth Century*. Boston: Harvard University Press, 1977.

Duffy, John, "Eighteenth Century Carolina Health Conditions," *The Journal of Southern History* 18, no. 3 (August 1952), pp. 289–302.

Duleep, Harriet Orcutt, "Measuring Socioeconomic Mortality Differentials Over Time," *Demography* 26, no. 2 (May 1989), pp. 345–51.

Earle, Carville V., "Environment, Disease and Mortality in Early Virginia," in Thad W. Tate and David L. Ammerman, eds., *The Chesapeake in the Seventeenth Century*. Boston: W. W. Norton, 1979, pp. 96–125.

Easterlin, Richard A., "The American Baby Boom in Historical Perspective," *American Economic Review*, LI, no. 5 (December 1961), pp. 869–911.

　Population, Labor Force and Long Swings in Economic Growth. The American Experience. New York: Columbia University Press, 1968.

　"Does Human Fertility Adjust to the Environment?" *The American Economic Review* 61, no. 2 (May 1971), pp. 399–407.

　"An Economic Framework for Fertility Analysis," *Studies in Family Planning*, 6, no. 3 (March 1975), pp. 54–63.

　"Population Change and Farm Settlement in the Northern United States," *The Journal of Economic History* 36, no. 1 (March 1976), pp. 45–75.

　"Factors in the Decline of Farm Family Fertility in the United States: Some Preliminary Research Results," *The Journal of American History* 63, no. 3 (December 1976), pp. 600–14.

　"The Economics and Sociology of Fertility, A Synthesis," in Charles Tilly, ed., *Historical Studies of Changing Fertility*. Princeton: Princeton University Press, 1978, pp. 57–134.

　"Twentieth-Century American Population Growth," in Stanley L. Engerman and Robert E. Gallman, eds., *The Cambridge Economic History of the United States*, 3 vols. Cambridge: Cambridge University Press, 1996–2000, vol. 3, pp. 505–48.

Easterlin, Richard A., George Alter, and Gretchen A. Condran, "Farms and Farm Families in Old and New Areas: The Northern States in 1860," in Tamara K. Hareven and Maris A. Vinovskis, eds., *Family and Population in Nineteenth-Century America*. Princeton: Princeton University Press, 1978, pp. 23–84.

Eblen, Jack E., "An Analysis of Nineteenth-Century Frontier Populations," *Demography* 2 (1965), pp. 399–413.

　"Growth of the Black Population in Antebellum America, 1820–1860," *Population Studies* 26, no. 2 (July 1972), pp. 273–89.

　"New Estimates of the Vital Rates of the United States Black Population During the Nineteenth Century," *Demography* 11, no. 2 (May 1974), pp. 301–19.

　"On the Natural Increase of Slave Populations: The Example of the Cuban Black Population, 1775–1900," in Stanley L. Engerman and Eugene Genovese, eds., *Race and Slavery in the Western Hemisphere*. Princeton: Princeton University Press, 1975, pp. 211–47.

Eltis, David, and Stanley L. Engerman, "Was the Slave Trade Dominated by Men?" *Journal of Interdisciplinary History* 23, no. 2 (Autumn 1992), pp. 237–57.

"Fluctuations in Sex and Age Ratios in the Transatlantic Slave Trade, 1663–1864," *The Economic History Review*, New Series, 46, no. 2 (May 1993), pp. 308–23.

Engerman, Stanley L., "The Economic Impact of the Civil War," in Ralph Andreano, ed., *The Economic Impact of the American Civil War*. 2d ed. Cambridge, Mass.: Schenkman, 1967, pp. 188–209.

"Changes in Black Fertility, 1880–1940," in Tamara K. Hareven and Maris A. Vinovskis, eds., *Family and Population in Nineteenth-Century America*. Princeton: Princeton University Press, 1978, pp. 126–53.

Erickson, Charlotte J., "Emigration from the British Isles to the USA in 1841: Part 1. Emigration from the British Isles," *Population Studies* 43 (1989), pp. 347–67.

Evans, Sara M., *Tidal Wave: How Women Changed America at Century's End*. New York: Free Press, 2003.

Farley, Reynolds, "The Demographic Rates and Social Institutions of the Nineteenth Century Negro Population: A Stable Population Analysis," *Demography*, 2 (1965), pp. 386–98.

Ferenczi, Imre, and Walter F. Willcox, *International Migrations*, 2 vols. New York: National Bureau of Economic Research, 1929.

Fiedel Stuart J., *Prehistory of the Americas*. 2d ed. Cambridge: Cambridge University Press, 1992.

"Older Than We Thought: Implications of Corrected Dates for Paleoindians," *American Antiquity* 64, no. 1 (1999), pp. 95–116.

Fields, Jason, and Lynne M. Casper, *America's Families and Living Arrangements: Population Characteristics*. Washington, D.C.: U.S. Census Bureau, Current Population Reports, P20-537. June 2001.

Fix, Alan G., "Colonization Models and Initial Genetic Diversity in the Americas," *Human Biology*, 74, no. 1 (February 2002), pp. 1–10.

Flandrin, Jean-Lous, *Families in Former Times: Kinship, Household and Sexuality*. Cambridge: Cambridge University Press, 1976.

Fligstein, Neil, *Going North. Migration of Blacks and Whites from the South, 1900–1950*. New York: Academic Press, 1981.

Flinn, Michael W., *The European Demographic System, 1500–1820*. Baltimore, Md.: Johns Hopkins University Press, 1981.

Fogel, Robert William, "Nutrition and the Decline in Mortality since 1700: Some Preliminary Findings," in Stanley L. Engerman and Robert E. Gallman, eds., *Long-Term Factors in American Economic Growth*. Chicago: University of Chicago Press, 1986, pp. 439–556.

Fogel, Robert William, and Stanley L. Engerman, *Time on the Cross: The Economics of American Negro Slavery*. Boston, Mass.: Little, Brown, 1974.

Fogelman, Aaron, "Migrations to the Thirteen British North American Colonies, 1700–1775: New Estimates," *Journal of Interdisciplinary History*, XXII, no. 4 (Spring 1992), pp. 691–709.

"From Slaves, Convicts and Servants to Free Passengers: The Transformation of Immigration in the Era of the American Revolution," *Journal of American History* 85, no. 1 (June 1998), pp. 43–76.

Forster, Colin, and G. S. L. Tucker, *Economic Opportunity and White American Fertility Ratios, 1800–1860*. New Haven, Conn.: Yale University Press, 1972.

Frey, William H., "Immigration, Domestic Migration and Demographic Balkanization in America: New Evidence for the 1990s," *Population and Development Review* 22, no. 4 (December 1996), pp. 741–63.

Galenson, David W., *White Servitude in Colonial America: An Economic Analysis*. Cambridge: Cambridge University Press, 1981.

"White Servitude and the Growth of Black Slavery in Colonial America," *The Journal of Economic History* 41, no. 1 (March 1981), pp. 39–47.

"The Rise and Fall of Indentured Servitude in the Americas: An Economic Analysis," *The Journal of Economic History* 44, no. 1 (March 1984), pp. 1–26.

"Economic Opportunity on the Urban Frontier: Nativity, Work, and Wealth in Early Chicago," *The Journal of Economic History* 51, no. 3 (September 1991), pp. 581–603.

"Population Turnover in the English West Indies in the Late Seventeenth Century: A Comparative Perspective," *The Journal of Economic History* 45, no. 2 (June 1985), pp. 227–35.

"Settlement and Growth of the Colonies: Population, Labor and Economic Development," in Stanley L. Engerman and Robert E. Gallman, eds., *The Cambridge Economic History of the United States*, 3 vols. Cambridge: Cambridge University Press, 1996–2000, vol. 1, pp. 135–207.

Galenson, David W., and Clayne L. Pope, "Economic and Geographic Mobility on the Farming Frontier: Evidence from Appanoose Country, Iowa, 1850–1870," *The Journal of Economic History*, 49, no. 3 (September 1989), pp. 635–55.

Gallman, James M., "Determinants of Age at Marriage in Colonial Perquimans County, North Carolina," *William and Mary Quarterly*, 3d ser., 39, no. 1, (January 1982), pp. 176–91.

Gallman, Robert E., "Dietary Change in Antebellum America," *The Journal of Economic History* 56, no. 1 (March 1996), pp. 193–201.

"Economic Growth and Structural Change in the Long Nineteenth Century," in Stanley L. Engerman and Robert E. Gallman, eds., *The Cambridge Economic History of the United States*, 3 vols. Cambridge: Cambridge University Press, 1996–2000, vol. 2, pp. 1–55.

Gaspari, K. Celese, and Arthur G. Woolf, "Income, Public Works and Mortality in Early Twentieth-Century American Cities," *Journal of Economic History* 45, no. 2 (June 1985), pp. 355–61.

Geggus, David, "Sex Ratio, Age and Ethnicity in the Atlantic Slave Trade: Data from French Shipping and Plantation Records," *The Journal of African History* 30, no. 1 (1989), pp. 23–44.

Gemery, Henry A., "Emigration from the British Isles to the New World: 1630–1700: Inferences from Colonial Populations," *Research in Economic History*, 5 (1980), pp. 179–231.

"The White Population of the Colonial United States, 1670–1790," in Michael R. Haines and Richard H. Steckel, eds., *A Population History of North America*. Cambridge: Cambridge University Press, 2000, pp. 143–90.

Geronimus, Arline T., John Bound, Timothy A. Waidmann, Cynthia G. Colen, and Dianne Steffick, "Inequality in Life Expectancy, Functional Status, and Active Life Expectancy Across Selected Black and White Populations in the United States," *Demography* 38, no. 2 (May 2001), pp. 227–51.

Gibson, Campbell J., "The Contribution of Immigration to United States Population Growth: 1790–1970," *International Migration Review* 9, no. 2 (Summer 1975), pp. 157–77.

"The Population in Large Urban Concentrations in the United States, 1790–1980: A Delineation Using Highly Urbanized Counties (in Measurement Issues)," *Demography* 24, no. 4 (November 1987), pp. 601–14.

Population of the 100 Largest Cities And Other Urban Places in the United States: 1790 to 1990, Population Division Working Paper No. 27; Washington, D.C.: U.S. Bureau of the Census, Population Division, June 1998.

Gibson, Campbell J., and Kay Jung, *Historical Census Statistics on Population Totals By Race, 1790 to 1990, and By Hispanic Origin, 1970 to 1990, for the United States, Regions, Divisions, and States*. Population Division Working Paper No. 56, Washington, D.C.: U.S. Census Bureau, September 2002.

Gibson, Campbell J., and Emily Lennon, *Historical Census Statistics on the Foreign-born Population of the United States: 1850–1990*, Population Division Working Paper No. 29; Washington, D.C.: U.S. Bureau of the Census, Population Division, February 1999.

Glick, Paul C., and Robert Parke, Jr., "New Approaches in Studying the Life Cycle of the Family," *Demography* 2 (1965), pp. 187–202.

Goldin, Claudia Dale, "The Economics of Emancipation," *The Journal of Economic History* 33, no. 1 (March 1973), pp. 66–85.

  Understanding the Gender Gap. An Economic History of American Women. New York: Oxford University Press, 1990.

Goldin, Claudia D., and Frank D. Lewis, "The Economic Cost of the American Civil War: Estimates and Implications," *The Journal of Economic History* 35, no. 2 (June 1975), pp. 299–326.

Goldin, Claudia, and Robert A. Margo, "Wages, Prices, and Labor Markets before the Civil War," in Claudia Goldin and Hugh Rockoff, eds., *Strategic Factors in Nineteenth Century American Economic History*. Chicago: University of Chicago Press, 1992, pp. 67–104.

Goldscheider, Frances K., and Regina M. Bures, "The Racial Crossover in Family Complexity in the United States," *Demography* 40, no. 3 (August 2003), pp. 569–87.

Goody, Jack, *The European Family: An Historico-Anthropological Essay*. Oxford: Blackwell Publishers, 2000.

Gordon, Linda, *The Moral Property of Women: A History of Birth Control Politics in America*. Urbana, Ill.: University of Illinois Press, 2002.

Greene, Evarts B., and Virginia D. Harrington, *American Population before the Federal Census of 1790*. New York: Columbia University Press, 1932.

Greenberg, Joseph H., Christy G. Turner II and Stephen L. Zegura, "The Settlement of the Americas: A Comparison of the Linguistic, Dental and Genetic Evidence," *Current Antrhopology* 27, no. 5 (December 1986), pp. 477–97.

Greven, Jr., Philip J., "Family Structure in Seventeenth-Century Andover, Massachusetts," *William and Mary Quarterly*, 3d ser., 23, no. 2 (April 1966), pp. 234–56.

  Four Generations: Population, Land and Family in Colonial Andover, Massachusetts. Ithaca, N.Y.: Cornell University Press, 1970.

Grubb, Farley, "The Market for Indentured Immigrants: Evidence on the Efficiency of Forward-Labor Contracting in Philadelphia, 1745–1773," *The Journal of Economic History* 45, no. 4 (December 1985), pp. 855–68.

  "Morbidity and Mortality on the North Atlantic Passage: Eighteenth-Century German Immigration," *Journal of Interdisciplinary History* 17, no. 3 (Winter 1987), pp. 565–85.

  "The Auction of Redemptioner Servants, Philadelphia, 1771–1804: An Economic Analysis," *The Journal of Economic History* 48, no. 3 (September 1988), pp. 583–603.

  "German Immigration to Pennsylvania, 1709 to 1820," *Journal of Interdisciplinary History* 20, no. 3 (Winter 1990), pp. 417–36.

  "Fatherless and Friendless: Factors Influencing the Flow of English Emigrant Servants," *Journal of Economic History* 52, no. 1 (March 1992), pp. 85–108.

"The End of European Immigrant Servitude in the United States: An Economic Analysis of Market Collapse, 1772–1835," *The Journal of Economic History* 54, no. 4 (December 1994), pp. 794–824.

Gutmann, Myron P., and Kenneth H. Fliess, "The Determinants of Early Fertility Decline in Texas," *Demography* 30, no. 3 (August 1993), pp. 443–57.

"The Social Context of Child Mortality in the American Southwest," *Journal of Interdisciplinary History* 26, no. 4 (Spring 1996), pp. 589–618.

Gutmann, Myron P., Michael R. Haines, W. Parker Frisbie, and K. Stephen Blanchard, "Intra-Ethnic Diversity in Hispanic Child Mortality, 1890–1910," *Demography* 37, no. 4 (November 2000), pp. 467–75.

Haines, Michael R., "Fertility, Nuptiality, and Occupation: A Study of Coal Mining Populations and Regions in England and Wales in the Mid-Nineteenth Century," *Journal of Interdisciplinary History* 8, no. 2 (Autumn 1977), pp. 245–80.

"Mortality in Nineteenth Century America: Estimates From New York and Pennsylvania Census Data, 1865 and 1900," *Demography* 14, no. 3 (August 1977), pp. 311–31.

"Fertility Decline in Industrial America: An Analysis of the Pennsylvania Anthracite Region, 1850–1900, Using 'Own Children' Methods," *Population Studies* 32, no. 2 (July 1978), pp. 327–54.

"The Use of Model Life Tables to Estimate Mortality for the United States in the Late Nineteenth Century," *Demography* 16, no. 2 (May 1979), 289–312.

"Inequality and Childhood Mortality: A Comparison of England and Wales, 1911, and the United States, 1900," *The Journal of Economic History* 45, no. 4 (December 1985), pp. 885–912.

"Social Class Differentials during Fertility Decline: England and Wales Revisited," *Population Studies* 43, no. 2 (July 1989), pp. 305–23.

"American Fertility in Transition: New Estimates of Birth Rates in the United States, 1900–1910," *Demography* 26, no. 1 (February 1989), pp. 137–48.

"Socio-Economic Differentials in Infant and Child Mortality During Mortality Decline: England and Wales, 1890–1911," *Population Studies* 49, no. 2 (July 1995), pp. 297–315.

"Long-Term Marriage Patterns in the United States from Colonial Times to the Present," Working Paper Series, Historical Paper 80. Cambridge, Mass.: National Bureau of Economic Research, March 1996.

"The White Population of the United States, 1790–1920, in Michael R. Haines and Richard H. Steckel, *A Population History of North America*. Cambridge: Cambridge University Press, 2000, pp. 305–70.

"The Population of the United States, 1790–1920," in Stanley L. Engerman and Robert E. Gallman, *The Cambridge Economic History of the United States*, 3 vols. Cambridge: Cambridge University Press, 1996–2000, vol. 2, pp. 143–206.

"The Urban Mortality Transition in the United States, 1800–1940," Historical Research, Paper no. 134. Cambridge, Mass.: National Bureau of Economic Research, July 2001.

"Ethnic Differences in Demographic Behavior in the United States: Has There Been Convergence?," Working Paper no. 9042. Cambridge, Mass.: National Bureau of Economic Research, July 2002.

Haynes, Gary, *The Early Settlement of North America. The Clovis Era*. Cambridge: Cambridge University Press, 2003.

Hajnal, J., "European Marriage Patterns in Perspective," in D. V. Glass and D. E. C. Eversley, eds., *Population in History, Essays in Historical Demography*. London: Edward Arnold, 1965, pp. 101–46.

"Two Kinds of Preindustrial Household Formation Systems," *Population and Development Review* 8, no. 3 (September 1982), pp. 449–94.

Hecht, Irene W. D., "The Virginia Muster of 1624/5 As a Source for Demographic History," *William and Mary Quarterly*, 3d ser., 30, no. 1 (January 1973), pp. 65–92.

Higgs, Robert, "Cycles and Trends of Mortality in 18 Large American Cities, 1871–1900," *Explorations in Economic History* 16, no. 4 (October 1979), pp. 381–408.

Higham, John, *Strangers in the Land: Patterns of American Nativism, 1860–1925*. New York: Atheneum Press, 1963.

Higman, B. W., *Slave Populations of the British Caribbean, 1807–1834*. Baltimore: Johns Hopkins University Press, 1984.

Himmer, Robert A., Richard G. Rogers, and Isaac W. Eberstein, "Sociodemographic Differentials in Adult Mortality: A Review of Analytical Approaches," *Population and Development Review* 23, no. 3 (September 1998), pp. 553–78.

Hobbs, Frank, and Nicole Stoops, "Demographic Trends in the 20th Century," U.S. Census Bureau, Census 2000, Special Reports, Series CENSR-4. Washington, D.C.: U.S. Government Printing Office, 2002.

Horn, James, "Servant Emigration to the Chesapeake in the Seventeenth Century," in Thad W. Tate and David L. Ammerman, eds., *The Chesapeake in the Seventeenth Century*. Boston: W. W. Norton, 1979, pp. 51–95.

Hutton, Timothy J., and Jeffrey G. Williamson, "What Drove Mass Migrations from Europe in the Late Nineteenth Century," *Population and Development Review* 20, no. 3 (September 1994), pp. 533–59.

Iceland, John, Daniel H. Weinberg, and Erika Steinmetz, *Racial and Ethnic Residential Segregation in the United States: 1980–2000* U.S. Census Bureau, Series CENSR-3. Washington, D.C.: U.S. Government Printing Office, 2002.

Irving, William N., "Context and Chronology of Early Man in the Americas," *American Review of Anthropology* 14 (1985), pp. 529–55.

Johnson, Daniel M., and Rex R. Campbell, *Black Migration in America: A Socio-Demographic History* Durham, N.C.: Duke University Press, 1981.

Josephy, Alvin M., Jr., *The Indian Heritage of America*. Boston: Houghton Mifflin Co, 1991.

Katz, Michael B., and Mark J. Stern, "Fertility, Class and Industrial Capitalism, Erie County, New York, 1855–1915," *American Quarterly* 33, no. 1 (Spring 1981), pp. 63–92.

Kessler-Harris, Alice, *Out to Work: A History of Wage-Earning Women in the United States*. New York: Oxford University Press, 1982.

Kinsella, Kevin, and Victoria A. Velkoff, *An Aging World: 2001*. U.S. Census Bureau, Series P95/01-1. Washington, D.C.: U.S. Government Printing Office, 2001.

Kitagawa, Evelyn M., "Differential Fertility in Chicago, 1920–40," *American Journal of Sociology* 58, no. 5 (March 1953), 481–92.

Kitagawa, Evelyn M., and Philio M. Hauser, *Differential Mortality in the United States: A Study in Socioeconomic Epidemiology*. Cambridge, Mass.: Harvard University Press, 1973.

Klein, Herbert S., "Slaves and Shipping in Eighteenth Century Virginia," *Journal of Interdisciplinary History*, V (Winter 1975), pp. 383–411.

The Middle Passage: Comparative Studies in the Atlantic Slave Trade. Princeton: Princeton University Press, 1978.

African Slavery in Latin America and the Caribbean. New York: Oxford University Press, 1986.

"The Demographic Structure of Mexico City in 1811," *Journal of Urban History* 23, no.1 (November 1996), pp. 66–93.

The American Finances of the Spanish Empire, 1680–1809. Albuquerque: University of New Mexico Press, 1998.

The Atlantic Slave Trade, revised ed.Cambridge: Cambridge University Press, 2002.

Klein, Herbert S. and Stanley L. Engerman, "The Transition from Slave to Free Labor: Notes on a Comparative Economic Model," in M. Moreno Fraginals, Frank Moya Pons, and Stanley L. Engerman, eds., *Between Slavery and Free Labor: The Spanish Speaking Caribbean in the Nineteenth Century*. Baltimore: Johns Hopkins University Press, 1985, pp. 255–69.

"Fertility Differentials between Slaves in the United States and the British West Indies: A Note on Lactation Practices and their

Implications," *William and Mary Quarterly*, 3d ser. 35, no. 2 (April 1978), 357–74.

"Long-term Trends in African Mortality in the Transatlantic Slave Trade," *Slavery and Abolition* 18, no. 1 (April 1997), pp. 59–71.

Klein, Herbert S., Stanley L. Engerman, Robin Haines, and Ralph Schlomowitz, "Transoceanic Mortality: The Slave Trade in Comparative Perspective," *William and Mary Quarterly*, 3d ser. 58, no. 1 (January 2001), pp. 93–118.

Klein, Herbert S., and Daniel C. Schiffner, "The Current Debate about the Origins of the Paleoindians of America," *Journal of Social History* 37, no. 2 (Winter 2003), pp. 169–78.

Klepp, Susan E., "Seasoning and Society: Racial Differences in Mortality in Eighteenth-Century Philadelphia," *William and Mary Quarterly*, 3d ser. 51, no. 3 (July 1994), pp. 473–506.

"Revolutionary Bodies: Women and the Fertility Transition in the Mid-Atlantic Region, 1760–1820," *The Journal of American History*, 85, no. 3 (December 1998), pp. 910–45.

Komlos, John, "The Height and Weight of West Point Cadets: Dietary Change in Antebellum America," *The Journal of Economic History* 47, no. 4 (December 1987), pp. 897–927.

"Anomalies in Economic History: Toward a Resolution of the "Antebellum Puzzle," *The Journal of Economic History* 56, no. 1 (March 1996), pp. 202–14.

Kramarow, Ellen A., "The Elderly Who Live Alone in the United States: Historical Perspectives on Household Change," *Demography* 32, no. 3 (August 1995), pp. 335–52.

Kulikoff. Allan, "A 'Prolific' People: Black Population Growth in the Chesapeake Colonies, 1700–1790," *Southern Studies* (Winter 1977), pp. 391–428.

Larsen, Clark Spencer, and George R. Milner, eds., *In the Wake of Contact: Biological Responses to Conquest*. New York: Wiley-Liss, 1994.

Lee, Everett S., Ann Ratner, Carol P. Brainerd, and Richard A. Easterlin, *Population Redistribution and Economic Growth in the United States, 1870–1950*. 2 vols. Philadelphia: The American Philosophical Society, 1957.

Leet, Dan R., "The Determinants of the Fertility in Antebellum Ohio," *Journal of Economic History* 36, no. 2 (June 1976), pp. 359–378.

Lell, Jeffry T., Rem I. Sukernik, Yelena B. Starikouskaya, Bing Su, Li Jin, Theodore G. Schurr, Peter A. Underhill, and Douglas C. Wallace, "The Dual Origin and Siberian Affinities of Native American Y Chromosomes," *American Journal of Human Genetics* 70 (2002), pp. 192–206.

Lindert, Peter H., *Fertility and Scarcity in America*. Princeton: Princeton University Press, 1978.

Lesthaeghe, Ron, "On The Social Control of Human Reproduction," *Population and Development Review* 6, no. 4 (December 1980), pp. 527–48.

Livi Bacci, Massimo, *L'immigrazione e l'assimilazione degli italiani negli Stati Uniti secondo le statistiche demografiche americane*. Milan: Giuffrè, 1961.

The Population of Europe: A History. Oxford: Blackwell Publishers, 2000.

Lockridge, Kenneth A., "The Population of Dedham, Massachusetts, 1636–1736," *The Economic History Review*, New Series 19, no. 2 (1966), pp. 318–44.

Logan, John R, "Hispanic Populations and Their Residential Patterns in the Metropolis," Albany: Lewis Mumford Center for Comparative Urban and Regional Research, SUNY Albany, May 8, 2002.

"The Suburban Advantage: New Census Data Show Unyielding City-Suburb Economic Gap, and Surprising Shifts in Some Places," Albany: Lewis Mumford Center for Comparative Urban and Regional Research, SUNY Albany, June 24, 2002.

Lollock, Lisa, *The Foreign Born Population in the United States: March 2000*, Current Population Reports, P20-534, Washington, D.C.: U.S. Census Bureau, 2001.

Maddison, Angus, *The World Economy: A Millennial Perpective*. Paris: Development Centre of the Organisation for Economic Co-operation and Development, 2001.

Massey, Douglas S., "The New Immigration and Ethnicity in the United States," *Population and Development Review* 21, no. 3 (September 1995), pp. 646–47.

Massey, Douglas S., and Nancy A. Denton, *American Apartheid: Segregation and the Making of the Underclass*. Cambridge, Mass.: Harvard University Press, 1993.

Massey, Douglas S., Jorge Durand, and Nolan J. Malone, *Beyond Smoke and Mirrors: Mexican Immigration in an Era of Economic Integration*. New York: Russell Sage Foundation, 1992.

Mathews, T. J., and Brady E. Hamilton, "Mean Age of Mother, 1970–2000," *National Vital Statistics Reports* 51, no. 1 (December 11, 2002).

May, Elaine Tyler, *Homeward Bound. American Families in the Cold War Era*. New York: Basic Books, 1988.

Mayer, Albert, and Carol Klapprodt, "Fertility Differentials in Detroit, 1920–1950," *Population Studies* 9, no. 2 (November 1955), pp. 148–58.

McClelland, Peter D., and Richard J. Zeckhauser, *Demographic Dimensions of the New Republic: American Interregional Migration, Vital Statistics and Manumissions, 1800–1860*. Cambridge: Cambridge University Press, 1982.

McCusker, John J., and Russell R. Menard, *The Economy of British America, 1607–1789*. Chapel Hill, N.C.: University of North Carolina Press, 1985, p. 154, tab 7.2.

McKinnon, Jesse, and Karen Humes, "The Black Population in the United States: March, 1999," U.S. Census Bureau, Current Population Reports, Series P20-530. Washington, D.C.: U.S. Government Printing Office, 2000.

Meckel, Richard A., "Immigration, Mortality and Population Growth in Boston, 1840–1880," *Journal of Interdisciplinary History* XV, no. 3 (Winter 1985), pp. 393–417.

Meeker, Edward, "The Social Rate of Return on Investment in Public Health, 1880–1910," *The Journal of Economic History* 34, no. 2 (June 1974), pp. 392–421.

Meltzer, David J., "Clocking the First Americans," *Annual Review of Anthropology*, 24 (1995) pp. 21–45.

Menard, Russell R., "The Maryland Slave Population, 1658 to 1730: A Demographic Profile of Blacks in Four Counties," *William and Mary Quarterly*, 3d ser., 32, no. 1 (January 1975), pp. 29–54.

"Five Maryland Censuses, 1700 to 1712: A Note on the Quality of the Quantities," *William and Mary Quarterly*, 3d ser. 37, no. 4 (October 1980), pp. 616–26.

"Financing the Lowcountry Export Boom: Capital and Growth in Early South Carolina," *William and Mary Quarterly*, 3d ser. 51, no. 4 (October 1994), pp. 659–76.

"Economic and Social Development of the South," in Stanley L. Engerman and Robert E. Gallman, eds., *The Cambridge Economic History of the United States*, 3 vols. Cambridge: Cambridge University Press, 1996–2000, vol. 1, pp. 249–95.

Meyer, Jean, *Histoire du Sucre*. Paris: Editions Desjonquères, 1989.

Mitchell, B. R., *International Historical Statistics: Europe, 1750–1993*. 3rd ed. New York: Stockton Press, 1992.

Modell, John, "Family and Fertility on the Indian Frontier, 1820," *American Quarterly* 23, no. 5 (December 1971), pp. 615–34.

Morgan, Edmund S., *American Slavery, American Freedom: The Ordeal of Colonial Virginia*. Boston: W. W. Norton, 1975.

Morgan, S. Philip, Antonio McDaniel, Andrew T. Miller, and Samuel Preston, "Racial Differences in Household and Family Structure at the Turn of the Century," *American Journal of Sociology* 98, no. 4 (January 1993), pp. 799–828.

Morgan, S. Philip, Susan Cotts Watkins, and Douglas Ewbank, "Generating Americans: Ethnic Differences in Fertility," in Susan Cotts Watkins, ed., *After Ellis Island: Newcomers and Natives in the 1910 Census*. New York: Russell Sage Foundation, 1994.

Nadal, Jordi, *La población española (siglos xvi a xx)*, 2nd rev ed. Barcelona: Editorial Ariel, 1986.

Norton, Susan L., "Population Growth in Colonial America: A Study of Ipswich, Massachusetts," *Population Studies* 25, no. 3 (November 1971),
pp. 433–52.

"Marital Migration in Essex County, Massachusetts, in the Colonial and Early
Federal Periods," *Journal of Marriage and the Family* 35, no. 3 (August 1973),
pp. 406–18.

Nugent, Walter, *Crossings: The Great Transatlantic Migrations, 1870–1914*.
Bloomington, Ind.: Indiana University Press, 1992.

Into the West: The Story of Its People. New York: Alfred A. Knopf, 1999.

Pappas, Gregory, Susan Queen, Wilbur Hadden, and Gail Fisher, "The Increasing Disparity in Mortality between Socioeconomic Groups in the United
States, 1960 and 1986," *New England Journal of Medicine* 329, no. 2 (July
8, 1993), pp. 103–09.

Pelletier, François, Jacques Légaré, and Robert Vourbeau, "Mortality in Quebec
During the Nineteenth Century: From the State to the Cities," *Population
Studies* 51 (1997), pp. 93–103.

Phillips, Seymour, "The Medieval Background," in Nicolas Canny, ed., *Europeans on the Move: Studies on European Migration, 1500–1800*. Oxford:
Clarendon Press 1994, pp. 9–25.

Pinnelli, Antonella, Hans Joachim Hoffman-Nowotny, and Beat Fux, *Fertility
and new types of households and family formation in Europe*. Population Studies, no. 35; Strasbourg: Council of Europe, 2001.

Polenberg, Richard, *One Nation Divisible: Class, Race and Ethnicity in the United
States Since 1938*. New York: The Viking Press, 1980.

Pope, Clyde L., "Adult Mortality in America before 1900: A View from Family
Histories," in Claudia Goldin & Hugh Rockoff, *Strategic Factors in Nine-
teenth Century American Economic History*. Chicago: University of Chicago
Press, 1992, pp. 267–96.

Potter, J., "The Growth of Population In America, 1700–1860," in D. V. Glass
and D. E. C. Eversley, eds., *Population in History, Essays in Historical Demography*. London: Edward Arnold, 1965, pp. 631–88.

Powell Joseph F., and Walter A. Neves, "Craniofacial Morphology of the First
Americans: Pattern and Process in the Peopling of the New World," *Yearbook of Physical Anthropology* 42 (1999), pp. 153–88.

Preston, Samuel H., and Michael R. Haines, *Fatal Years: Child Mortality in
Late Nineteenth-Century America*. Princeton: Princeton University Press,
1991.

Rao, S. L. N., "On Long-Term Mortality Trends in the United States: 1850–
1968," *Demography* 10, no. 3 (August 1973), pp. 405–19.

Rosenberg, Charles E., *The Cholera Years: The United States in 1832,
1849 and 1866*. 2nd ed. Chicago: University of Chicago Press,
1987.

Rossiter, W. S., A Century of Population Growth. From the First to the Twelfth Census of the United States: 1790–1900. Washington, D.C.: U.S. Government Printing Office, 1909.

Rothenbacher, Franz, The Societies of Europe: The European Population 1845–1945. New York: Palgrave-MacMillan, 2002.

Ruggles, Steven, "The Transformation of American Family Structure," American Historical Review 99, no. 1 (February 1994), pp. 103–28.

"The Rise of Divorce and Separation in the United States, 1880–1990," Demography 34, no. 4 (November 1997), pp. 455–66.

Rutman, Darrett B., and Anita H. Rutman, "Of Agues and Fevers: Malaria in the Early Chesapeake," William and Mary Quarterly, 3d ser. 33, no. 1 (January 1976), pp. 31–60.

"Non-Wives and Sons-in-Law: Parental Death in a Seventeenth Century Virginia County," in Thad W. Tate and David L. Ammerman, eds. The Chesapeake in the Seventeenth Century. Boston: W. W. Norton, 1979, pp. 153–82.

Rutman, Darrett B., Charles Wetherell, and Anita H. Rutman, "Rhythms of Life: Black and White Seasonality in the Early Chesapeake," Journal of Interdisciplinary History 11, no. 1 (Summer 1980), pp. 29–53.

Salinger, Sharon V., "To Serve Well and Faithfully" Labor and Indentured Servants in Pennsylvania, 1682–1800." Cambridge: Cambridge University Press, 1987.

Sánchez-Albornoz, Nicolás, La poblacion de América Latina desde los tiempos precolombinos al año 2025, 2nd ed. Madrid: Alianza Editorial, 1994.

"The First Transatlantic Transfer: Spanish Migration to the New World, 1493–1810," in Nicolas Canny, ed., Europeans on the Move: Studies on European Migration, 1500–1800. Oxford: Clarendon Press 1994, pp. 26–38.

Sanderson, Warren C., "Quantitative Aspects of Marriage, Fertility and Family Limitation in Nineteenth Century America: Another Application of the Coale Specifications," Demography 16, no. 3 (August 1979), pp. 339–58.

"Below-Replacement Fertility in Nineteenth Century America," Population and Development Review 13, no. 2 (June 1987), pp. 305–313.

Santos, Eduardo Tarazona, and Fabrício R. Santos, "The Peopling of the Americas: A Second Major Migration," American Journal of Human Genetics 70 (2002), pp. 1377–80.

Schapiro, Morton Owen, "Land Availability and Fertility in the United States, 1760–1860," Journal of Economic History 42, no. 3 (September 1982), pp. 577–600.

Filling Up America: An Economic-Demographic Model of Population Growth and Distribution in the Nineteenth-Century United States. Greenwich, Conn.: JAI Press, 1986.

Schofield, Roger, "Family Structure, Demographic Behavior, and Economic Growth," in John Walter and Roger Schofield, eds., *Famine, Disease and the Social Order in Modern Society*. Cambridge: Cambridge University Press, 1989, pp. 305–30.

Shoemaker, Nancy, *American Indian Population Recovery in the Twenteith Century*. Albuquerque, N.M.: University of New Mexico Press, 1999.

Shryock, Henry S, Jacob S. Siegel, and Associates, *The Methods and Materials of Demography*. New York: Academic Press, 1976.

Silva, Wilson A., et. al., "Mitochondrial Genome Diversity of Native Americans Supports a Single Early Entry of Founder Populations into America," *American Journal of Human Genetics* 71 (2002) pp. 187–92.

Smith, Billy G., "Death and Life in a Colonial Immigrant City: A Demographic Analysis of Philadelphia," *The Journal of Economic History* 37, no. 4 (December 1977), pp. 863–89.

Smith, Daniel Blake, "Mortality and Family in the Colonial Chesapeake," *Journal of Interdisciplinary History* 8, no. 3 (Winter 1978), pp. 403–27.

Smith, Daniel Scott, "Parental Power and Marriage Patterns: An Analysis of Historical Trends in Hingham, Massachusetts," *Journal of Marriage and the Family* 35, no. 3 (August 1973), pp. 419–28.

Steckel, Richard H., "Nutritional Status in the Colonial American Economy," *William and Mary Quarterly*, 3d ser., 56, no. 1 (January 1999), pp. 31–52.

"The African American Population of the United States, 1790–1920," in Michael R. Haines and Richard H. Steckel, eds., *A Population History of North America* Cambridge: Cambridge University Press, 2000, pp. 433–81.

Stone, Anne C., and Mark Stoneking, "mtDNA analysis of a prehistoric Oneota population: Implications for the peopling of the New World," *American Journal of Human Genetics*, 62 (1998), pp. 1153–70.

Taeuber, Irene B., and Conrad Taeuber, *People of the United States in the 20th Century*. Washington, D.C.: U.S. Bureau of the Census, U.S. Government Printing Office, 1971.

Temkin-Greener, H., and A. C. Swedlund, "Fertility Transition in the Connecticut Valley, 1740–1850," *Population Studies* 32, no. 1 (March 1978), pp. 27–41.

Thernstrom, Stephan, *Poverty and Progress: Social Mobility in a Nineteenth Century City*. Cambridge, Mass.: Harvard University Press, 1964.

Thompson, Warren S., and P. K. Whelpton, *Population Trends in the United States*. New York: McGraw-Hill, 1933.

Thornton, Russell, "Population History of Native North Americas," in Michael R. Haines and Richard H. Steckel, eds., *A Population History of North America*. Cambridge: Cambridge University Press, 2000, pp. 9–50.

U.S. Immigration and Naturalization Service, *Statistical Yearbook of the Immigration and Naturalization Service, 1998*. Washington, D.C.: U.S. Government Printing Office, 2000.

    Statistical Yearbook of the Immigration and Naturalization Service, 2000. Washington, D.C.: U.S. Government Printing Office: 2002.

U.S. Bureau of the Census, *Historical Statistics of the United States, Colonial Times to 1970*. CD edition. New York: Cambridge University Press, 1997. Original edition, Washington: U.S. Dept. of Commerce, Bureau of the Census, 1975.

    The Social and Economic Status of the Black Population in the United States, 1790–1978: An Historical View. Current Population Reports, P-23, no. 80. Washington: U.S. Government Printing Office, 1978.

    Statistical Abstract of the United States, 1995. Washington, D.C.: U.S. Government Printing Office, 1996.

    Statistical Abstract of the United States, 2002. Washington D.C.: U.S. Government Printing Office, 2002.

U.S. Department of Education, National Center of Educational Statistics, *The Digest of Educational Statistics 2001*. Washington D.C.: U.S. Government Printing Office, 2002.

U.S. Department of Labor, *Report on the American Workforce, 2001*. Washington: D.C.: U.S. Government Printing Office, 2001.

University of California, Berkeley and Max Planck Institute for Demographic Research. *Human Mortality Database*, accessed at http://www.demog.berkeley.edu/wilmoth/mortality/

Ubelaker, Douglas H., "North American Indian Population Size, A.D. 1500 to 1985," *American Journal of Physical Anthropology* 77, no. 3 (November 1988), pp. 289–94.

    "Patterns of Disease in Early North American Populations," in Michael R. Haines and Richard H. Steckel, eds., *A Population History of North America*. Cambridge: Cambridge University Press, 2000, pp. 51–98.

Uhlenberg, Peter R., "A Study of Cohort Life Cycles: Cohorts of Native Born Massachusetts Women, 1830–1920," *Population Studies* 23, no. 3 (November 1969), pp. 407–20.

Underhill, P. A., Jin L., Zemans R., Oefner P. J., and Cavalli-Sforza L. L., "A pre-Columbian Y chromosome-specific transition and its implications for human evolutionary history," *Proceedings of the National Academy of Science USA* 93 (1996), pp. 196–200.

United Nations, *Demographic Yearbook, Historical Supplement*. New York: United Nations Publications, 2000.

Vallin, Jacques, France Meslé and Tapani Valkonen, *Trends in Mortality and Differential Mortality*. Population Studies, no. 36; Strasbourg: Council of Europe, 2001.

Van de Walle, Etienne, "Alone in Europe: The French Fertility Decline until 1850," in Charles Tilly, ed., *Historical Studies of Changing Fertility*. Princeton: Princeton University Press, 1978, pp. 257–88.

Vázquez Calzada, José L., *La población de Puerto Rico y su trayectoria histórica*. Rio Piedras: Raga Printing, 1988.

Vinovskis, Maris A., "Mortality Rates and Trends in Massachusetts Before 1860," *The Journal of Economic History* 32, no. 1 (March 1972), pp. 184–213.

   Fertility in Massachusetts from the Revolution to the Civil War. New York: Academic Press, 1981.

Waldinger, Roger, "From Ellis Island to LAX: Immigrant Prospects in the American City," *International Migration Review* 30, no. 4 (Winter 1996), pp. 1078–1086.

Walsh, Lorena S., "'Till Death Us Do Part': Marriage and Family in Seventeenth-Century Maryland," in Thad W. Tate and David L. Ammerman, eds., *The Chesapeake in the Seventeenth Century*. Boston: W.W. Norton, 1979, pp. 126–52.

Wells, Robert V., "Family Size and Fertility Control in Eighteenth-Century America: A Study of Quaker Families," *Population Studies* 25, no. 1 (March 1971), pp. 73–82.

   The Population of the British Colonies before 1776: A Survey of the Census Data. Princeton: Princeton University Press, 1975.

   "The Population of England's Colonies in America: Old English or New Americans?" *Population Studies* 46, no. 1 (March 1992), pp. 85–102.

Wells, Robert V., and Michael Zuckerman, "Quaker Marriage Patterns in a Colonial Perspective," *William and Mary Quarterly* 3d ser. 29, no. 3 (July 1972), pp. 415–42.

Woodbury, Robert M., *Infant Mortality and Its Causes*. Baltimore: Williams and Wilkins, 1926.

Wright, Chester W., "The More Enduring Economic Consequences of America's Wars," *The Journal of Economic History* 3, Supplement (December 1943) pp. 9–26.

Wrigley, E. A., and R. S. Schofield, *The Population History of England, 1541–1871: A Reconstruction*. Cambridge: Cambridge University Press, 1989.

Yasuba, Yasukichi, *Birth Rates of the White Population in the United States, 1800–1860: An Economic Study*. Baltimore: Johns Hopkins University, 1962.

Zopf, Paul E., Jr., *Mortality Patterns and Trends in the United States*. Westport, Conn: Greenwood Press, 1992.

INDEX